Vaccination panic in Australia

Brian Martin

Published 2018 by Irene Publishing
Sparsnäs, Sweden
http://www.irenepublishing.com/
irene.publishing@gmail.com

ISBN 978-91-88061-24-9

Contents

Glossary *v*

1 Introduction *1*

2 The vaccination issue *6*

3 The vaccination debate in Australia *31*

4 Denigration *47*

5 Harassment *101*

6 Censorship *152*

7 Defending *208*

8 Contexts *245*

9 Moral panics *310*

10 Conclusion *358*

Index *363*

Acknowledgements

When writing on a controversial topic, obtaining feedback on drafts is especially important.

Over several years I presented extracts from work in progress to members of the high-output writing group at the University of Wollongong. For helpful textual suggestions and feedback on content, I thank Tonya Agostini, Anu Bissoonauth-Bedford, Zhuqin Feng, Kathy Flynn, Anneleis Humphries, Michael Matteson, Anne Melano, Ben Morris, Adrian Mozejko, Zhuoling Tian and Jody Watts.

For valuable comments on specific points or on portions of the draft text, I thank Sudeepa Abeysinghe, Gabriele Bammer, Lee Basham, Daniel Beckman, Stuart Blume, Elena Conis, Michelle Crino, Goodarz Danaei, Evelyne de Leeuw, Mark Diesendorf, Meryl Dorey, Don Eldridge, Kurtis Hagen, Jaron Harambam, David Hess, Pru Hobson-West, Graham Howard, Sue Curry Jansen, Tim Marchant, Sarah Wright Monod, Melissa Raven, Jennifer Reich, Patrick Stokes, Kenneth Thompson, Samantha Vanderslott, Kevin White, Trevor Wilson and half a dozen others who prefer to remain anonymous. None of these readers necessarily agrees with anything I've written. I especially appreciate those readers who generously offered comments despite reservations about my perspective.

I also thank the numerous colleagues, friends and correspondents who have shared with me their ideas, observations, information and opinions about the topics covered in this book. For me, it has been an experience of continual learning.

Glossary

AVN
A citizens' group critical of Australian government vaccination policy and supportive of choice in vaccination decisions. Formed in the mid 1990s by Meryl Dorey, after a few years the group's name became the Australian Vaccination Network. In 2014, it was forced to change its name, and changed it to the Australian Vaccination-skeptics Network, retaining the abbreviation AVN.

Fair Trading
A government agency in the state of New South Wales, responsible for incorporated associations.

HCCC
Health Care Complaints Commission, a government agency in the state of New South Wales set up to receive complaints about healthcare workers.

Meryl Dorey
Founder of the AVN and for many years its prime mover.

NSW
New South Wales, one of Australia's six states.

OLGR
Office of Liquor, Gaming and Racing, a government agency in the state of New South Wales, responsible for charitable status of incorporated associations.

Reasonable Hank
A blog run by Peter Tierney containing many attacks on vaccine critics.

SAVN
A citizens' group set up to silence and destroy the AVN and other vaccine critics. Established in 2009, its initial name was Stop the Australian Vaccination Network. In 2014 it changed its name to Stop the Australian (Anti)Vaccination Network.

1
Introduction

On 15 March 2010, I received a call from Meryl Dorey. Some sixteen years earlier, she had set up the precursor of the Australian Vaccination Network (AVN), a group critical of vaccination and the Australian government's vaccination policy, and supportive of parental choice concerning children's vaccination. She told me that starting in 2009, the AVN had been targeted by a group calling itself Stop the Australian Vaccination Network (SAVN), which was using tactics of verbal abuse, derogatory claims, censorship and complaints to attempt to shut down the AVN.[1]

Dorey's concerns resonated with two areas with which I had long been involved. Since the mid 1970s I had studied a variety of public scientific controversies, including nuclear power, pesticides, fluoridation, nuclear winter and the origin of AIDS.[2] In these sorts of controversies, the struggles between contending parties involve both power and knowledge.

---

1 The names of the AVN and SAVN have changed over the years. For details, see the glossary and chapter 5.

2 "Brian Martin: publications on scientific and technological controversies," http://www.bmartin.cc/pubs/controversy.html. Unless otherwise indicated, all URLs were accessed in February 2018.

The second area in which I'd long had a keen interest is suppression of dissent. I started studying this topic in the late 1970s. In a typical scenario, a scientist questions an orthodox position, for example on forestry — this is the dissent — and comes under attack, for example being censored, denied research funding, denied access to research materials, or dismissed. These methods of attack I called "suppression."[3]

Through my studies of scientific controversies, I discovered predictable patterns of suppression. Most commonly, when anyone with scientific credibility challenged orthodoxy through research, teaching or public statements, they were susceptible to reprisals from those in positions of authority. I documented numerous instances in the controversies over nuclear power, forestry, pesticides and fluoridation.

In each of these controversies, the dominant scientific position is aligned with groups with considerable power. For example, in the pesticide controversy, the dominant scientific position, that most pesticides are safe and beneficial, lines up with the interests of the chemical companies that produce pesticides. The climate change controversy, in contrast, is different in that the orthodox scientific position, that global warming is real and mostly caused by human activity, clashes with the interests of the most powerful groups affected, the coal, oil and gas industries.

---

3 "Brian Martin: publications on whistleblowing and suppression of dissent," http://www.bmartin.cc/pubs/supp.html

In most such public controversies, citizen campaigners are usually left alone. They are not considered to have much expertise or scientific credibility, so for them to speak out is less threatening to those with power. In a few cases, citizen campaigners have been targets when they are involved in direct action. For example, US forests campaigner Judi Bari was the target of a bomb attack. She had been prominent in leading direct action campaigns. Citizen activists who rely on more conventional methods such as writing letters, organising petitions, lobbying and joining rallies were unlikely to become targets of attack. Or so I thought, until Dorey's call.

On further investigation, I found that the AVN was a typical citizens' group presenting a minority view on a contested public policy.[4] It was like many other such vaccine-critical groups in various countries,[5] and was like groups on a range of other issues, from genetic engineering to climate change. Since its formation in the mid 1990s, it had used typical methods to present its views: a magazine, email lists, a website, submissions to official inquiries, letters to politicians, occasional rallies and so forth.

---

4 To say that a policy is contested is not to make a judgement about the merits of the cases for and against the policy.

5 Pru Hobson-West, "'Trusting blindly can be the biggest risk of all': organised resistance to childhood vaccination in the UK," *Sociology of Health & Illness*, Vol. 29, No. 2, 2007, pp. 198–215. I have adopted Hobson-West's useful expression "vaccine-critical group" and refer throughout to "vaccine critics." See chapter 3 for more on vaccine-critical groups.

What was different from the usual scenario was the creation of SAVN, which introduced a new dynamic into the debate. SAVN's agenda was to suppress public criticism of vaccination and specifically to destroy the AVN. No longer were the key issues just vaccination and vaccination policy. To these were added the question of whether it was possible to openly question vaccination and standard government vaccination policy without being subject to ridicule, abuse, complaints and censorship.

I've long been concerned about free speech, in particular the ability to express unpopular ideas without reprisals. For me, the attack on the AVN was an issue of free speech, and I decided to become involved on that basis.

Personally, I do not have strong views about vaccination. I have no children and have never made a decision about anyone else's vaccination. My interest in the vaccination issue is as a social scientist and defender of free speech.

In getting involved with the struggle between SAVN and the AVN, I had two goals. One was to offer ideas to participants for countering attacks and enabling free speech. My second goal was to gain and share insights about the dynamics of scientific controversy. The Australian vaccination debate promised to be a fruitful source of material. As it turned out, there was far more material involved than I anticipated. For me, it was a researcher's dream being in the middle of an evolving controversy in which amazingly diverse methods were deployed, many of them unusual or even unprecedented in the controversies with which I was familiar.

In chapter 2, I give a brief overview of the vaccination issue. Chapter 3 looks at vaccination in Australia and introduces the AVN and SAVN. Chapters 4 to 6 examine SAVN's attack techniques of denigration, harassment and censorship. Chapter 7 addresses some ways of defending. In the remaining chapters, I look at the bigger picture. Chapter 8 offers a number of wider perspectives on the struggle and chapter 9 looks at moral panics. The final chapter presents a few lessons from this analysis.

I've written this book to highlight the extraordinary range of methods used to curtail free speech in a public scientific controversy. Some readers will be most interested in how to resist these methods. Even for those who are fully supportive of current vaccination recommendations, it can be useful to understand free speech dynamics, because attacks on vaccine critics have the potential to be counterproductive. However, it is not obvious how best to intervene in the debate to foster a more respectful and productive discussion of the issues.

2
The vaccination issue

One of my primary aims in this book is to provide insights about struggles over free speech. The Australian public debate over vaccination happens to provide an extraordinary amount of rich material for understanding such struggles. To appreciate what is involved, it is not necessary to know a whole lot about vaccination, but it is useful to understand a few basics. In this chapter, I begin by explaining the rationale for vaccination, including both stimulation of immunity and the phenomenon of herd immunity. Then I outline the main points raised by critics of vaccination. This leads into a discussion of "absent viewpoints," which are ideas that are usually missing from the public debate because neither side can easily use them to advantage.

My account here is oriented to issues relevant to the Australian situation and omits many complexities. My generalisations about the stances of campaigners are based on years of reading commentary in news and social media as well as contact with individuals. Others might make different assessments.

Vaccination
Vaccination is a procedure designed to reduce the risk of infectious disease, such as polio, measles and whooping cough. It typically involves exposing a person to a small

dose of an agent designed to stimulate the person's immune system. The basic idea is that a limited exposure is enough to develop immunity so that you are not susceptible to the full-blown disease.[1]

The agent used to stimulate immunity is usually a version of the agent that causes the disease. For example, there are several variants of what is called the polio virus that are implicated in the development of the disease polio. Scientists, through experimentation, developed versions of the polio virus designed to stimulate immunity — the body's immune system recognises the alien invader virus and prepares defences against it — but not so strong that they actually cause polio. One method is to use killed versions of the virus, as in the Salk vaccine, named after pioneer polio researcher Jonas Salk. Another common method is to develop a live virus, but one genetically different so that it stimulates the immune system but doesn't cause the disease. The Sabin polio vaccine, named after pioneer polio researcher Albert Sabin, is a live virus vaccine. The live virus is weakened and changed, a process called "attenuation." When Sabin developed his vaccine during the 1950s, it was long before the emergence of genetic engineering. The attenuated strains were

---

[1] Sources presenting information about and the case for vaccination include F. E. Andre, R. Booy, H. L. Bock, et al., "Vaccination greatly reduces disease, disability, death and inequity worldwide," *Journal of the World Health Organization*, Vol. 86, No. 2, 2008, pp. 140–146; Paul A. Offit and Louis M. Bell, *Vaccines: What You Should Know*, 3rd edition (Hoboken, NJ: John Wiley, 2003); Stanley A. Plotkin, Walter A. Orenstein and Paul A. Offit, *Vaccines*, 6th edition (Elsevier, 2013).

developed by "passing" them through various species. For example, the virus would be given to chickens and then extracted from the chickens' faeces. In the passage through the chicken, the virus's genetic structure would be altered. This process would be repeated until the desired level of attenuation was reached. Today, more direct methods of genetic modification of viruses and bacteria can be used.

To understand the dynamics of the vaccination debate, you don't need to understand lots of technical details about vaccines. But it is useful to know that vaccines are designed to stimulate the immune system to prevent full-blown disease. When a one-year-old baby is given a measles vaccine, the goal is for the baby's immune system to be triggered so that if the child later is exposed to measles virus in "the wild" — for example by coming in contact with someone who has measles and is shedding the measles virus — then the child will not contract the disease. If a vaccine does this, it is said to "take." However, sometimes the vaccine does not stimulate increased immunity in an individual, even after receiving several doses. Vaccines can produce immunity in most or nearly all of those who receive them, but some percentage of individuals will not be immune. They have been vaccinated but not immunised.

Imagine that you've been exposed to an infectious disease, maybe mumps or chickenpox, and have become a carrier. Your body sheds viruses, and others you come in contact with are exposed to the virus. Suppose you go to a party where you are hugging and kissing your friends. If they are exposed to the virus, they might catch the disease

— but only if they have insufficient immunity. If everyone at the party is immune, no one will catch the disease. Suppose 48 of 50 people there are immune: two have low immunity, for whatever reason. Suppose you have close contact with ten others, exposing them to the virus. Depending on which ones they are, no one might catch the disease. At worst, the two with low immunity catch it. This is largely a matter of chance. It should be obvious that when fewer people have low immunity, it is less likely that you'll spread the disease.

When a disease has difficulty spreading because lots of people are immune, this is called herd immunity. The basic idea is that when enough individuals have immunity, this protects those who don't: the entire group or herd is protected.

Because each disease has a different level of infectiousness, the percentage of people with individual immunity needed to protect the community depends on the disease. For highly infectious diseases like measles and whooping cough, herd immunity requires something like 95% of individuals to be immune. For less infectious diseases like polio or hepatitis B, a lower percentage of population immunity is required. But any such percentage is only an approximation, because so much depends on chance. If you're contagious, you might go to a large party or attend a school and expose dozens or hundreds of others, or you might stay among a small circle of immune friends.

There are two basic sorts of herd immunity. It can be "natural" when most people have had the disease and developed immunity as a result. When speaking about vaccination, herd immunity usually refers to vaccine-induced herd immunity. Most individuals have been vaccinated and most of those vaccinated have developed immunity, so disease can't easily spread, because too few individuals are susceptible.

Herd immunity introduces a collective dimension to the issue of vaccination. By being vaccinated and becoming immune, you help to protect others who are not immune. Several groups are protected this way. Babies may lack immunity because their immune systems are undeveloped, and not have acquired immunity from their mothers. Some people have compromised immune systems, for example due to carrying HIV. There are people who have no immunity because they have never had the disease and they have not been vaccinated, or perhaps they were vaccinated but the vaccine didn't take: it didn't stimulate an adequate immune system response.

There are further complications. Viruses can evolve, changing their genetic structure, and thus elude the immune system. This is a special problem for the flu virus, which is constantly changing. Hence the flu vaccine needs to be different each year in anticipation of the most likely forms of the virus, and it seldom can protect against all strains. So the flu vaccine can only provide selective protection, against some strains but not others. There is a continuing struggle between the flu virus and its human opponents. Seen in evolutionary terms, the flu virus is trying to reproduce itself by finding susceptible hosts, and to do so it must mutate to escape host immune systems.

Behind every vaccination, there has been a vast amount of research, development and testing. Billions of dollars are spent to develop vaccines and implement vaccination programmes. In medical journals, there are thousands of articles about every aspect of vaccination, including virus genetics, the distribution of disease, immune system function, and education of health professionals. Within hospitals and other health system organisations, there is an immense amount of training and accumulated practical skills. Within pharmaceutical companies, there is practical knowledge of how to produce, verify, distribute and document vaccines. Having a vaccination is to be part of a huge industrial enterprise.

Vaccination is also a dominant belief system. It can be called a paradigm: it is a way of understanding the world, shaping perceptions, maintained within a "thought collective."[2] To call something a belief system is not a criticism but rather a description. It calls attention to the way beliefs perpetuate themselves. If infectious disease is a problem, vaccination is seen as a solution — not the only solution, but an important one. Researchers are keen on improving current vaccines and on developing new ones to tackle additional diseases. Practitioners want to ensure that vaccination rates are high, in order to minimise the ravages of deadly diseases.

---

2 Two classic references are Ludwik Fleck, *Genesis and Development of a Scientific Fact* (Chicago: University of Chicago Press, 1979; originally published in 1935), on thought collectives, and Thomas S. Kuhn, *The Structure of Scientific Revolutions* (Chicago: University of Chicago Press, 1962), on paradigms. There is a huge body of subsequent research and commentary, especially about paradigms.

Although it is possible to refer to the vaccination paradigm, a dominant set of beliefs and practices, it is only unified over some essentials, and there is considerable disagreement about various aspects of belief and implementation. Some countries differ from others in the number and type of vaccines recommended. For example, in Germany, 44 doses of vaccines are recommended before the age of 2; in Japan, the figure is 34.[3] To a degree, this can be attributed to differences in health conditions, but it also reflects different assessments by health authorities, who may judge that for a particular vaccine the benefits are not sufficiently great to outweigh the costs.

Disagreements occur about how vaccination is to be promoted. Should the government subsidise the cost, perhaps making some vaccines free to users? Should financial incentives be given to doctors to maintain high vaccination rates among their patients? Should children be required to be vaccinated before attending school? Should parents be allowed to exempt their children from vaccination requirements on conscientious or religious grounds? These and many other questions can divide supporters of vaccination. They agree that vaccination is a worthwhile, indeed vital, public health measure, but may disagree about the details.

---

3 See "Calling the shots," an infographic published by *BMJ*, "Visualising childhood vaccination schedules across G8 countries," 2015, http://www.bmj.com/content/351/bmj.h5966/infographic. The figures in the text were current as of March 2017.

Vaccination criticism
In the face of this dominant paradigm and massive enterprise, there are critics and opponents of vaccination.[4] They question the benefits, raise concern about the risks, and support choice in whether to vaccinate. Like proponents, there are many differences among critics. Also like proponents, they regularly refer to scientific research that supports their views.[5]

Many critics say that the benefits of vaccination have been oversold. Vaccination is regularly cited as one of the most significant health measures in the past century. Critics say that the huge death rates from most infectious diseases, such as measles and diphtheria, had declined dramatically prior to the introduction of mass vaccination. The implication is that much of the decline was due to improved sanitation, nutrition and living standards, and that death rates would have continued to decline even without mass vaccination, as in the case of scarlet fever, previously a major killer but now rare even though there is no vaccine.

---

4 See for example Louise Kuo Habakus and Mary Holland (eds.), *Vaccine Epidemic: How Corporate Greed, Biased Science, and Coercive Government Threaten Our Human Rights, Our Health, and Our Children* (New York: Skyhorse, 2011); Richard Halvorsen, *The Truth about Vaccines: How We Are Used as Guinea Pigs without Knowing It* (London: Gibson Square, 2007).

5 For readable summaries of articles from the scientific literature that raise questions about vaccination, see Neil Z. Miller, *Miller's Review of Critical Vaccine Studies* (Santa Fe, NM: New Atlantean Press, 2016).

Nearly all critics raise concern about the adverse effects of vaccination, citing seizures and other immediate effects and long-term consequences including disability and death. Most controversially, critics raise concerns about vaccines contributing to autism spectrum disorders. Critics refer to studies showing that only a small proportion of adverse effects are officially reported.

Most critics argue in favour of parental choice in making decisions about whether and when their children are vaccinated. Some critics question the theory of vaccine-based herd immunity,[6] but in any case the argument for choice runs head-on against arguments that vaccination is an ethical imperative because it protects others.

Criticism of vaccination is a minority position. In many countries, vaccination rates are high, with 90% or more of children receiving all the recommended vaccines by the scheduled times. This suggests that most parents

---

6 For example, Tetyana Obukhanych says that for most communicable viral diseases, vaccine-induced immunity wears off, so only some adults are immune, hence herd immunity doesn't apply: not enough of the herd is immune. She says the reason why there are so few outbreaks is due to lack of *"endemic viral exposure."* Basically, when a virus has been mostly eliminated from a region, that is what protects people, not herd immunity. Outbreaks can occur when the virus is imported, even in communities with 100% childhood vaccinations. In contrast, when a virus is endemic — widely prevalent — then attaining herd immunity can contribute to eliminating it. See Tetyana Obukhanych, *Vaccine Illusion: How Vaccination Compromises Our Natural Immunity and What We Can Do to Regain Our Health* (US: Tetyana Obukhanych, 2012), pp. 105–107.

believe vaccination is beneficial or at least do not want to challenge the advice of their doctors or health authorities. Very few doctors, researchers or health officials make public criticisms of vaccination. There are a few, though, and they help sustain citizen opposition.

Most vaccine critics share several basic concerns: that the benefits of vaccines are exaggerated, that the risks are greater than officially stated, and that individual choice is vital. Outside of this, there is considerable diversity of views. For example, some parents are selective vaccinators: they want their children to have some recommended vaccines but not others. Then there are those opposed to vaccination altogether.

Absent viewpoints[7]
In the public debate over vaccination, the two sides become polarised, in rigid positions at opposite ends of a spectrum of belief. This is typical of scientific controversies, and applies to debates over nuclear power, pesticides, genetic modification and others. What happens is that each side probes for weak points in the other side, looking for "concessions" that can be used to support their own case. The result is that each side becomes reluctant to express any doubt about core beliefs.

Potentially, there can be a range of beliefs about three different aspects of the vaccination issue.

---

7 An alternative term is "missing middle." However, this might be taken to imply that all views are located on a one-dimensional continuum, whereas actual views potentially can be anywhere in a multi-dimensional conceptual space.

• Benefits. At one end, every recommended vaccine is beneficial to nearly everyone. At the other end, no recommended vaccine is beneficial to anyone.

• Risks. At one end, the risks of vaccination are rare. At the other end, the risks are significant.

• Ethics. At one end, there is an ethical imperative for universal vaccination. At the other end, there is a right for individual choice.

Most vocal proponents are at the same end of each of these spectrums and most vocal critics are at the other end. It is rare to hear anyone say the risks are sizeable, far greater than usually acknowledged, yet still say the benefits are greater than the risks. The reason is that any proponent who says the risks are significant is likely to be quoted by opponents — and this is not a comfortable position.

Much of the public debate, carried out in the mass and social media, treats vaccination as a single undifferentiated measure, either supported or opposed.[8] Campaigners in this public debate do sometimes talk about different vaccines, but seldom do they present separate arguments about specific vaccines. The reason, presumably, is that examining the case for or against specific vaccines would undermine the general argument.

A central argument for mass vaccination is that the community benefits from herd immunity. In Australia, there is an aspirational target of having 95% of children

---

8 Discussions in scientific and clinical forums can be much more nuanced.

fully vaccinated.[9] This is considered more than enough to achieve herd immunity for measles, the most infectious vaccine-preventable disease, and therefore is enough to prevent transmission of all other vaccine-preventable diseases. Vaccination coverage considerably lower than 95% would be adequate to provide herd immunity for some diseases, for example polio. Then there is tetanus, which is not contagious at all: there is no benefit to an individual due to others having immunity.

The implication is that target vaccination coverage could be different for different vaccines. For measles, there might be a high target and special measures to encourage vaccination. For less contagious diseases like polio and mumps, targets could be lower and opting out could be made much easier. Of course, people could be urged to vaccinate for the personal protection provided. The difference is that high vaccination rates would be justified by herd immunity arguments only for some diseases.

So why are there targets for the proportion of children being *fully* vaccinated — namely having all recommended vaccines at the scheduled times — rather than separate targets for different vaccines? The possibility of having different target vaccination rates for different diseases is never discussed openly by health departments, but the reason is easy to see: it would be an administrative and public relations nightmare. Some parents might seek exemptions for specific vaccines, and record keeping

---

9 Australian Government, Department of Health, Immunise Australia Program, "Immunisation coverage targets," 16 February 2016, http://goo.gl/eWcVkW.

would be more complex. More importantly, though, the vaccination message would be muddled. Rather than saying to parents, "Now's the time for your child's MMR, and then it's time for polio" and so forth, the message might be "It's really important that your child receives the measles vaccine on schedule, but for tetanus it's less urgent."

The bundling of different vaccines into a single concept of vaccination is aided by multivalent vaccines, in which two more vaccines are combined in a single injection, for example measles, mumps and rubella in MMR and diphtheria, pertussis and tetanus in DPT. This means a parent can't come along and say, "Let's have measles and whooping cough (pertussis), but postpone the others."

Another option missing from the public debate is the possibility of replacing repeat vaccinations with antibody testing. Children are given repeat doses of several vaccines, for example measles and hepatitis B. This is not because the immunity wears off quickly, but rather to ensure that nearly everyone who is vaccinated develops immunity. With live virus vaccines, most recipients develop long-term immunity after a single exposure. However, for various reasons, a small number do not. To increase the percentage of vaccine recipients who develop immunity to measles, a second or sometimes a third vaccination is recommended, even though it is superfluous for maybe 90% of those who receive it, because their immune systems have already been primed.

Whether a vaccine produces immunity is normally determined by an antibody test: has the person's body developed antibodies to the virus? So, for those who would prefer not to have an unnecessary repeat dose of a vaccine but otherwise subscribe to the vaccination paradigm, it should be satisfactory to have an antibody test with a positive result.

However, this option is not available. It is easy to see why: it is an extra administrative hassle and, more importantly, it might encourage people to ask more questions about vaccination. Keeping track of both vaccinations and antibody test results would be an administrative burden, though hardly difficult. The raising of questions is more important. Most people probably believe that children need all the recommended repeat doses of vaccines such as measles. To offer the option of antibody testing after the first dose might make more people realise that vaccination does not guarantee immunity, something seldom mentioned by health authorities. It might also make people ask, "Why is antibody testing an option? Does that mean there's an avoidable risk from being vaccinated?" On the other side, few critics of vaccination are keen on antibody testing.[10]

Robert Sears, a paediatrician working in California, describes himself as pro-vaccine. He believes that addressing parents' concerns is far better than stigmatising the parents, and he would rather children be partially vaccinated or have their vaccinations spaced out than for them to remain unvaccinated. To that end, he wrote *The Vaccine Book,* a compendium of information about each

---

10 Some critics say antibodies are due to exposure to a virus and do not necessarily provide immunity to disease.

vaccine in the US schedule.[11] There is a chapter on each vaccine and the disease it prevents, telling whether the disease is common, serious and treatable, describing how the vaccine is made, giving the brands available, listing side effects and giving both reasons to have the vaccine and reasons why some parents decide not to have it. For some vaccines, Sears' own advice is to deviate from the standard schedule. For example, for mothers and families not affected by hepatitis, he suggests that the hep B vaccine need not be administered at birth, but can be postponed.

Sears is thus pro-vaccine but not in conformity with government recommendations. In particular, by addressing each vaccine separately, he deviated from the approach dominant in vaccination policy. Because he questioned the official recommendations, Sears came under attack from Paul Offit, the most prominent pro-vaccination figure in the US, and other proponents.[12] On the other hand, leading vaccine-critical groups did not recruit Sears to be one of their spokespeople. Sears tried to adopt a position between

---

11 Robert W. Sears, *The Vaccine Book: Making the Right Decision for Your Child,* 2nd edition (New York: Little, Brown, 2011).

12 Paul A. Offit and Charlotte A. Moser, "The problem with Dr Bob's alternative vaccine schedule," *Pediatrics,* Vol. 123, No. 1, January 2009, pp. e164–e169. See also Steven Novella, "Paul Offit takes on Robert Sears," *Science-Based Medicine,* 7 January 2009, https://sciencebasedmedicine.org/paul-offit-takes-on-robert-sears/.

the two sides in the vaccination controversy, but it was not comfortable.[13]

In the 1990s, Andrew Wakefield was a medical researcher studying gastrointestinal syndromes at the Royal Free Hospital in London.[14] He was contacted by a mother who reported that her child's gastrointestinal problems and regression to autism seemed connected to a recent vaccination. Wakefield was intrigued and investigated further. In 1998, he and a dozen colleagues at the hospital published a paper in *The Lancet,* a leading medical journal. The paper was a case review study of a dozen children. It did not say there was a link between vaccination and autism, but rather said the possibility of a link should be further investigated. In a related media conference, Wakefield recommended use of a single

---

13 For informative discussions of Sears' role in the vaccination debate, see Mark A. Largent, *Vaccine: The Debate in Modern America* (Baltimore, MD: Johns Hopkins University Press, 2012), p. 167, and Jennifer A. Reich, *Calling the Shots: Why Parents Reject Vaccines* (New York: New York University Press, 2016), pp. 175–184.

14 Writing about Wakefield is highly polarised, so it is difficult to find accounts that are informative and balanced. One useful treatment is by Mark A. Largent, *Vaccine: The Debate in Modern America* (Baltimore, MD: Johns Hopkins University Press, 2012), pp. 94–137. I discuss Largent's book in chapter 8. For my own commentary, see "On the suppression of vaccination dissent," *Science and Engineering Ethics,* Vol. 21, No. 1, 2015, pp. 143–157, http://www.bmartin.cc/pubs/15see.html. My brief account here omits many details.

measles vaccine rather than the measles-mumps-rubella (MMR) triple vaccine.

The paper in *The Lancet* became a huge media story, leading many parents to avoid the MMR vaccine. Not long afterwards, the British government limited access to the single measles vaccine.[15] Wakefield was blamed for the decline in vaccination rates and increase in disease.[16] In 2004, journalist Brian Deer made allegations against Wakefield,[17] leading the General Medical Council to hold an inquiry and find Wakefield and two of his co-authors guilty of conflict of interest and abuse of children who were research subjects. Wakefield and co-author John Walker-Smith had their medical registrations withdrawn and the editor of *The Lancet* retracted their 1998 paper. After this, Wakefield's name and the retraction of the article in *The Lancet* were regularly invoked by proponents of vaccination as showing there is no link between

---

15 "Q&A: MMR and the single vaccine," *BBC News*, 4 January 2001, http://news.bbc.co.uk/2/hi/health/1100489.stm.

16 Prominent commentator Ben Goldacre, *Bad Science* (London: Fourth Estate, 2009), pp. 290–331, instead blames media coverage for the decline in vaccination rates. According to F. Edward Yazbak, "Measles in the United Kingdom: the 'Wakefield factor'," *Vaccination News*, 2010, https://www.vaccinationnews.org/measles-united-kingdom-wakefield-factor, there were fewer recorded cases of measles in Britain in the five years after Wakefield et al.'s 1998 *Lancet* paper than in the five years before, and no deaths.

17 Brian Deer, "Revealed: MMR research scandal," *Sunday Times*, 22 February 2004.

vaccination and autism, with the further implication that any scientific criticism of vaccination is wrong or even fraudulent.

The condemnation of Wakefield has been extreme and persistent. He is widely reported as being found guilty of scientific fraud. However, although Deer later made allegations of fraud, published in the *British Medical Journal*, they have been contested.[18] The General Medical Council, in deregistering Wakefield, did not allege scientific fraud.

Wakefield has been categorised as "anti-vax"[19] and used as an example of what is wrong with opposition to vaccination. However, Wakefield then and ever since has not been an opponent of vaccination. His concern is about the MMR vaccine and he continues to support single vaccines for measles, mumps and rubella.[20] Wakefield, like Sears, adopted a position deviating from the official vaccination policy.

---

18 Brian Deer, "Piltdown medicine: the missing link between MMR and autism," *BMJ Blogs,* 6 January 2011. For an independent analysis contesting Deer's claims, see David L. Lewis, *Science for Sale* (New York: Skyhorse, 2014), pp. 111–147.

19 On Wikipedia he is categorised as an "anti-vaccination activist."

20 For Wakefield's perspective, see Andrew J. Wakefield, *Callous Disregard: Autism and Vaccines — The Truth behind a Tragedy* (New York: Skyhorse Publishing, 2010) and, more concisely and accessibly, "Dr Andrew Wakefield deals with allegations," *Vaxxed the Movie,* 2016, http://bit.ly/2BSLoJT.

The absent viewpoints in the public vaccination debate thus encompass a number of options, including disease-specific vaccination targets, antibody testing, spacing out vaccinations, and using single rather than multivalent vaccines, each of them with different implications for different children. That such options are seldom raised in the public debate highlights the rigidities of the positions on each side. An option in between seems like a concession to the proponents or the opponents or even both.[21] For proponents, it is far easier to sell a fixed vaccination schedule, aiming at the same coverage for all vaccines and with the same expectations for every child. For opponents, it is easier to question vaccination in general than to say something like "Most vaccinations are beneficial most of the time, but several are questionable and their risks may outweigh their benefits for some individuals in some circumstances."

Vaccination rhetoric

As noted, vaccination does not guarantee the development of immunity. Nevertheless, in everyday parlance, the terms "vaccination" and "immunisation" are often used interchangeably.

---

21 Jacob Heller, *The Vaccine Narrative* (Nashville, TN: Vanderbilt University Press, 2008), says the polarisation of viewpoints makes it difficult to study vaccination from a social or political perspective. Because studies can be castigated or co-opted, "The overall result is a chilling effect on open discussion and research about vaccines; one must be for them or against them, whole hog." (p. 23). See chapter 8 for more on *The Vaccine Narrative*.

A common slogan by proponents is "Vaccination saves lives." Even accepting that the sum total of vaccinations leads to less loss of life from disease than not having any vaccinations, the slogan implicitly groups all vaccines into one package, thereby obscuring the possibility that some vaccines save lives but others do not, depending on the time, place and populations involved.

Vaccination proponents often refer to infectious diseases as vaccine-preventable diseases, thereby affirming through language the effectiveness of vaccination. On the other hand, the expression "vaccine-preventable disease" also distinguishes such diseases from others for which there is no vaccine. In some circumstances "infectious disease" is more stable in meaning: when a new vaccine is developed, a disease can become vaccine-preventable whereas previously it was not. AIDS, for example, is not currently vaccine-preventable. But there are also vaccines in development for diseases that are not contagious, so the expression "infectious disease" has its limitations.

Proponents commonly refer to critics as anti-vaxxers, but I have never seen a careful definition of this term. Does it include only people who oppose all vaccinations? Does it include people who selectively vaccinate? Does it include people who are fully vaccinated themselves, and have their children fully vaccinated, but who voice criticisms of particular vaccines? Applying the label "anti-vaxxer" often serves to dismiss anything a person has to say. It is a stigmatising term.

Even more stigmatising is "vaccination denier."[22] This trades on the more common expression "Holocaust denier," referring to someone who believes the Holocaust, the genocide of the Jews under Hitler, did not occur. More generally, "denier" refers to someone who rejects something that is unarguably true. "Denier," like the term "anti-vaxxer," puts every critic into a single category so that differences in belief are skated over, and moreover implies that the only truth is on the other side.

Interestingly, there is no standard term for those who subscribe to the standard set of vaccination recommendations. "Believer" would not be flattering, as it might suggest support is based on belief rather than scientific fact. In the climate change debate, sceptics about global warming sometimes refer to those subscribing to the mainstream view held by climate scientists as "alarmists." However, in the vaccination debate, it would probably be more accurate to refer to partisans on both sides as alarmists: supporters raise the alarm about the hazards of infectious diseases whereas critics raise the alarm about the hazards of vaccination.

Proponents of vaccination often say that parents should trust the experts, namely doctors, medical authorities and government health departments. Often this is accompanied by an assumption that vaccination is a scientific issue, so the views of scientific experts should be heeded. However, scientific controversies are never just

---

22 See my discussion in "Debating vaccination," *Living Wisdom*, Issue 8, February 2011, pp. 14–40, http://goo.gl/3GkMPz, at pp. 24–26.

about science, and the vaccination controversy is not an exception. This is obvious enough when concerns about herd immunity are raised: the collective benefits of vaccination are not just about science but also about ethics. Likewise, a key argument by critics, that people should have a choice about whether to vaccinate, without coercion, is about liberty, again involving ethics. So when proponents say that science supports vaccination, this is actually presenting a non-scientific decision, namely about policy, as if it were purely about science.

A full treatment of the issues concerning vaccination would cover many dimensions and options, and would bring in various sorts of evidence and a range of arguments. The public debate, especially as conducted in the mass media and social media, misses much of this complexity. Furthermore, partisans usually stick to their own favoured claims and angles. For example, proponents seldom mention the importance of individual choice while critics seldom accept the benefits of herd immunity. The absent viewpoints are those left off the public agenda due to the extreme polarisation of the controversy.

Goals and motivations
It is important to recognise, and to acknowledge, that in the public vaccination debate the two opposed sides share a common goal: to benefit public health and, more specifically, children's health. What differentiates the two sides is not the goal but rather the method to help achieve it, namely whether vaccination is the most appropriate means. In chapter 9 I comment on the way the fixation on

vaccination as either solution or problem can overshadow other means of improving health.

Related to goals are the motivations of the leading public campaigners. On each side, some campaigners attribute bad motives to their opponents. Some critics of vaccination see proponents as being driven by money and careers, with funding by pharmaceutical companies believed to shape beliefs and actions. Proponents are more likely to see critics as misguided, as being driven by false beliefs. It is important to note that many campaigners seek to engage in debate respectfully and refrain from attributing bad motives to opponents.

My working assumption in analysing the vaccination debate is that all participants have the best of intentions. In most cases, this means that ultimately they are concerned with children's lives. Of course, individuals can have baser motives, such as obtaining a higher salary, looking good in the eyes of peers or gaining satisfaction by attacking opponents. However, whether such motives are consciously acknowledged is another matter. Studies of perpetrators of the most heinous crimes show that nearly all of them feel justified in what they do.[23]

There is a widespread presumption that when people do bad things, they must have bad motives, a feature of thinking called correspondence bias.[24] For example,

---

23 Roy F. Baumeister, *Evil: Inside Human Violence and Cruelty* (New York: Freeman, 1997).

24 See for example Nicholas Epley, *Mindwise: how we understand what others think, believe, feel and want* (London: Penguin, 2014), p. 142.

following the 9/11 attacks, President George W. Bush and many US citizens believed that the attackers hated America and its freedoms.[25] They saw the action — a horrific attack— and assumed that the goals and motivations of the attackers corresponded with it. Actually, the goals of al Qaeda were different, a central one being the removal of Western troops from Saudi Arabia.[26]

The same psychological dynamics are involved in the vaccination debate. When those on the other side are perceived to be doing something wrong, their motives are assumed to correspond to their actions. When vaccine critics are believed to be endangering children's lives, vaccine proponents see them as malevolent, and when proponents attempt to silence critics, many of the critics assume the proponents are motivated by hate.

Conclusion

Support for vaccination is the overwhelmingly dominant position, contested by a small number of critics. The debate is highly polarised because opponents may exploit any concession from the standard line, seeing it as an admission of weakness. The result is that neither side welcomes intermediate positions, which are largely

---

25 Ziauddin Sardar and Merryl Wyn Davies, *Why Do People Hate America?* (Cambridge: Icon, 2002).

26 Robert Pape, *Dying to Win: The Strategic Logic of Suicide Terrorism* (New York: Random House, 2005). For an analysis of 9/11 using the concept of correspondence bias, see Max Abrahms, "Why terrorism does not work," *International Security*, Vol. 31, No. 2, 2006, pp. 42–78, http://goo.gl/SPM456.

missing from the public debate. One manifestation of these absent viewpoints is that the debate is primarily carried out using the blanket term "vaccination" rather than in terms of individual vaccines.

Some campaigners on each side apply stigmatising labels to their opponents. It is important to remember that campaigners share a common goal — health, especially children's health — and differ only in their preferred means to achieve it.

3
The vaccination debate in Australia

The Australian government, via its health departments, promotes mass vaccination. Drawing on expert advice, recommendations are made about vaccines and vaccination schedules, most of which are similar to recommendations in other high-income countries. The Australian government began introducing vaccination for the general population in the 1950s and 1960s, and added a great number of additional vaccinations in the 1990s and thereafter.[1] It begins with hepatitis B at birth, then at two months eight vaccines (hepatitis B, diphtheria, tetanus, pertussis, haemophilus influenzae type b, polio, pneumococcal conjugate and rotavirus), and so on for later ages.

Government endorsement combined with support from nearly all doctors and other health practitioners has led to widespread public acceptance of vaccination. Furthermore, the government has introduced measures to encourage universal vaccination, for example offering vaccines free of charge. (The government pays the manufacturers.)

---

1 See Australian Government, Department of Health, Immunise Australia Program, National Immunisation Program Schedule.

Vaccination rates in Australia have been high for many years.[2] A typical figure is that 92% of children are fully vaccinated, namely have had all the recommended vaccines by the scheduled times.[3] The percentage varies a bit across the country. Some of the areas with lower average vaccination rates are referred to in the media as "hot spots" and are presumed to carry a higher risk of infectious diseases.

The high vaccination rates are stable: they have not changed much in recent years.[4] The high rates have been maintained even with the introduction of additional vaccines in the schedule. From this perspective, it can be said that promoters of vaccination have been highly successful in achieving their aims. Of course, it is always possible to say that vaccination rates should be higher still, and that special efforts are needed to prevent outbreaks and declines in coverage in particular populations and areas.

---

2 Frank H. Beard, Brynley P. Hull, Julie Leask, Aditi Dey and Peter B. McIntyre, "Trends and Patterns in Vaccination Objection, Australia, 2002–2013," *Medical Journal of Australia*, Vol. 204, No. 7, 18 April 2016, pp. 275.e1–275.e6.

3 There are many complications. Figures are calculated for children aged one, two and five, and vary somewhat from year to year. Furthermore, the definition of "fully immunised" can change over time. See for example Brynley P. Hull et al., "Immunisation coverage annual report, 2014," *Communicable Diseases Intelligence*, Vol. 41, No. 1, 2017, pp. E68–E90.

4 Beard et al., 2016, op. cit.

Parents and vaccination

Proponents of vaccination are especially concerned about parents whose children are not fully vaccinated according to the government's schedule. However, it is misleading to divide parents into being either for or against vaccination. A more nuanced classification is needed.

Parents whose children are fully vaccinated can be called vaccination-compliant: they follow the advice of health professionals. Some of these parents simply do what their doctor recommends, without question. Others, though, search out information and become informed about arguments on both sides, and decide to have their children fully vaccinated. So the category vaccination-compliant includes a range of attitudes and levels of understanding.

For parents whose children are not fully vaccinated, there are three main categories. First are parents opposed to all vaccines, who can be called vaccine refusers.

Second are parents who decide to have their children partially vaccinated or vaccinated on a non-standard schedule. For example, they might select pertussis but not polio. They might choose single vaccines of measles, mumps and rubella rather than the triple vaccine MMR.[5] They might choose to have a single dose of MMR vaccine and not a second one. They might space out the vaccines that are given, so their children eventually obtain all the recommended vaccines but not as soon as provided in the

---

5 In many countries, single vaccines for measles, mumps and rubella are not available. Still, there may be other options for having fewer rather than more vaccines at a time.

government schedule. Or they might adopt more than one of these deviations from the recommended schedule. These parents have been called vaccine-hesitant. They accept some vaccinations but choose to deviate from the standard path.

There is a third category of parents whose children are not fully vaccinated. Parents in this group support vaccination or have no objections, but encounter obstacles that prevent their children from being fully vaccinated. The obstacles include childhood illness, limited access to transportation, and parents' unawareness or forgetfulness about appointments, vaccination schedules or vaccination status.[6]

In Australia, vaccine refusers are the smallest group of parents whose children are not fully vaccinated. Some proponents argue that efforts to increase vaccination coverage should give most attention to the third group, the parents facing obstacles.[7]

The AVN

In a number of countries, there are groups critical of vaccination. Typically they are composed of citizens without advanced qualifications though, as in a number of

---

6 Matthew E. Falagas and Effie Zarkadoulia, "Factors associated with suboptimal compliance to vaccinations in children in developed countries: a systematic review," *Current Medical Research and Opinion,* Vol. 24, No. 6, 2008, pp. 1719–1741.

7 Frank H. Beard, Julie Leask and Peter B. McIntyre, "No Jab, No Pay and vaccine refusal in Australia: the jury is out," *Medical Journal of Australia,* Vol. 206, No. 9, 15 May 2017, pp. 381–384.

such issues, it is possible for citizen campaigners to develop sophisticated understandings of technical matters without being professional practitioners in the field.[8] Aligned with these groups are a few doctors and scientists who are openly critical of vaccination or whose research lends support to critics.[9]

These vaccine-critical groups typically rely mainly on conventional campaigning methods: producing leaflets, magazines and websites; holding group meetings; giving talks; hosting public meetings; organising visits by noteworthy critics; seeking media coverage; meeting with politicians; writing letters to government officials and making submissions to government inquiries; and sometimes participating in election campaigning. In some cases they may hold rallies and other forms of public protest. Compared to some of the direct action tactics used by peace and environmental groups, such as blockades, entry to restricted areas, and sabotage, contemporary vaccine-critical groups have mostly operated at the conventional, non-disruptive end of the activist spectrum. Their methods are designed to change public opinion and

---

8 Steven Epstein, *Impure Science: AIDS, Activism, and the Politics of Knowledge* (Berkeley: University of California Press, 1996).

9 As noted in chapter 1, I refer throughout to "vaccine critics," inspired by the term "vaccine-critical group" introduced by Pru Hobson-West, "'Trusting blindly can be the biggest risk of all': organised resistance to childhood vaccination in the UK," *Sociology of Health & Illness*, Vol. 29, No. 2, 2007, pp. 198–215.

influence political decision-making through provision of information and showing their concern.

Members of vaccine-critical groups are drawn from a range of occupations. Some individuals have personal experience with injuries from vaccines, most commonly their own children. Others express concerns about vaccination to their doctors and, as a result of being treated arrogantly, become more sceptical. Yet others read about problems with vaccination, investigate further, and discover the existence of groups sharing their concerns. There has not been a great deal of study of vaccine-critical groups, but the available evidence suggests they are similar to citizen groups on a range of issues. There is an overlap between members of vaccine-critical groups and people who are called vaccine-hesitant, namely having some concerns or reservations about vaccination, some of whom deviate from the recommended vaccination schedule. There are many more vaccine-hesitant parents than members of vaccine-critical groups.

In Australia in the mid 1990s, Meryl Dorey set up a group critical of vaccination. She did this after her son experienced adverse reactions to vaccines. The group eventually took the name Australian Vaccination Network or AVN.[10] Dorey had enormous energy and propelled the AVN into becoming the most significant vaccine-critical group in Australia. By the year 2009, it had some 2000 members, ran a large website, sold a variety of merchandise (especially books), produced a glossy magazine

---

10 The AVN changed its name in 2014. See the glossary and the discussion in chapter 5.

called *Living Wisdom* that covered a range of alternative health topics, and was frequently reported in the media.

Subscribing to *Living Wisdom* automatically meant becoming a member of the AVN, so the 2000 members actually were 2000 subscribers. The number of these active in the group was far smaller. The AVN was an incorporated body, with a constitution, elected committee members and an annual general meeting, as is typical of numerous other such organisations. Dorey was the driving force and most commonly in the public eye, with other committee members taking supporting roles, usually in the background. Subscriptions and sales of products brought in enough money to pay some office staff and pay Dorey for her work editing *Living Wisdom*.

The AVN was just one of several Australian vaccine-critical groups,[11] but by the 2000s it had become the most prominent. Yet despite its activity and public visibility, it seemed to have little impact on vaccination policy. New vaccines were added to the government's schedule. As noted, vaccination rates remained high and stable. The vaccination debate also seemed stable, in the sense that health departments and leaders of the medical profession dominated vaccination policy and most members of the public supported vaccination despite persistent criticism

---

11 Other Australian vaccine-critical groups established in the 1990s include Vaccination Information Serving Australia (key figure: Kathy Scarborough), Vaccination Information Service (key figure: Bronwyn Hancock) and Vaccination Awareness and Information Service (key figure: Stephanie Messenger). Some group names have changed over the years.

from the AVN and other vaccine-critical groups. This is the sort of configuration found in many other countries.

SAVN

As discussed in chapter 1, in 2009 the dynamics of the Australian vaccination debate changed dramatically. The reason was the formation of a pro-vaccination group with the express purpose of discrediting and destroying the AVN. The group's name was Stop the Australian Vaccination Network or SAVN.[12] The Australian vaccination struggle was converted to a massive attack by SAVN against the AVN, with the AVN struggling to survive. One of my main purposes in this book is learning from SAVN's attack.

The events leading to the formation of SAVN involved the death of a baby from pertussis. According to its own self-description, SAVN was set up in 2009

> ... when Australian Vaccination Network (AVN) supporters harassed a grieving family and AVN President Ms Meryl Dorey demanded the baby's medical records from the Health Service ... [13]

Dorey gives a very different account. Concerning these events, I have not attempted to reconcile the wildly diver-

---

12 SAVN changed its name in 2014. See the glossary and the discussion in chapter 5.

13 Stop the Australian (Anti)Vaccination Network, "About," https://www.facebook.com/pg/stopavn/about/, accessed 7 July 2017.

gent accounts by SAVNers, Dorey and others.[14] Suffice it to say that some people believed Dorey behaved badly and this was the trigger or rationale for initiating a campaign to destroy the AVN.

SAVN is best described as a network or amorphous group built around a Facebook page. Technically, SAVN has no membership, only Facebook friends. The administrators of the Facebook page might be considered its core figures, roughly corresponding to office bearers in a more formal organisation. A number of SAVN members run their own separate blogs. Most prominent of these is "Reasonable Hank," run by Peter Tierney, one of SAVN's Facebook administrators. A Reasonable Hank blog post often leads to comments on the SAVN Facebook page.

---

14 Among the accounts addressing events surrounding the death of Dana McCaffery are (in chronological order) Maggie, "Toni McCaffery has had enough," *The Sceptics' Book of Pooh-Pooh*, 18 June 2009, http://scepticsbook.com/2009/06/18/toni-mccaffery-has-had-enough/; Meryl Dorey, "Why I did what I did — why I do what I do," *No Compulsory Vaccination*, 14 February 2010, http://nocompulsoryvaccination.com/2010/02/14/why-i-did-what-i-did-why-i-do-what-i-do/; Meryl Dorey, "A grieving family and baseless accusations," *No Compulsory Vaccination*, 30 July 2010, http://nocompulsoryvaccination.com/2010/07/30/a-grieving-family-and-baseless-accusations/; Peter Tierney, "Meryl Dorey: when is repeating a lie about a grieving family okay?", *Reasonable Hank*, 24 June 2012, https://reasonablehank.com/2012/06/24/meryl-dorey-when-is-repeating-a-lie-about-a-grieving-family-okay/; Jane Hansen, "Grieving mother Toni McCaffery was vilified by anti-vaccination bullies," *Daily Telegraph*, 26 May 2013.

It is not easy to characterise SAVNers. Only some of them are readily identifiable offline, for example Ken McLeod, Sue Ieraci and Rachael Dunlop. The identity of Peter Tierney is unclear, and some have speculated that Reasonable Hank's activities are actually the work of several people. In the online world, identities can be masked. A recurring issue is the presence of contributors with fake identities, called sock puppets. In some cases, outrageous statements might be made to discredit the side apparently making them. In one instance, a provocative contributor to SAVN's Facebook page was disowned by both the AVN and SAVN.

Since 2009, the primary confrontation in the Australian vaccination debate has been between SAVN and the AVN, and it will be the focus of much of my attention. SAVN has gradually increased its influence, inducing journalists, government agencies, doctors and politicians to join its campaign against the AVN. Meanwhile, SAVN has always seen the AVN as just one of its targets, though the central one. Other targets have included vaccination critics separate from the AVN, and homoeopaths and chiropractors. As the AVN has been beaten down, losing members and influence, others have become more prominent as vaccination critics, for example Stephanie Messenger, author and campaigner.

My main focus is on the methods used by SAVN and its allies against the AVN and other vaccination critics. This may seem a narrow topic, but actually it is a remarkably rich area, because SAVN has deployed an extraordinarily diverse set of tactics, and the AVN has used a variety of means of defence. Although this engagement is about vaccination, the same sorts of tactics are found in many other struggles, in scientific controversies and other domains.

Dorey claimed that within a year of SAVN's formation, the AVN was subject to the following.

- Setting up of websites and blogs attacking the AVN
- Accusations that the AVN believes in conspiracy theories, such as the Illuminati
- Allegations that the AVN are child murderers
- Complaints to the Health Care Complaints Commission
- Complaints to the Office of Liquor, Gaming and Racing
- Complaints to the Australian Securities and Investments Commission
- Complaints to the Department of Fair Trading
- Complaints to the Internet Service Provider hosting the AVN's website
- Harassment of businesses advertising in *Living Wisdom*
- Harassment of AVN members, especially those with professional practices
- Harassment of families of AVN supporters
- Harassment of donors to the AVN
- Threats of legal action for defamation
- Attempts to stop AVN seminars
- Hacking of the AVN's website
- Death threats by telephone and email.[15]

---

15 Adapted from a list circulated by Meryl Dorey.

This is a considerable number of methods, yet many others have been used against the AVN.

For some of these actions, it is not clear whether SAVNers were responsible or involved. Some actions, such as conspiracy allegations, were on SAVN's Facebook page. Complaints to government regulatory bodies have been endorsed on SAVN's Facebook page, and many complainants are prominent SAVNers. Years later, SAVN proudly took responsibility for quite a few actions taken against the AVN.

- Complaint to the Health Care Complaints Commission (HCCC)
- Complaint to the Office of Liquor, Gaming and Racing
- Protest to the Australian Tax Office
- Lobbying of the NSW government for the AVN to change its name
- Investigation by the Australian Communications and Media Authority into a television report on Meryl Dorey's claims
- The NSW government increasing the power of the HCCC, enabling it to initiate investigations without a complaint
- Discouraging a folk festival from inviting Dorey from giving any more talks
- Cancellation of AVN seminars

- The mass media "referring to the AVN, Ms Dorey and other cranks as 'anti-vaccine' 'nutjobs'"[16]

Other actions, such as threatening phone calls to advertisers in the AVN's magazine *Living Wisdom,* are not announced as SAVN's responsibility, but they fit within SAVN's overall approach. SAVNers might or might not be responsible for some actions. SAVN administrators have formally denounced the making of death threats. Even if these are not undertaken by SAVNers, they might be inspired by SAVN's campaigning.

In the following chapters, I try to make clear when SAVNers are directly involved. In ambiguous situations, it is possible to refer to SAVN-inspired actions. In the years after 2009, as SAVN had more influence with mass media and politicians, the scope of SAVN-inspired actions expanded, so sometimes I use SAVN to include this wider pattern of action.

It is important to note that quite a few SAVNers would reject some or even most of the methods used against the AVN. Some SAVNers are always polite, oppose abusive language and attempt to engage in respectful conversations with vaccine critics. However, from the point of view of the AVN and others subject to attack, it is often the more extreme SAVN tactics that capture attention and drive emotional responses, making it exceedingly difficult to recognise good will among SAVNers.

---

16 Stop the Australian (Anti)Vaccination Network, "About, " https://www.facebook.com/pg/stopavn/about/?ref=page_internal, accessed 11 July 2017.

It would be possible to do a parallel examination of techniques of abuse and censorship used by vaccine critics. For several reasons, I have restricted most of my attention to attacks by SAVN and its allies. One reason is that vaccination is the dominant position in Australia, backed by government health authorities, associations of doctors, nurses and other health professionals, and pharmaceutical companies, as well as SAVN-type citizen campaigners. This means the power of the attackers is far greater than that of the AVN and its supporters. The struggle is asymmetrical: the AVN has little capacity to counterattack effectively, and most of its methods involve defence. SAVN has used a much wider range of methods than the AVN.

Another reason is that the evidence for abusive and censorious tactics by vaccine critics is limited. I have read quite a number of claims, by SAVN and in news commentary, about nasty tactics by vaccine critics, but seldom do critics openly engage in abuse under their own names. The AVN disowns such techniques. In contrast, SAVN is quite open about how it proceeds, with some exceptions.

My focus here is on free speech and how to defend it, rather than trying to pass judgement on the merits of the claims about science and ethics made by campaigners in the vaccination debate. The AVN has had almost no impact on the capacity of SAVNers and others to express their views,[17] and hence there is less to be learned by

---

17 The major exception is making comments on the AVN's blog, as discussed in chapter 6.

looking at efforts by vaccine critics to censor proponents. However, if roles were reversed, it would be a different story. My assumption is that if vaccine critics were in power, with the tools of government and the backing of major corporations, many of them would be just as intolerant of criticism as vaccination proponents are now. That at least is what I have observed in looking at many fierce debates over the years. Nat Hentoff, a free speech commentator in the US, observed the way political partisans on the left and right each tried to censor their opponents. The title of one of Hentoff's books sums up his conclusion: *Free Speech for Me — But Not for Thee*.[18] Unfortunately, there seem to be relatively few people with strong views who will defend the free speech of their opponents, especially if this means challenging the censorious activities of those on their own side.

In chapters 4 to 6, I analyse three types of SAVN's attack techniques: denigration, harassment and censorship. Chapter 7 covers methods of defending. This is not a comprehensive account of the campaign by SAVN against the AVN, much less of the wider struggle over vaccination in Australia. My aim is to look at methods of attack and defence, and for this a focus on selected methods is adequate.[19]

---

18 Nat Hentoff, Nat. 1992. *Free Speech for Me — But Not for Thee: How the American Left and Right Relentlessly Censor Each Other* (New York: HarperCollins, 1992).

19 Among the topics not addressed in the following chapters are Side Wikis and online petitions. I give only brief attention to allegations about improprieties in AVN finances and disputes

Chapter 8 steps back from the details of attack and defence, giving wider perspectives on the debate. One particular wider perspective is addressed in chapter 9: the idea of moral panics, and how this can be applied to the Australian vaccination debate. Chapter 10 presents a few conclusions from the saga.

There is no sign the public debate over vaccination will be over any time soon. It has been continuing for decades in its contemporary stage — in which numerous childhood vaccines are recommended — and before this there was opposition to vaccination from its earliest days, centuries ago. However, SAVN-style attacks are new, and may reflect capacities for online campaigning. So even though the vaccination debate is likely to be continuing decades from now, it is worth examining the techniques used to wage it.

---

over apprehended violence orders. I give limited attention to media coverage of the vaccination issue and of the AVN; this topic warrants a separate investigation.

4
Denigration

Denigration is a technique of attack. It aims to harm reputations, reduce credibility and foster negative mental images. Rather than address the evidence and arguments that a person presents, instead the person is the target. Other targets include organisations, beliefs and actions.

Denigration is a widespread technique, used regularly in politics, inside organisations, in neighbourhood disputes, families and elsewhere. In fact, it is so common that it deserves detailed analysis.

What is the purpose of denigrating someone or something? An obvious answer is to lower their status or reputation, so that others think less of them. This has a spin-off consequence: if you think less of someone, then you might not care as much about harm done to them. An assault on a child is more shocking than an assault on a murderer.

As a result, there is a curious recursive process involved in denigration: the more someone is denigrated, and the lower their status, the less others are likely to see any problem with the denigration process itself. If you make nasty comments about a respected, altruistic surgeon, people may think this is unjustified, even disgusting: the comments may reflect more on you than on the surgeon. But if you make nasty comments about someone who has a low reputation — a paedophile or a terrorist, for example — then less offence will be caused by your comments, and others may join in.

Denigration thus can be part of a cycle of putting down a person or group. If unemployed people are called no-hopers, welfare spongers, whiners or cheats, this lowers their status and sets the stage for harsher treatment, for example greater surveillance, lower unemployment payments or tighter controls over spending.

There seems to be no standard way of classifying methods of denigration.[1] To provide a framework, I allocate the many types of denigration into four categories.

> 1. Exposing and hiding information. The usual method is to highlight negative information about the target and to hide or ignore positive information.

> 2. Devaluation. There are many methods here, including verbal abuse, false claims about beliefs,

---

1 Writings on denigration can be found in a range of fields. See for example Sharyl Attkisson, *The Smear: How Shady Political Operatives and Fake News Control What You See, What You Think, and How You Vote* (New York: HarperCollins, 2017) on denigration as a tool in US political campaigning; Sam Keen, *Faces of the Enemy: Reflections of the Hostile Imagination* (San Francisco: Harper & Row, 1986) on derogatory images of the enemy in wartime; Wolf Wolfensberger, *A Brief Introduction to Social Role Valorization: A High-Level Concept for Addressing the Plight of Societally Devalued People, and for Structuring Human Services*, 3d ed. (Syracuse, NY: Training Institute for Human Service Planning, Leadership & Change Agentry (Syracuse University), 1998) on devaluation of people with disabilities.

guilt by association, demeaning pictures, and negative labelling. The key feature of these devaluation techniques is the fostering of negative images in people's minds.

3. Explanation. This involves an explicit justification for thinking badly about a target. An example is providing information about wrongdoing; another is blaming the target for something bad. Explanation, when it is balanced and honest, is the most legitimate of denigration techniques. If explanation is accompanied by opportunities for the target to reply, then this can morph into a genuine dialogue.

4. Endorsement. When others, especially high-status individuals or groups, support a negative evaluation, this gives it greater credibility.

These four categories overlap in several ways. For example, when negative information is exaggerated or fabricated, this is a combination of the techniques of exposing information and devaluation. In this chapter, I present a range of examples roughly following the sequence of these four categories. After this, I describe the impact of denigration and then outline some ways to respond.

EXPOSING AND HIDING INFORMATION

There are two basic ways to use information to lower someone's reputation. The first is to highlight negative information, for example by constantly mentioning it. The second is to ignore, hide or disguise positive information. If a person has some good and some bad attributes, or has some notable accomplishments and some failures, attacking the person's reputation can proceed by ignoring their good attributes and their notable accomplishments and instead constantly drawing attention to their bad attributes and their failures. Note that in deploying information this way, there is no need to manufacture dirt or distort the record. The treatment can be entirely factual. Denigration occurs through the selection of which facts to highlight and how much attention to pay to them.

The target might have made one thousand posts on a blog. To attack, it is only necessary to pick one or two ill-judged posts, refer to them over and over, and never mention any of the high-quality posts, nor indeed the large numbers of sensible posts.

In order for this technique to be credible, it should never draw attention to itself. It would not work to say, "I'm now going to point to Meryl's two most egregious posts." That would signal that there are other posts, perhaps a lot of other posts, that are not as bad and indeed may be quite good. The technique of highlighting negative information operates through the implication that these particular negatives reflect the essence of the person. The atypical is presented as the typical or as the essence.

Everyone in the world is a mixture of positives and negatives. They do some things well, others not so well. A successful basketball coach might be a bully towards poor performers. A big-time criminal might be generous to friends. Hitler was a vegetarian.

However, it is possible to treat the world as composed of goodies and baddies, as white and black. In this picture, those on our side — "we" — are of course the goodies and those on the other side are the baddies. In the psychological process called projection, one's own bad elements are denied and attributed to (projected onto) others, and then attacked.[2] A man might refuse to accept his own feminine side and homosexual urges and instead project them onto gay men, and be hostile towards them.

SAVNers, in their comments on vaccine critics, are relentlessly negative. They find fault with everything to do with Meryl Dorey, the AVN and other vaccine critics, and rarely mention a single positive.[3] It would be possible to comment, for example, that vaccine critics are concerned, in their own way, about children's lives, or that some of them care for their own children by encouraging exercise and a healthy diet. But such comments are rare. To mention positives would be to humanise vaccine critics, to recognise them as concerned parents and citizens who, in the eyes of SAVNers, are unfortunately misguided. Instead, most SAVNers ignore any positives and comment exclusively on negatives, everything from appearance to personal integrity. It needs to be said that many vaccine critics do exactly the same thing about SAVNers.

---

2 There are many studies of projection. I especially like Philip Lichtenberg, *Community and Confluence: Undoing the Clinch of Oppression,* 2d ed. (Cleveland, OH: Gestalt Institute of Cleveland Press, 1994).

3 See chapter 3 for introductory comments about SAVN, the AVN and Dorey.

Next I turn to the denigration technique of devaluation, addressing verbal abuse, conspiracy attributions, guilt by association, derogatory pictures and labelling.

DEVALUATION

Verbal abuse

Here's an exchange on the SAVN Facebook page, from 2011, about Dorey.

> **Carol Calderwood**: Meryl now claims that Smallpox has not been eradicated...
> **Peter Tierney**: Oh crap she's finally gone and broken that medical qualification of hers
> **Rhianna Miles**: I may be drunk — but Meryl is a belligerent fool
> **Rhianna Miles**: And a cunt
> **Rhianna Miles**: "Did I say that? I don't believe I did..."
> **Amy Ives**: Do I see? Yes, I see she's a fucking idiot.
> **Scott Lewis**: One thing that is becoming even more apparent is that the views of Meryl and Greg will never be changed and will never be able to be argued with. The responses have been to make claims (AKA make shit up) that we can't disprove, despite [...].
> **Simon Vincent**: Two for 'Cunt'. I had to promote her from 'Thief'.
> **Simon Vincent**: Pardon the language, apologies etc... but seriously... I'm having trouble finding another word. 'Disgraceful mealymouthed nonsensical science-bastardizing dangerous deceitful behaviour' is

too long to type each time. She should hang her head in shame.[4]

Here's the beginning of a blog post by Rebecca Fisher:

That evil hag Meryl Dorey's at it again, trying to spread her pro-infectious disease, child killing agenda around Australia. This time she's organised a bunch of seminars throughout Central / Western New South Wales in August, mainly at ex-services clubs, where she and some cockend called Greg Beattie (Author of a probably self-published bound together collection of used fucking bog roll entitled "Vaccination, why I'm full of shit" or something - can't be bothered to look up the actual title right now) will bang on for bloody ages about the evils of **TEH VACCINES - OH NOES!!** Oh - and she's going to charge you fifteen Australian Dollars for the privilege of hearing her fucking whiny, nasal tones for god knows how long.[5]

---

4 This commentary is no longer available on the SAVN Facebook page. Dorey reproduced it in "Poor skeptics — and their right to be cyberbullies," *No Compulsory Vaccination*, 6 November 2011, http://bit.ly/2EDaW0B.

5 Rebecca Fisher, "Australian Vaccination Network seminars," *JABS Loonies — Justice, Awareness, Basic Support and Mind Blowing Stupidity*, 28 June 2012, http://jabsloonies.blogspot.com.au/2012/06/australian-vaccination-network-seminars.html.

From the time of SAVN's formation and for many years afterwards, Dorey was its primary target. There are hundreds of possible examples, though only some are as abusive as the two I've quoted.

Others besides Dorey have been attacked as well. In November 2011, Mina Hunt made a post on the AVN's page. SAVNer Peter Tierney took a screenshot of Hunt's comment and posted it on SAVN's Facebook page, adding his own commentary:

> Here is the repugnant Mina Hunt blaming parents whose babies die of VPD [vaccine-preventable disease], citing the villain Scheibner. This is one of the reasons I fight so hard against the vileness and cruelty which is the cult of anti-vaccination.

Various SAVN contributors added comments, such as:

> **Ken McLeod**: 10/10 crank, and here's me thinking she was a nice girl. I'm such a sucker for a pretty face. [...].
> **Ilijas Milisic**: I agree, a vicious, callout and contemptible individual who has earned the disrespect of the public.
> **Daniel Raffaele**: Four letter word. Starts with C. That's right, she's a cram.[6]

Hunt is referred to as repugnant, a crank, callous, contemptible and a cram (a humorous replacement for the expected word cunt). These commenters do not attempt to

---

6 http://www.facebook.com/stopavn, 30 November 2011.

analyse what Hunt said, much less to understand it within its context. They simply condemn her. A reader might assume that what she has said must be terrible to deserve such abuse.

Peter Bowditch is a prominent SAVNer. In a 2012 Twitter exchange with a woman (with Twitter handle @SAVNGodComplex) who was a member of the AVN's Facebook page, Bowditch (as @RatbagsDotCom) made these tweets, among others:

> @SAVNGodComplex Questions for anti-vax liars: 1) How many dead children in a pile do you need to trigger a spontaneous orgasm? #StopAVN

> @SAVNGodComplex And your loins are where you must get a tingle every time you hear of another death from measles or whooping cough. #StopAVN[7]

Some denigration is directed towards vaccine critics in general. A flowery example is the beginning of a 2017 post by Reasonable Hank:

> Picture a round-table populated by untreated, angry perianal abscesses, each with their own internet connection. That's the Australian anti-vaccination movement: infected; weeping offensive, purulent exudate; ready to explode at the slightest of prodding;

---

7 Reproduced in Meryl Dorey, "Pseudo-Skeptics behaving badly," *No Compulsory Vaccination,* 28 July 2012, http://nocompulsoryvaccination.com/2012/07/28/pseudo-skeptics-behaving-badly/.

causing excruciating pain; adjacent to faeces and often indistinguishable from it; carving out distressing fistulas from where its festering message can newly seep.[8]

On the SAVN Facebook page, Ken McLeod posted a link to this Reasonable Hank blog post, noting: "What we do best is expose the antivax cranks for what they are with a little bit of humour." This was followed by numerous comments. The first few were:

> **Kathryn Nowland** Can't stand the (insert swear word here) ignorance of these morons.
> **Kate Golder** Just so sad that a grieving family trying to prevent other families from going through the pain of losing a child are treated like this.
> **Annora Farstad** Pretty soon this behaviour will become illegal like it is in the U.K.
> **Tony Davidovski** Yes ... the sooner the better!! Evil AVN people must be curbed by law.[9]

Whether or not one judges vaccine critics to have behaved badly, the language used by these SAVNers denigrates them as people.

---

8 Reasonable Hank, "Light for Riley attacked in official Vaxxed group run by AVN president," 29 June 2017, https://reasonablehank.com/2017/06/29/light-for-riley-attacked-in-official-vaxxed-group-run-by-avn-president/.

9 Stop the Australian (Anti)Vaccination Network, https://www.facebook.com/stopavn/, 29 June 2017.

Conspiracy attributions
SAVN's primary manifestation has always been its Facebook page. The page has an "about" tab, enabling SAVN to provide a self-description. In the first few years of its existence, SAVN's self-description included a claim about the AVN's beliefs, worth quoting:

> Name: Stop the Australian Vaccination Network
> Category: Organizations - Advocacy Organizations
> Description: The Australian Vaccination Network propagates misinformation, telling parents they should not vaccinate their children against such killer diseases as measles, mumps, rubella, whooping cough and polio.
> They believe that vaccines are part of a global conspiracy to implant mind control chips into every man, woman and child and that the "illuminati" plan a mass cull of humans.
> They use the line that "vaccines cause injury" as a cover for their conspiracy theory.
> They lie to their members and the general public and after the death of a 4 week old child from whooping cough their members allegedly sent a barrage of hate mail to the child's grieving parents.
> The dangerous rhetoric and lies of the AVN must be stopped. They must be held responsible for their campaign of misinformation.[10]

---

10 Stop the Australian Vaccination Network Facebook page, accessed 13 October 2010. This text was later removed. Note that the claim that "They lie to their members and the general public," which implies the existence of a core group in the AVN with a

Most readers would assume it is simply absurd to believe that vaccination is a means for implanting mind-control chips, indeed absurd to believe that mind-control chips even exist, or that vaccinations would be a means for surreptitiously implanting anything, or even containing anything other than vaccines and adjuvants. So absurd is this belief that SAVN didn't feel the need to argue against it. Simply spelling out the belief is enough to discredit it in most people's eyes, and by association anyone who believes it is discredited too.

The basic technique here is straightforward: attribute a belief to others and hold it up for ridicule and contempt. The belief needs to be one that is widely rejected. For example, in many circles racism is taboo, so claiming that a person believes blacks are inferior to whites can be a way of discrediting them. There is not seen to be any need to present a careful exposition of the views of the alleged racist, which might be nuanced and defendable. The technique involves discrediting without giving an argument.

Although many people believe in conspiracies, many others — especially scientists and academics — dismiss them out of hand. Saying that someone believes in a conspiracy theory thus can be a way of discrediting them and excluding them from the realm of scientific thinking, something important in the vaccination debate.[11]

---

secret agenda to mislead members and the public. This, ironically, is itself a conspiracy theory.

11 Jaron Harambam and Stef Aupers, "Contesting epistemic authority: conspiracy theories on the boundaries of science," *Public Understanding of Science,* Vol. 24, No. 4, 2015, pp. 466–

SAVN provided no evidence that members of the AVN believed in a global conspiracy to implant mind-control chips. In my first piece of writing about the attack on the AVN, I described this as an unsupported claim.[12] In a subsequent exchange on the Reasonable Hank blog, I was surprised that SAVNers defended their absurd claim about the AVN.[13] I pointed out there was no evidence that members of the AVN believed in such a conspiracy. SAVNers said Meryl Dorey believed in it, implying this was sufficient to support their claim about the AVN. (For them, it seemed Dorey and the AVN were identical, even though the AVN had thousands of members.) I talked with Dorey; she denied having any such belief. So what evidence did SAVNers have that she believed in this conspiracy theory? It was once she had made a link to an article on David Icke's website. Icke apparently has some strange beliefs concerning the Illuminati and reptilian

480. They argue that disqualifying conspiracy theories and theorists is a type of "boundary work": see chapter 8 for more on boundary work. See also Ginna Husting and Martin Orr, "Dangerous machinery: 'conspiracy theorist' as a transpersonal strategy of exclusion," *Symbolic Interaction*, Vol. 30, No. 2, 2007, pp. 127–150, who write that "If I call you a 'conspiracy theorist'," then I avoid the need to respond to your claims, and "I strategically exclude you from the sphere where public speech, debate, and conflict occur." (p. 127).

12 Brian Martin, "Debating vaccination: understanding the attack on the Australian Vaccination Network," *Living Wisdom*, No. 8, 2011, pp. 14–40, http://goo.gl/3GkMPz.

13 Brian Martin, "Caught in the vaccination wars, part 3," http://www.bmartin.cc/pubs/12hpi-comments.html

aliens. However, the article to which Dorey linked was by a journalist, not Icke; it was about vaccination and did not discuss any of Icke's views.[14]

It is absurd to suggest that making a link to an article means subscribing to the beliefs of the administrator of the website hosting the article. Yet this single link by Dorey was apparently the way SAVNers justified claiming that the AVN (not just Dorey) believed in a global conspiracy to implant mind-control chips via vaccination.

In my exchange on the Reasonable Hank blog, the SAVNers continued with their claims. I then offered them the opportunity for peer review: we would each prepare documents spelling out our case about the AVN's belief in a conspiracy theory and send them to independent experts on conspiracy theories. (There are quite a number of scholars who have analysed conspiracy theories.[15]) At this

---

14 On this point see Meryl Dorey, "Dossier of attacks on the AVN: censorship and suppression," 26 August 2012, http://goo.gl/j8iZJo.

15 For a range of views, see for example Jack Z. Bratich, *Conspiracy Panics: Political Rationality and Popular Culture* (Albany, NY: State of New York University Press, 2008); Lance deHaven-Smith, *Conspiracy Theory in America* (Austin, TX: University of Texas Press, 2013); Mark Fenster, *Conspiracy Theories: Secrecy and Power in American Culture,* revised and updated edition (Minneapolis, MN: University of Minnesota Press, 2008); Kurtis Hagen, "Conspiracy theories and the paranoid style: do conspiracy theories posit implausibly vast and evil conspiracies?" *Social Epistemology,* 2017, https://doi.org/10.1080/02691728.2017.1352625; Jaron Harambam, *"The Truth Is Out There": Conspiracy Culture in an*

point, I was blocked from the blog and my final comment deleted. However, the exchange apparently had some effect: SAVN changed its description of the AVN, no longer mentioning anything about belief in conspiracy theories.

Guilt by association
The SAVN conspiracy-theory claim can be seen as an example of attributing guilt by association. SAVNers assumed David Icke was totally without credibility because of some of his beliefs. Dorey linked to an article on Icke's website and therefore was tarred by association. SAVNers went beyond guilt by association in this case: association was enough to claim that Dorey believed in an Icke-type conspiracy. Then, on top of this, the entire membership of the AVN was tarnished by association with Dorey. This is guilt by association with someone portrayed as guilty by association.

The logic of guilt by association does not stand up under scrutiny. It operates by insinuation, rather than evidence and argument.

Age of Epistemic Instability (PhD dissertation, Erasmus University Rotterdam, 2017); Ginna Husting and Martin Orr, "Dangerous machinery: 'conspiracy theorist' as a transpersonal strategy of exclusion," *Symbolic Interaction*, Vol. 30, No. 2, 2007, pp. 127–150; Peter Knight, *Conspiracy Culture: from the Kennedy Assassination to the X-Files* (London: Routledge, 2000); Timothy Melley, *Empire of Conspiracy: The Culture of Paranoia in Postwar America* (Ithaca, NY: Cornell University Press, 2000). Thanks to Jaron Harambam for advice about scholarly analyses of conspiracy theories.

After my student Judy Wilyman received her PhD, there was a massive attack on her, on me as her supervisor, and on the University of Wollongong for granting her PhD.[16] The outrage over her receiving a PhD revealed a cascade of guilt-by-association links. The first step was to discredit her thesis by falsely claiming that it involved a conspiracy theory. I was attacked for being Judy's supervisor: she was guilty, so by association so was I. And likewise the university, even though no one presented any evidence for any shortcoming in my supervision or in the university's procedures.[17]

There was another fascinating example of guilt by association in newspaper articles criticising Judy's work. It was reported, correctly, that I had supervised Michael Primero, who in the 1990s undertook but did not complete a PhD involving a critique of vaccination. Referring to Michael, but not mentioning the two dozen other PhD students I had supervised, none of whom researched vaccination, made it seem like I made a specialty of supervising students critical of vaccination, with the implication that there was a problem with this. Then Michael was discredited by mentioning his connection with the journal *Medical Veritas,* and *Medical Veritas* was discredited by mentioning one article published in it about an alleged conspiracy involving musical tones. In none of

---

16 For my analyses of the attack, see http://www.bmartin.cc/pubs/controversy.html#Wilyman.

17 My account of the university's role: "Defending university integrity," *International Journal for Educational Integrity,* Vol. 13, No. 1, 2017, pp. 1–14, http://goo.gl/3y4QMH.

these associations was any argument made.[18] There is no sensible logic involved in drawing a link between an article in *Medical Veritas* and Judy's thesis.[19] This was an exercise in denigration using the technique of guilt by association, operating through several links.

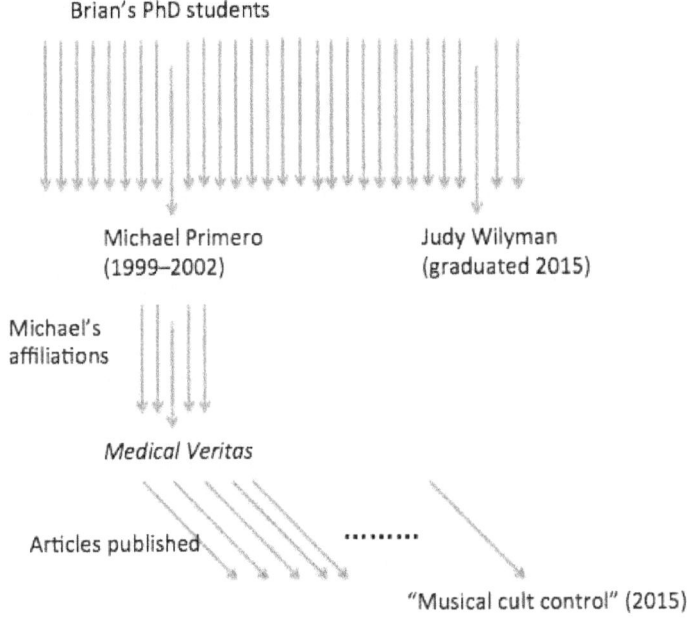

18 Incidentally, Michael had never even mentioned to me his involvement with *Medical Veritas*.

19 Furthermore, the article "Musical cult control" in *Medical Veritas* was published in 2015, more than a decade after Michael discontinued his PhD candidature.

Philosophers who analyse statements uniformly reject guilt by association as a valid form of logic. Just because *Medical Veritas* published an allegedly kooky article does not mean that everything in the journal is irretrievably tainted. With the same logic, it might be said that the prestigious scientific journals *Science* and *Nature* are tainted because they have published articles by authors later exposed as engaging in scientific fraud.

Guilt by association operates by bypassing the rational mind. Rationally, there is no reason to dismiss *Medical Veritas* on the basis of an association with a supposedly goofy article; what's required is a careful analysis of the journal. Indeed, just because an article sounds goofy on the basis of a brief summary does not mean it actually is goofy. After all, the summary might be misleading.

Suppose you meet a businessman at a social function. It turns out he's a crime boss, but you didn't know it. Using the technique of guilt by association, it would be easy to smear you. Imagine the text underneath your picture: "Seen consorting with crime boss."

Derogatory pictures
Some SAVNers delighted in composing images to make fun of the AVN and, most commonly, Dorey. This was more common in SAVN's early years, when there was a sense of playfulness, though with a nasty twinge.

To appreciate this graphics about nuts, it is useful to know that Dorey's husband is a macadamia nut farmer.

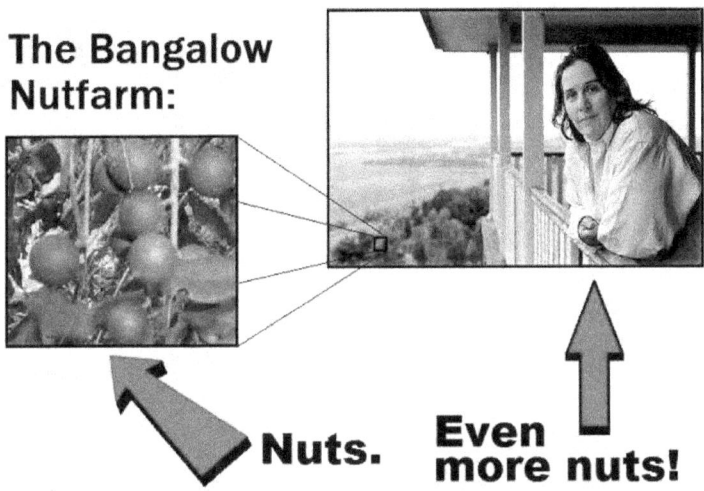

In the film *V for Vendetta*, a self-described anarchist sets out to bring down the British establishment. He wears a stylised mask that has been adopted by activists worldwide as a symbol of resistance. In some images composed by SAVNers, they put the V mask on a picture of Dorey, not to suggest that she has the capacity of V, but ironically to suggest that she is challenging the establishment with no chance of success.[20] This, at least, is one interpretation. None of SAVN's images intend to portray Dorey or the AVN positively.

---

20 Image added to SAVN Facebook page by David Romeo, 1 February 2011.

As a spin-off from the V mask, one SAVNer composed a picture titled "W for windowlickers."[21] According to the Urban Dictionary, "A windowlicker is a derogatory, informal description of someone with severe learning disabilities and/or a physical incapacity which renders them helpless when faced with the prospect of seeing a stranger through a window without smearing their mucus covered tongues all over the glass, possibly as some kind of retard greeting."

These three graphics might be taken to suggest that Dorey is insane and a caricature of an anti-establishment rebel and that vaccine critics have intellectual disabilities. The playful aspect of such graphics suggests they are intended to be ironic rather than interpreted literally. The

---

21 This image was added to the SAVN Facebook page by Liam Skoda, 1 February 2011.

precise meanings are less important than the general sentiment behind these and other such images, which is that vaccine critics are not to be taken seriously, and indeed are so misguided that they are fair game for humorous dismissals.

Labelling

Applying a label to someone is a way of categorising them, of assigning them to a group. Once the label is applied, it can be taken as representing a person's identity.

Labels are used all the time and it is hard to imagine operating without them. A news headline says "Protesters clash with police," thereby drawing on each reader's ideas about the categories of protester and police. The group labelled protesters might include a diversity of individuals, young and old, dishevelled and well-dressed, doctors and mechanics, and so forth, but these differences are ignored for the purposes of the headline, and likewise differences among the police. Another headline says "Mother of two drowns." The person who drowns might be an executive, a benefactor, a criminal or a musician, but instead is put in the category of mother, which has a set of connotations different from her other roles.

Derogatory labelling involves assigning a person or activity or belief to a negative category. If the label sticks, the target can have a hard time escaping the category's associated meanings. SAVNers have used the label "anti-vaxxer" as a key derogatory label, and it has been taken up by many others, including doctors, journalists and even some vaccine critics. Though "anti-vaxxer" is not inherently derogatory, SAVNers have made concerted efforts to make it strongly negative, so it becomes almost a term of abuse.[22]

As noted in chapter 1, personally I do not have a strong view about vaccination. I do not campaign for or

---

22 For commentary from within the medical establishment critical of labelling anyone who raises concerns about vaccination as "anti-vaccine," see Peter Doshi, "Medical response to Trump requires truth seeking and respect for patients," *BMJ*, Vol. 356, 7 February 2017: j661.

against vaccination. In my writings I present the arguments both for and against vaccination. I defend the right of vaccine critics to express their views without censorship or harassment, but this does not mean I necessarily endorse their views. In other contexts, I have argued for free speech for climate sceptics and Holocaust deniers, who hold views with which I disagree.[23]

Nevertheless, SAVNers for years have tried to find a reason to label me "anti-vax." In February 2016, I received an email, ostensibly from someone in Pakistan, asking for help in making arguments against the polio vaccine. I assumed this email was written by SAVNers or other Australian pro-vaccination campaigners in an attempt to induce me to send material critical of vaccination so I then could be labelled "anti-vax." In January 2016, one of the changes to my Wikipedia entry was to include me in the category "Anti-vaccination activists."[24]

When SAVNers label someone as an "anti-vaxxer," it seems to provide a way to avoid discussing their views. For example, Lucija Tomljenovic, a scientist, has pub-

---

23 "Monckton and Notre Dame: a case for free speech?" *The Conversation*, 30 June 2011, https://theconversation.com/monckton-and-notre-dame-a-case-for-free-speech-2104; "Statement regarding the complaint by Jeremy Jones about the Adelaide Institute web site," 30 October 1997, http://www.bmartin.cc/pubs/97Toben.pdf.

24 Brian Martin, "Persistent bias on Wikipedia: methods and responses," *Social Science Computer Review*, 2017, http://www.bmartin.cc/pubs/17sscr.html; "'Brian Martin: social scientist': a Wikipedia entry annotated by its subject," 26 October 2016, http://www.bmartin.cc/pubs/16wp.pdf.

lished various papers with findings critical of certain vaccines. Here are some comments by SAVNers in response to a paragraph of text by Tomljenovic, followed by "Lucija Tomljenovic, PhD, Molecular Biochemist."

> **Sue Ieraci** So, a molecular biochemist in an academic ophthalmology dept is not an immunologist after all. Just an ordinary anti-vaxer. Surprise!
>
> **Vanessa Young** Maybe we are confused and 'molecular biochemist' is her surname, not her job.
>
> **Tony Davidovski** These people should be banned from making any type of pseudoscientific statements that are false, misleading and potentially fatal to newborns...this should be considered as criminal acts!
>
> **Ilijas Milišić** Lucija is a new Dr Andrew Wakefield.
>
> **Anne Blake** Even less qualified and not medically qualified at all[25]

Rather than analysing the substance of her papers, SAVNer Sue Ieraci uses an alleged mistake by Tomljenovic to dismiss her as an "anti-vaxer," and other SAVNers add their own dismissive comments. Applying a stigmatising label seems to absolve SAVNers of addressing Tomljenovic's evidence and arguments; instead, she is simply dismissed as not worthy of consideration.[26]

---

25 SAVN Facebook page, 3 January 2016.

26 See also Nicola Luigi Bragazzi, Abdulla Watad, Howard Amital and Yehuda Shoenfeld, "Debate on vaccines and autoimmunity: do not attack the author, yet discuss it

Viera Scheibner is an earth scientist who began studying the adverse effects of vaccines and became a prominent vaccine critic, one of the few with scholarly credentials.[27] She was an inspiration and mentor for several later vaccine critics. Earlier, I cited Peter Tierney: "Here is the repugnant Mina Hunt blaming parents whose babies die of VPD [vaccine-preventable disease], citing the villain Scheibner." Tierney dismisses Scheibner using the label "villain," putting her in a reject category without any effort to analyse her work or cite any studies analysing her work.

Another label is "liar," frequently applied to Dorey. This is most floridly displayed in the title of a document written by SAVNer Ken McLeod: "Meryl Dorey's trouble with the truth, part 1: how Meryl Dorey lies, obfuscates, prevaricates, exaggerates, confabulates and confuses in promoting her anti-vaccination agenda."[28] Many instances of Dorey's alleged lies are actually her persistence in

---

methodologically," *Vaccine*, 2017, http://dx.doi.org/10.1016/j.vaccine.2017.08.018.

27 Viera Scheibner, *Vaccination: 100 Years of Orthodox Research Shows that Vaccines Represent a Medical Assault on the Immune System* (Blackheath, NSW: Viera Scheibner, 1993).

28 Ken McLeod, "Meryl Dorey's trouble with the truth, part 1: how Meryl Dorey lies, obfuscates, prevaricates, exaggerates, confabulates and confuses in promoting her anti-vaccination agenda," 2010, http://www.scribd.com/doc/47704677/Meryl-Doreys-Trouble-With-the-Truth-Part-1.

presenting views that McLeod believes are wrong.²⁹ This is not lying in the normal definition of the word, namely consciously being deceptive. Hence, saying she is a liar is a way of negatively categorising her.

SAVNers have invested considerable effort in catching out Dorey in alleged lies. Some of them tried to obtain personal information about her, including her statement that she had worked as a stockbroker in the US before immigrating to Australia. Not being able to verify her claim, they demanded that she provide proof, with the implication that she was lying about having been a stockbroker. SAVNers seemed to believe that if she could be proved to have lied about stockbroking, her credibility about vaccination would be undermined. However, there is little logic in such a belief, because many people who lie in one domain, for example in preparing their income tax returns, are truthful in another, such as doing scientific research. SAVNers never produced evidence that Dorey had lied about her stockbroking background. Their search for it reveals their agenda of trying to justify derogatory labelling.

---

29 I analysed some of McLeod's argumentation — in his complaint to the HCCC — in "Debating vaccination," *Living Wisdom,* Issue 8, February 2011, pp. 14–40, http://goo.gl/3GkMPz, at pp. 24–30.

EXPLANATION

Pointing to discrediting information

One of SAVN's allegations against the AVN was that it was misusing its money. Basically this was a claim that the AVN was involved in fraud. Some SAVNers pored through the AVN's financial statements looking for discrepancies. They also made complaints to various organisations asking that the AVN's records be scrutinised. In one instance, the health editor for the *Sydney Morning Herald* hired an independent auditor to go through the AVN's financial records.[30]

The AVN's annual income for the decade before SAVN's creation was between $50,000 and $400,000. Although it is legitimate to raise concerns about financial mismanagement and fraud, SAVN's continued attention to alleged problems with the AVN's finances has no point except to discredit the AVN. Conveniently, SAVN, with no declared income, itself seems safe from complaints about mismanaging finances.

Blaming
Blaming is a process of attributing agency and guilt for outcomes: someone was responsible for what went wrong. They are to blame.

---

30 For a response, see Meryl Dorey, "The AVN — our finances are an open book," *No Compulsory Vaccination*, 13 March 2014, http://nocompulsoryvaccination.com/2014/03/13/the-avn-our-finances-are-an-open-book/.

Blaming can be used as a method of denigration. It can contain several components, including labelling, guilt by association, and false or unproven allegations.

One of SAVN's central contentions — often treated as a given — is that Dorey and the AVN are responsible for the illnesses and deaths of children from vaccine-preventable diseases. The logic behind this view is that the AVN discourages parents from having their children vaccinated, and lower vaccination rates mean higher disease rates, including some deaths.[31] Blaming is encapsulated in the label "baby-killer" applied to Dorey and others.

ENDORSEMENTS

One of the most powerful tools of denigration is to obtain official endorsements. For SAVNers to say that the AVN is dangerous is one thing; more discrediting is when a government agency says the AVN is dangerous.

One of the main techniques used by SAVN is making complaints about the AVN and about vaccine critics to various government agencies. I discuss this in more detail in chapter 4 on harassment. In a few cases, agencies have launched investigations into the AVN and made pronouncements about the AVN.

---

31 As discussed in chapter 8, it is possible that the AVN is a consequence, rather than a primary cause, of some parents' concerns about vaccination, in which case SAVN's blaming of the AVN is misdirected.

The Health Care Complaints Commission (HCCC) is a government-funded agency in the state of New South Wales, where the AVN is incorporated. In 2010, Ken McLeod made a lengthy complaint to the HCCC about the AVN, and the HCCC began an investigation. This was enough for SAVNers to denigrate the AVN: it was being investigated, suggesting that there was something wrong. This is analogous to the way that someone being arrested and charged with a crime can harm their reputation. Even if they are found not guilty, the stigma of possible guilt remains. This is in part guilt by association, except even stronger.

So SAVNers make complaints and then highlight the fact that the AVN is under investigation. Even better, though, from SAVN's point of view, is when a government agency finds something wrong. The HCCC requested that the AVN put a disclaimer on its website. After the AVN refused — it already had a disclaimer on its site, and its lawyers advised against accepting the HCCC's disclaimer — the HCCC issued a public warning about the AVN. The warning stated that the AVN provided inaccurate and misleading information and that because it did not post the disclaimer demanded by the HCCC, the AVN was a risk to public health and safety.

Ever after, SAVNers cited the HCCC's public warning. It was a potent tool to discredit the AVN.

In 2013, Senator Richard Di Natale, the leader of the Australian Greens, put a motion to the federal senate:

That the Senate –
(a) notes the low vaccination rates in certain parts of

Australia, and the threat this poses to the health of Australian children;
(b) notes the irresponsible campaign run by the Australian Vaccination Network, which is spreading misinformation about the risks of vaccination and discouraging parents from vaccinating their children;
(c) calls on the AVN to immediately disband and cease their harmful and unscientific scare campaign against vaccines.[32]

The Senate passed this motion unanimously, showing that SAVN and its allies had convinced federal politicians from all parties to condemn the AVN. It was a symbolic gesture: it did not require any action by the AVN. Nevertheless, it provided a significant endorsement of SAVN's campaign.

Web of Trust
The Web of Trust (WoT) is a browser extension. You can download it and add it to your web browser. When you visit a WoT-endorsed website, a gold WoT icon may appear. For some sites, though, WoT generates a pop-up alert about the site in relation to trustworthiness and child safety. You can still click through for access if you want.

The WoT is set up for child protection, to give warnings about pornography and other sites seen as

---

32 Richard Di Natale, "Senate to anti-vax group: pack up and go home," media release, 25 June 2013, http://richard-di-natale.greensmps.org.au/articles/senate-anti-vax-group-pack-and-go-home.

undesirable. The ratings are largely based on user inputs. You can submit your ratings of any site. This opens them to manipulation: a campaigning group can submit numerous negative ratings of a target website, thereby harming its reputation.

That is exactly what has happened with the AVN's website (https://avn.org.au). With WoT installed on my browser, visiting the AVN's website triggers a pop-up saying "Warning! This website has a poor reputation based on user ratings."[33] Both trustworthiness and child safety are rated as "very poor." The user comments reveal a preponderance of vaccination supporters who consider that the AVN's site is misleading and dangerous.

From the point of view of SAVNers, the AVN is indeed dangerous to child health, so their ratings on the WoT are legitimate in their eyes. However, to see vaccine criticism as a matter of child safety is different from seeing the AVN's website as unsuitable for children. In this case, WoT has been used as a tool by SAVNers as part of its campaign against the AVN.

AVN members, if they were sufficiently organised and concerned, could try to counter the WoT ratings by putting in their own favourable ratings, but this is a losing proposition because SAVNers have far greater numbers and energy for engaging in this sort of online reputation management.

The WoT warning serves as an endorsement of SAVN's view of the AVN. In as much as the WoT warning results from ratings by SAVNers and their allies,

---

33 Accessed 8 August 2017.

this is a case of SAVNers manipulating a rating system to provide an apparent endorsement of their own views.

Wikipedia

The online encyclopaedia called Wikipedia is one of the most widely used sites on the Internet. Started in 2001 and produced by volunteers, it is by far the largest encyclopaedia available, with millions of entries in numerous languages. Wikipedia is one of the best-known success stories of voluntary cooperative work, along with free software such as the operating system Linux. Considering the scale of Wikipedia and that editing is carried out entirely by volunteers, the result is a remarkable achievement.

Wikipedia has had its share of problems. Entries on some contentious topics, such as abortion and the Israel-Palestine conflict, have been the subject of acrimonious editing "wars," in which partisans seek to impose their own perspectives. There are vandals who seek to deface Wikipedia entries. Some companies and governments pay staff to edit entries to create desirably favourable or unfavourable treatments. In these and other areas, Wikipedia managers have worked out various responses.

An ongoing problem is biased editing. On contentious issues when there are large numbers of partisans on each side, the result can be an entry that reconciles different views, or at least represents a stalemate in a struggle. On some issues, though, one group can shape entries to serve an agenda.

Years ago, SAVNers essentially took control over the Wikipedia entry about the AVN. Given a superficial adherence to Wikipedia guidelines, the entry has been written to present the AVN in a negative light. Meanwhile, there is a Wikipedia entry about SAVN itself, presented in a very positive light, obviously reflecting editing by SAVNers.

On Wikipedia, there is no independent tribunal to which to appeal in the face of hostile editing. To counter bias in the AVN entry, AVN supporters can do their own editing, but this is futile in the face of larger numbers of SAVNers doing editing, and higher level administrators (with greater power over editing) supportive of SAVN's agenda.[34]

As in the case of the Web of Trust, when Wikipedia entries are colonised by SAVNers and their allies, these entries give an endorsement of SAVN viewpoints that seems to be independent but isn't.

EFFECTS OF DENIGRATION

Verbal abuse, misrepresentations and other forms of denigration can have powerful effects on people involved. These vary from individual to individual. For those who are the targets of abuse, some laugh it off, others are bemused, and yet others are embarrassed, distressed or angry. Though there are no studies of the effects on vaccine critics of continual denigration, I know from

---

34 See Brian Martin, "Persistent bias on Wikipedia: methods and responses," *Social Science Computer Review*, 2017, http://www.bmartin.cc/pubs/17sscr.html for an analysis and additional references.

various conversations that quite a few are negatively affected. It is a rare person who is unaffected by being called a liar or a baby-killer, or who doesn't feel upset when others misrepresent their beliefs.

Participating in verbal abuse of others has an effect too. As already noted, when done in a group, it can be a means of building or reaffirming a sense of community, of solidarity of the in-group against the stigmatised out-group. When the techniques of denigration are used repeatedly, they become normalised: participants see them as legitimate. When others in the group regularly use these methods, joining in may feel like an expectation or even an obligation. Attitudes towards opponents or the enemy — members of the out-group being denigrated — become fixed, and generic: everyone in the out-group is seen in the same way.

These processes are well known from studies of racism, but are more widespread. Group identification can be created from the most trivial of differences, for example blue eyes versus brown eyes or assignment to a team with a name. Attitudes towards out-group members are easier to maintain when there is little or no personal interaction with them.

These considerations suggest that many SAVNers may gain a sense of group identification through their ridicule and condemnation of vaccine critics. It is also likely that they do not see what they do as inappropriate: condemning the AVN and making fun of vaccine critics is seen as legitimate: "they deserve it" because of their misguided and dangerous views, not to mention their lies and fraudulent activities.

In the SAVN-versus-AVN struggle, it is reasonable to believe that attitudes towards the techniques of denigration differ dramatically, with most SAVNers seeing them as legitimate and justified and not that serious while many of the targets of abuse feeling violated and distressed.

Verbal abuse, misrepresentation and other forms of denigration involve a lack of respect for others. They make it far more difficult to build a relationship based on trust. That indeed may be the goal of some SAVNers: to so stigmatise and distance vaccine critics from themselves, and from others, that no one would want to establish a trusting relationship with them. This can be considered the tactic of social ostracism, though in practice it only operates to the extent that others take up SAVN's approach.

This leads to another important issue: the effect of abuse on bystanders. The denigration of vaccine critics occurs on the SAVN Facebook page, on SAVNer blogs and in media stories that adopt the negative framing modelled or inspired by SAVN. So how do others respond to this campaign of denigration? To my knowledge, there has been no empirical research on this question, so it is only possible to make some general comments.

Some bystanders will adopt SAVN's attitudes towards vaccine critics. This is most likely among those who strongly support vaccination and who are already hostile towards vaccine critics. After all, SAVN is not the only influence on attitudes. Many doctors and others in mainstream medicine have long promoted vaccination and raised the alarm about non-vaccinators, so it is a short step from concern to attitudes that support abuse.

On the other hand, some bystanders will be alienated by SAVN's approach, for example seeing abusive language as unfair, disgusting or childish. I've talked with several people, supportive of vaccination, who have looked at SAVN's Facebook page and been repelled by the attitudes displayed.

Some bystanders may decide to stay away from the issue, for fear of encountering abuse themselves. This choice contributes to the polarisation of the debate: only those with the most passionately held views are likely to want to stay in an arena in which nastiness is more likely than considered debate. To the extent that this choice prevails, SAVN's approach drives away those who might pursue options involving respect and dialogue.

Responses

How can vaccine critics, the targets of SAVN's attacks, respond? What can Meryl Dorey, for years SAVN's prime target, do? What about one of the nurses identified in a Reasonable Hank blog and targeted for verbal abuse? There are several possibilities, including ignoring, defending, counterattacking, analysing and exposing.

Ignoring
In the face of abuse, saying nothing and seeming to pay no notice can be a powerful response. It sends an implicit signal to the attackers that their nasty comments seem not to have caused any distress. Without a response, attackers may tire of their game, because part of the fun is seeing

the victim squirm in discomfort. Not responding can signal that the abuse is not worthy of comment.

William Irvine in his book *A Slap in the Face* recommends not responding to insults, or in a face-to-face encounter, saying "Thank you."[35] This can disconcert the person making the insult, who expected a response, either defence or counterattack. In formulating the strategy of non-response to insults, Irvine drew inspiration from the Stoics in ancient Greece, and to follow the Stoics there is another dimension to non-response: it is to not respond emotionally. This can be difficult, but can be developed as an emotional skill. It involves observing the insult and deciding how to feel about it. Just as an experienced meditator can maintain mental focus, for example paying attention to every breath, and not be distracted by extraneous thoughts, so someone who has developed the skills sought by Stoics can avoid being caught in emotional turmoil and instead examine the insult and make a decision about how to respond, for example setting it aside or choosing to react in some way.

For those who are subject to continual abuse, maintaining emotional balance can be difficult. Cultivating a stoic response can be the foundation of surviving and even thriving in such circumstances.

Although ignoring abuse can be effective for some purposes, it may be inadequate when the abuse is influencing others. While personally pursuing a stoic emotional response, it is worth considering other responses.

---

35 William B. Irvine, *A Slap in the Face: Why Insults Hurt — and Why They Shouldn't* (New York: Oxford University Press, 2013).

Defending

For many people, a natural response to criticism is to defend. If someone says, "You're a liar!" you may want to say, "No, I'm not a liar" or "No, I'm telling the truth" and launch into a justification.

Defending by presenting a contrary view can be important in order to prevent false claims becoming accepted by others. You might know the claims are wrong or misleading, but do others? If they are being seriously misled, then setting the record straight can be important.

For example, consider a nurse attacked on Reasonable Hank's blog. If some of the claims on the blog are false, it might be worth preparing a factual, unemotional response and giving it to co-workers and bosses, assuming they know about the blog and are being influenced by it. A good part of the effectiveness of such a response is in its style, which is why I recommend preparing a response that is factual and unemotional.[36]

Defending makes most sense when there are actual claims involved. When SAVN said that Dorey was extracting large amounts of money from the AVN, she can present the AVN's accounts. However, the more absurd the claims, the harder it is to defend using facts and logical arguments. SAVN's initial claim that the AVN believed in a global conspiracy to implant mind control chips was a slur, with only the slimmest of evidence as a pretext. Should Dorey and other members have said, "No, of

---

36 Brian Martin, "When you're criticized," *Journal of Scholarly Publishing,* Vol. 43, No. 2, 2012, pp. 230–237, http://www.bmartin.cc/pubs/12jsp.html.

course we don't believe in any such conspiracy"? Or would such a response give the claim unwarranted credibility, as something to be debated rather than dismissed as silly?

Defending makes even less sense in the face of ridicule and abuse. When SAVNers call Dorey a baby-killer, should she respond, "I'm actually concerned about the health of babies"? And what should she say when SAVNers call her a cunt?

In the face of abusive verbal attacks, a potent way to defend is to behave rationally and sensibly, without getting angry and defensive. Instead of taking the bait and getting into an argument or counterattacking, the response could be to refer to the evidence and arguments. This sends a message to observers that you are the sensible one and your attackers are emotional and nasty.

Remaining calm in the face of attack is not easy. If you are easily upset, it may be better to do nothing until you feel ready to respond in a suitable way. In a face-to-face situation, for example at a workplace, typical advice is to take 10 breaths, allowing emotions to settle. Online, it is important not to respond quickly, in the heat of emotion. Waiting an hour or a day or even longer can be worthwhile. Seldom is it necessary to make an immediate reply.

When possible, it is highly worthwhile to seek advice from friends and supporters before replying. For example, if you are subject to abuse on a blog, by all means write a response. Then wait for a while and revise the response when you're feeling less agitated. Then give your response to a friend or supporter, seeking their advice and input. Even better is for them to write their own response to defend you. Having a defender, especially someone with credibility and who is seen as independent, speak on your behalf is often more effective than replying yourself.

The problem with defending is that your attackers have set the agenda. They made accusations and you feel obliged to defend against them. In attacking, SAVNers concentrate on negatives and ignore positives. Part of a good response is to turn the agenda around. So rather than simply addressing the points raised by the attacker, it can be valuable to present different issues. When SAVNers raise only negatives, it can be worthwhile highlighting things they ignore.

There's something else that SAVNers ignore: their own shortcomings. This brings up counterattacking as an option.

Counterattacking

In response to being attacked, one option is to counterattack. Rather than or in addition to defending against criticisms, it's possible to make criticisms of the attackers.

There are various forms of counterattack. One is to reply in kind, using the same sorts of claims and the same style. If SAVNers make accusations about believing in conspiracy theories, then accuse them of believing in conspiracy theories. If they allege vaccine critics ignore the evidence, then point out how SAVNers ignore the evidence.

At the level of style, counterattacking can involve mimicking the attackers. When SAVNers use abusive language, counterattackers then verbally abuse SAVNers. When SAVNers use condescending humour, counterattackers might deploy their own condescending humour about SAVNers.

There is a great risk in counterattack, especially when the other side has more people, more energy and more skills. SAVNers have been far more active in using derogatory humour, put-downs and nasty comments than their targets. They have been doing this for years and refined their skills in these techniques. To get into a slanging match with SAVNers is likely to be a losing proposition.

Speaking generally — not just about SAVNers — many of those who use abusive language online get kicks out of seeing their targets squirm. For trolls, verbal abuse can be a game, and when a whole group joins in, there can be a competition to see who can be the most abusive or the most original in formulating a contemptuous comment.[37] This is an indication that counterattack can be extremely unwise: it is exactly what some attackers would like you to do. It gives them pleasure that they've caused distress, excitement in being able to continue the attacking game, and justification for their actions. It is for these reasons that quite a lot of verbal abuse is provocative. It is designed to maximise the likelihood the target will respond. Therefore, to respond is often to fall into a trap set by attackers. Furthermore, when trolls like this are involved, counterattacking runs the risk of causing a huge escalation of attacks.

---

37 For an illuminating study of trolling, see Whitney Phillips, *This Is Why We Can't Have Nice Things: Mapping the Relationship between Online Trolling and Mainstream Culture* (Cambridge, MA: MIT Press, 2015).

Another risk in counterattacking is that it helps legitimise the attacker's methods. On SAVN's Facebook page, sometimes a vaccine critic makes derogatory comments about SAVNers or about vaccination promotion. This is typically greeted with a combination of bile and glee, with an outpouring of hostility and a sense that SAVN had just been justified in its approach. Denigration is commonly seen as justifying counter-denigration, and on SAVN's page SAVNers always have the numbers and the last word.[38]

Analysing
Rather than engage in defending or counterattacking, another option is to analyse the methods used by attackers. This means stepping back from the give-and-take of the exchange and commenting on how it is proceeding. It means drawing attention to assumptions, language, connotations and other facets of the engagement. It involves stepping out of the debate and commenting on the debate itself.

Both sides in the debate use this technique at times, pointing out the methods used by their opponents. Usually this is done as a method for further attack or defence, as when pointing out the abuse used by the other side. Seldom does anyone critically evaluate the methods they use themselves. Analysis, if insightful and fair-minded, potentially can short-circuit hostile exchanges by making

---

38 Whether anti-SAVN commentary is actually due to AVN members, or even to actual vaccine critics, is unknown, because so few of these commentators use their real names.

participants reflect on their behaviour — though whether this actually occurs is something that needs to be determined on a case-by-case basis.

Many of my own interventions into the Australian vaccination debate can be classified as analysis. I have written about tactics used by SAVNers in quite a few articles, blogs and other commentary. For example, in response to the attack on Judy Wilyman's PhD thesis, I wrote a series of articles, for example a detailed critique of the initial attack article published in *The Australian*.[39]

Initially, from about 2011 to 2014, SAVNers responded to these articles by attacking me personally, for example verbal abuse or making complaints to my university. Only a few addressed the arguments I presented. In about 2014, most SAVNers instead began ignoring my new articles: rather than attacking, they made no comment. I interpreted this as them not wanting others to read my analyses, because these analyses made a convincing case against their methods.[40]

After writing a detailed analysis of the 13 January 2016 article in *The Australian* about Judy's thesis, I wrote to its author, Kylar Loussikian, inviting him to comment. He declined. Engaging with a careful analysis means departing from the attack mode. Those who use denigration as a primary tool are unlikely to want to shift from a technique they have practised and refined and instead

---

39 "News with a negative frame: a vaccination case study," 4 March 2016, http://www.bmartin.cc/pubs/16Loussikian.html.

40 "What SAVN doesn't want you to read," 14 July 2014, http://www.bmartin.cc/pubs/14savn/.

engage in a serious exchange. They are more comfortable in the realm of abuse than the scholarly realm of careful mustering of evidence and argument.

Exposing

If you make nasty, hostile comments about someone, this can seem rude and unfair, especially if they do not respond with similar comments. Verbal abuse thus can potentially be counterproductive in the eyes of independent observers.

When SAVNers make abusive comments about Dorey or some other vaccine critic, their main audience is themselves. If those who are denigrated are observing, they may be upset, and often are too embarrassed to want to respond.

Exposure is a potent means of challenging wrongdoing. In this case the wrongdoing is verbal abuse. Some people might see verbal abuse as a small problem, but for those targeted it is a serious matter.

However, exposure is not to be undertaken lightly. Some women, after being targeted in online campaigns of denigration, speak out about the abuse. In response, their attackers subject them to even more graphic threats of rape and murder, as well as threats to their family members.[41]

However, SAVN could not easily escalate its attacks without paying a serious cost in terms of reputation.

---

41 Danielle Keats Citron, *Hate Crimes in Cyberspace* (Cambridge, MA: Harvard University Press, 2014); Emma A. Jane, *Misogyny Online: A Short (and Brutish) History* (London: Sage, 2017); Bailey Poland, *Haters: Harassment, Abuse, and Violence Online* (Lincoln, NE: Potomac Press, 2016).

SAVNers see themselves as moral protectors of children's health against the threat of dangerous "anti-vaxxers." They regularly refer to scientific findings and contest challenges to their views through their own understanding of vaccination as well as by referring others to doctors and scientific experts. They thus present themselves, on some levels, as having credibility concerning vaccination, if only by aligning themselves with authorities in the field.

Thus, SAVNers are treading a fine line when they engage in verbal abuse. They regularly denigrate vaccine critics as a prime method of attack, but if they come across too crudely, this risks hurting their credibility. After all, very few doctors and scientists openly engage in sustained campaigns insulting those with whom they disagree. This would clash with their status as authorities. SAVNers need to feel and appear justified when they denigrate others, while keeping this technique sufficiently hidden from wider audiences to avoiding hurting their image as virtuous crusaders.

In response to cascades of abuse, Meryl Dorey set up a page on the AVN website exposing the prime perpetrators, giving examples.[42] She reproduced some of the most offensive comments, and importantly included the names of those who had made them, thus assigning responsibility. The page was not open for comment, so SAVNers could not swamp it with more abusive comments. What might have seemed like fun among other SAVNers instead seemed nasty and hurtful when presented in a forum for

---

42 "Dossier of attacks on the AVN," https://avn.org.au/dossier-of-attacks-on-the-avn/, 24 August 2012.

those who were the prime targets. Exposing abuse might seem like a method of counterattack. It certainly can discredit the attackers. However, counterattack involves verbal abuse of opponents, a type of tit for tat, whereas exposure involves letting people see what the opponents have done and making their own judgements about it.

SAVNers have also used the technique of exposure, presenting examples of verbal abuse and other inappropriate behaviours perpetrated by vaccine critics. Setting aside the credibility of the evidence, this can be effective in countering nasty comments, but it lacks persuasiveness for anyone familiar with SAVN's own regular use of denigration.

One of the complications of exposure versus counter-exposure is the difference between individual actions and actions attributed to groups. Dorey's list of verbal abuse by SAVNers gives names and details. It would lack impact if Dorey regularly used similar verbal abuse against SAVNers. (SAVNers seize on any comment by Dorey that they can paint as aggressive.) It is a different matter to attribute blame to an entire group for the actions of an individual, for example blaming the AVN for the abusive comments by one or two vaccine critics, especially if the AVN disowns the comments, or blaming SAVN for comments by a single SAVNer.

The difference between the two groups is most apparent in the pages they control. SAVN's Facebook page is filled with vitriol and humorous put-downs, which could be removed if SAVN administrators so desired. (No doubt some of the more extreme comments are removed.) The AVN's website lacks this sort of hostile commentary. So while there are some vaccine critics who make highly derogatory comments about SAVNers and other vaccination advocates, this is not endorsed or encouraged on AVN-controlled forums. In contrast, SAVN's hosting of hostile commentary might be said to provide tacit endorsement for using similar language outside SAVN's direct ambit.

Therefore, when looking at efforts to expose abuse by those on the other side, it is worth paying attention to the context. Is there a pattern of abuse or are there just a few isolated incidents? Is abuse endorsed or tolerated by administrators? Is it attributed to individuals or to groups?

Some of my articles about SAVN involve the technique of exposure. I have written about SAVN's attribution of beliefs to the AVN, SAVNers' verbal abuse and humorous put-downs, and other denigration techniques used by SAVN. In this, I try to be careful to focus on SAVN methods while acknowledging that SAVNers believe they are protecting public health. My aim is to describe and display SAVN methods so readers can understand them and, if desired, decide on ways to respond.

CONCLUSION

Denigration can be a powerful tool of attack, serving multiple functions. It can cause distress among targets, sometimes causing them to withdraw from debates. It angers some targets, leading them to lash out in ways that discredit them and provide an apparent justification for the attackers.

Among observers, denigration is sometimes enough to cause their opinion of targets to be reduced. This can occur through the information provided through attacks and, more potently, through the connotations and implications involved. As the saying goes, "Mud sticks." Hostile allegations, if repeated long and assertively enough, start to become the lens through which observers see the target.

There are numerous types of denigration tactics, for example attributing absurd or unsavoury beliefs to targets, suggesting guilt by association with low status groups or activities, selectively presenting negative information about targets and blowing it out of proportion while omitting any mention of positives, applying derogatory labels, making fun of targets, and subjecting targets to verbal abuse. The common theme in these tactics is to put the focus on the targets and to make them seem bad in some way: as strange, ignorant, malicious, criminal or dangerous.

Denigration, when carried out by a group, potentially has powerful effects on the perpetrators. It helps distinguish the group from its targets, relying on and reinforcing the sense that "we" are different from, and superior to, "them." This is the in-group versus out-group dynamic that is so easily invoked among humans. Denigration is a tool for accentuating similarities within the in-group and within the out-group while accentuating the gulf between the two groups.

Denigration potentially relies on both rational and intuitive parts of the mind. The rational mind is brought in when negative information is provided about targets, but in a misleading way, without proper context. However, the more powerful aspect of denigration is via the intuitive mind, which mostly operates automatically, unconsciously, rapidly and without careful consideration. The intuitive mind is highly accurate for many purposes but not when insults and negative associations trigger unconscious thought processes that lead to a negative image, without rational evaluation of the processes.[43]

SAVN, in its campaign against the AVN and other vaccine critics, has used a wide range of denigration tactics. Indeed, SAVN's campaign, along with others who have joined in, provides an illuminating showcase for how denigration tactics can operate. However, there are some limits to the effectiveness of such tactics.

Not everyone is taken in by denigration tactics. Some have information that makes them realise the allegations, implications and associations are wrong or misleading. Targets, and people who know them, are most likely to resist the tactics.

Some denigration tactics, because they are seen to be nasty or unfair, can cause disapproval of the attackers. Some of the mud being thrown by the attackers may stick to their hands, while missing the target.

SAVNers, when using denigration tactics, run the risk of going too far, of seeming to be the problem rather than the solution. If their verbal abuse is too extreme, and is exposed, they may hurt their own cause. Thoughtful observers may question why SAVNers need to deploy so

---

43 Mahzarin R. Banaji and Anthony G. Greenwald, *Blindspot: Hidden Biases of Good People* (New York: Delacorte Press, 2013).

many distasteful methods against apparently weak and misguided opponents when, as SAVNers proclaim, there is no debate and the evidence for vaccination is overwhelming. If the evidence is overwhelming, why cannot parents simply be allowed to make up their own minds? Why must critics be treated with contempt?

Denigration is one of the three main methods used against vaccine critics, the others being harassment and censorship. There is an overlap between these methods. For example, verbal abuse is a technique of denigration that also serves to harass targets. These connections will be covered in the next two chapters.

Appendix: on claims about abuse
The difficulties involved in getting to the bottom of claims about online abuse are illustrated in a case that occurred in October 2016. Jill Hennessy, the Minister of Health for the state of Victoria, claimed to have been subject to abusive tweets from vaccine critics. She produced a video in which she read out 14 abusive tweets.[44] One of them was:

> Go crawl back into the gutter from where you came, you malevolent ignorant mouthpiece for the corrupt and moronic pharmaceutical industry which for your edification is controlled by elitist Zionist jews and their minions.

---

44 "Vic MP reads mean tweets from anti-vaxxers," *News.com.au*, 21 October 2016, http://goo.gl/zyEh58.

In the video, some profanity that Hennessy reads is covered over by bleep sounds.

Hennessy's video, and the abusive tweets from vaccine critics, became the subject of a front-page story titled "Jill Hennessy gets abusive tweets from anti-vaccine campaigners" published on 20 October in the *Herald Sun*, a major Melbourne daily newspaper, which was picked up by major television stations and news sites on social media. The *Herald Sun* conveniently provided the text of some of the tweets, such as the one above.

Some vaccine critics became suspicious about Hennessy's claims. The alleged tweet above has 220 characters, more than Twitter's then maximum of 140 characters. A week after the *Herald Sun* story, an anonymous investigator posted an exposé on a site called *The Truth Library*.[45] The investigator was able to track down two of the tweets — the only two for which usernames were provided in Hennessy's video. One was made in the name of Irene Beune, a Dutch obstetrician and gynaecologist, who wrote to the investigator saying she had a Twitter account but had never made a tweet, and furthermore she was a supporter of vaccination. The implication is that someone had forged a tweet in the name of Irene Beune.

The investigator also determined that 10 of the 14 tweets read out by Hennessy were taken from comments

---

45 A Vaccine Injured Mum, "Abusive tweet drama: Health Minister Jill Hennessy busted fabricating lies," *The Truth Library*, 27 October 2016, http://www.truthlibrary.info/blog/hennessyliesexposed/.

made in a closed Facebook group. Because of the possibility of being attacked on social media, some vaccine critics — most commonly mothers, including those believing their children were damaged by vaccines — feel the need to share stories and feelings confidentially, so they join private Facebook groups.[46] However, some vaccination proponents portray themselves as vaccine critics, gain access to some of these groups and take screenshots of comments made. The blog Reasonable Hank specialises in exposing vaccine critics using such screenshots.[47]

Some of the comments were quite hostile towards Hennessy. These constituted 10 of the comments she read out. The point is that these were not tweets, and they were not sent to Hennessy. The investigator for *The Truth Library* believed Reasonable Hank had provided the screen shots to Hennessy (or, more likely, to staff in Hennessy's ministerial office), presenting them as tweets. She was so eager to discredit vaccine critics that care was not taken to check that the comments were genuine and made on Twitter.[48]

---

46 It's also possible that some vaccination supporters fear being attacked and set up private Facebook groups.

47 For Reasonable Hank's view of the Hennessy tweet affair, see "More ugly misogyny against Victorian Health Minister Jill Hennessy from the antivax movement," Reasonable Hank, 8 January 2017, https://reasonablehank.com/2017/01/08/more-ugly-misogyny-against-health-minister-jill-hennessy/.

48 A later story in the *Australian National Review* claimed that after the exposure in *The Truth Library*, the *Herald Sun* altered its original story: see "Victorian Health Minister And NewsCorp caught allegedly lying in order to attack parents with vaccine

If *The Truth Library* investigator's analysis is correct, this is an example of what Truda Gray and I have called "black backfire."[49] Hennessy attempted to use abuse by vaccine critics to discredit them, in other words to make their abusive comments backfire against the critics. But if the texts she read out were not actual tweets, they were not what she purported them to be: they were "black."

That such alleged tweets could become a significant news story shows the imbalance in media coverage of the Australian vaccination debate. Alleged abuse from vaccine critics was deemed newsworthy, whereas abuse from vaccination proponents over several years has never been covered by any major news outlet. Furthermore, I am not aware of instances of SAVNers or other vaccination proponents withdrawing their abusive comments.

Undoubtedly, some vaccine critics do make abusive comments about proponents. Indeed, that is exactly what commenters on the closed Facebook group were doing. For vaccine critics to use verbal abuse is likely to be counterproductive, because proponents have a far greater capacity to expose and denounce the abuse, making it backfire. However, according to *The Truth Library* investigator's analysis, it seems that Reasonable Hank or others considered there was not enough abuse from critics and so

---

injured children," *Australian National Review*, 11 April 2017, reproduced at http://goo.gl/PfhJ9p.

49 Truda Gray and Brian Martin, "Backfires: white, black and grey," *Journal of Information Warfare*, Vol. 7, Issue 1, 2007, pp. 7–16, http://www.bmartin.cc/pubs/07jiw.html.

decided to manufacture or misrepresent some for the purpose of discrediting them.

5
Harassment

The campaign against Australian vaccine critics has involved a variety of techniques of harassment, including making complaints to regulatory bodies, posting names in a "hall of shame," sending pornography, threatening legal action and infiltrating closed groups. Some of these techniques involve denigration, which overlaps with harassment.[1] Suffice it to say that in this chapter I address

---

[1] Techniques of denigration and harassment are closely related and overlapping. Verbal abuse, a technique of denigration, is also a form of harassment. So what's the difference? It's a matter of emphasis.

When SAVNers post nasty comments about the AVN on SAVN's Facebook page, it's possible to ignore the comments. The comments might be upsetting and can be considered harassment, but they are "out there," not in the personal space of AVNers. When anonymous callers leave threats on a target's phone, it is more personal.

Some forms of harassment cannot easily be ignored. When complaints to government agencies led to investigations of the AVN, the AVN felt obliged to respond in order to prevent adverse findings and actions. Complaints thus seemed to necessitate more efforts in response than adverse newspaper articles. But again, the difference is a matter of degree: some complaints are a minor nuisance whereas others require enormous effort; an adverse newspaper article can pass with little notice or can trigger additional attacks.

a number of additional techniques used by SAVNers and others to attack the AVN and other vaccine critics.[2]

COMPLAINTS

SLAPPs

It is quite legitimate to make complaints. Watchdog agencies such as ombudsmen's offices are set up to consider complaints, the rationale being that this would allow corruption and malpractice to be addressed through formal procedures. However, although many complaints are completely legitimate, complaint procedures can also be used for harassment.

In the US, researchers George Pring and Penelope Canan became aware of a disturbing pattern.[3] Various groups and individuals, for example corporations and police officers, were launching legal actions against citizens in ways that seemed like reprisals for exercising their right of free speech. For example, a local resident would write a letter to a local government body opposing a housing development, and the developer would sue the resident for defamation or economic damage. Or a citizen

---

Another possible contrast is that denigration targets reputation whereas harassment is designed to disturb and disrupt targets. Again, the contrast is not necessarily all that great. It might be said that denigration often serves to harass and harassment often serves to denigrate.

2 On SAVN and the AVN, see the glossary and chapter 3.

3 George Pring and Penelope Canan, *SLAPPs: Getting Sued for Speaking Out* (Philadelphia: Temple University Press, 1996).

would submit a complaint about a police officer and be sued by the officer. Some people were sued simply for signing a petition. The most common legal basis for these actions was defamation, which includes libel and slander. If you write something that harms someone's reputation, you have committed libel; if you say it, you have committed slander.

The reality is that people routinely defame others, for example in office gossip and in social media commentary, but seldom is anyone sued. Traditionally, legal action was reserved for cases involving significant damage to reputations, for example major media coverage that recklessly makes false allegations.

Pring and Canan observed something different: powerful groups using defamation law, and other torts, to intimidate ordinary citizens who were speaking out about matters of social concern. They coined an acronym to describe these legal actions: SLAPPs, standing for Strategic Lawsuits Against Public Participation.

In the US, the First Amendment to the Constitution is well known for protecting free speech. This amendment also contains a lesser known provision protecting the right to petition the government. In practical terms, this means that if a US citizen writes a letter to a politician or a government agency, it is considered speech protected by the First Amendment. So when a developer sued a citizen who wrote a letter to the local government, this legal action had no chance of success in court, because the constitution protected this form of speech.

However, having the constitution on your side is of little solace if you have to engage a lawyer, fork out thousands of dollars and wait months while the case slowly proceeds through the legal system. The whole process is frightening, and in many instances caused the citizens to withdraw from the issue about which they were concerned. This is why Pring and Canan called these legal actions SLAPPs: they discouraged legitimate public participation in matters affecting people's lives.

It is important to be aware of how SLAPPs work. In many instances, the corporations and other plaintiffs knew their legal actions had no chance of success. The point of these actions was not to win in court but to intimidate their targets, and often they were very effective in this goal.

When a citizen speaks out about commercial developments, police abuse or other social problems, they are engaging in public discourse, often in a public domain. SLAPPs move the issue out of the public domain into the legal arena. In the public domain, corporations and citizens each have to argue their case, and the evidence and arguments presented by corporations may come up short. In the legal system, on the other hand, the conflict is tilted in favour of the corporation, because it has a lot more money, and because the conflict is no longer about the issue — a development or a case of police use of force — but instead is about the legal issue at hand, for example damage to reputation. The issue is pulled out of the public arena and put into an arena where money and power favour one side.

Pring and Canan's writings helped raise awareness of the iniquity of what they called SLAPPs, and in the following years there was a push back against those who launched them. Defendants and lawyers better understood what was happening and how to invoke first-amendment defences. Furthermore, legislatures in many US states passed anti-SLAPP laws in an attempt to discourage these sorts of legal actions, though plaintiffs continue to use legal actions to intimidate opponents.

In Australia, activists have also been targets of legal actions seemingly designed to inhibit speech, including speech in the form of protest. Animal liberationists have been sued. Environmentalists critical of a bridge to Hindmarsh Island in South Australia were sued by the owners of a resort on the island. The most prominent Australian SLAPP was launched by the huge forestry company Gunns in Tasmania against a whole group of environmentalists and politicians.[4]

In Australia, defending against SLAPPs has to operate differently than in the US, because Australia has no bill of rights and no explicit constitutional protection for free speech or for petitioning the government. Furthermore, defamation laws in Australia are much tougher than in the US, in the sense that it is harder for defendants to prove their case. Therefore, in Australia it is more common for politically aware SLAPP defendants to use publicity and campaigning to increase the reputation costs to plaintiffs.

Scapps

It is not common for SLAPPs to be used in the Australian vaccination struggle. SAVN is not a wealthy group able to

---

4 Greg Ogle, *Gagged: The Gunns 20 and Other Law Suits* (Sydney: Envirobook, 2009).

afford the hundreds of thousands of dollars needed to run a defamation or other legal action. Instead, SAVN has relied on a related technique: making complaints to government agencies. This costs virtually nothing aside from the time and effort to formulate the complaints. If an agency acts on a complaint, this has much the same effect as a SLAPP: it takes the issue out of the domain of public debate about vaccination and into the formalities of complaint procedures; it soaks up time and energy of the target of the complaint; and it serves as a threat to the target about the possible consequences if the complaint is upheld by the agency. To label the strategy of making complaints as a form of harassment, by analogy with SLAPPs I coined the acronym SCAPPs: Strategic Complaints Against Public Participation.[5]

SAVN's complaint strategy has only been possible because there is overwhelming support for vaccination within the medical profession and relevant government departments. This makes it likely that government agencies, or at least some figures within them, will be hostile to vaccine critics and willing to take action against them. In the case of SLAPPs, only those with money and influence can use them effectively; for an ordinary citizen to sue a wealthy corporation would probably lead to financial ruin. Similarly, SCAPPs are likely to be effective only when serving dominant perspectives. For the AVN to appeal to government agencies to act against vaccination

---

5 Brian Martin, "Debating vaccination: understanding the attack on the Australian Vaccination Network," *Living Wisdom*, No. 8, 2011, pp. 14–40, http://goo.gl/3GkMPz.

providers would be futile. However, if we imagine a different world in which vaccination is a marginal and stigmatised practice, it is possible to imagine SCAPPs being used against vaccination proponents.

SCAPPs are not guaranteed to be effective, because agencies might decide that complaints have no merit and dismiss them without even notifying the target of the complaint. SAVN's strategy seems to have been to make numerous complaints in the hope that some of them will lead to investigations of or sanctions against the AVN and other targets.

There is no public record of the number of complaints filed by SAVNers over the years. Going by occasional comments on the SAVN Facebook page and information available to the AVN (including comments from agency staff) as well as the publicly announced investigations, a rough guess is that SAVNers and others have made dozens or even hundreds of complaints about the AVN to government bodies. Some of the complaints are quite long and involve detailed allegations: considerable effort is required to formulate such complaints. Detailed, well-referenced complaints that show an understanding of the relevant agency's rules are far more likely to be taken seriously than short, quickly drafted and poorly documented complaints. The complaint strategy, to be effective, thus requires both knowledge and hard work.

Effectiveness can be judged at several levels. For SAVN, a complaint that triggered a request to the AVN for information or response was effective in diverting the AVN from its normal activities into responding to the complaint; it might also cause some anxiety. This was the first level of success. If the agency announced an investigation, this was a greater impact, because SAVN could then trumpet that the AVN was being investigated, thus denigrating the AVN. Being investigated brings a taint, as many people may think there would be no reason to investigate unless something suspicious was going on. This was a second level of success. If the investigation led to adverse actions being taken against the AVN, this was an even greater level of success for SAVN. The AVN was tied up in dealing with the complaint, was discredited by the investigation and was sanctioned in a way that hurt its operations.

The HCCC
Ken McLeod has been a prominent figure in SAVN. One of his most high-impact actions was to submit a complaint about the AVN to the Health Care Complaints Commission (HCCC), alleging that the AVN "engages in misleading and deceptive conduct to dissuade people from vaccinating themselves and their children, and that consequently the AVN is a danger to public health and safety."[6]

The HCCC is an agency funded by the government of New South Wales, the state where the AVN is incorporated. The HCCC receives complaints about health care

---

6 Ken McLeod, "Complaint pursuant to the Health Care Complaints Act 1993 that the 'Australian Vaccination Network' is providing a health service that endangers public health," 14 July 2009, quote from p. 3. Available at https://www.scribd.com/document/34134349/Initial-Complaint-against-the-AVN-by-Ken-McLeod.

practitioners, typically complaints by patients about doctors and nurses.[7] McLeod's complaint about the AVN was unusual in that the AVN was not, in the usual way of looking at things, a health care provider.

The HCCC asked the AVN to respond to two complaints, McLeod's and one made by Toni and David McCaffery, whose baby daughter Dana had died from whooping cough, the death that triggered the formation of SAVN. The AVN was given a copy of McLeod's complaint but was not allowed to see the McCafferys'.

McLeod's complaint was long and detailed, with 23 pages and 39 footnotes.[8] The AVN's response was similarly lengthy and comprehensive, requiring a great deal of time and effort. That the AVN felt obliged to respond to the complaints was success for the complainants at level one.

Following the complaints, the HCCC initiated an investigation into the AVN. The existence of this investigation was a powerful rhetorical tool for SAVN. In all sorts of communications thereafter, SAVNers publicised

---

7 For some of the history of the HCCC, from a critical perspective, see Sue Williams, *Death of a Doctor: How the Medical Profession Turned on One of Their Own* (Sydney: Allen & Unwin, 2005), pp. 146–160. Williams tells the story of John Harrison, a charismatic alternative practitioner who was brought down by the HCCC on the basis of dodgy complaints of sexual misconduct. His deregistration for life was a convenient blow by the medical establishment against alternative practitioners.

8 I analysed several aspects of McLeod's complaint in "Debating vaccination," *Living Wisdom*, No. 8, 2011, pp. 14–40, http://goo.gl/3GkMPz.

that the AVN was under investigation by the HCCC. This was success at level two.

These two complaints to the HCCC turned out to be a big win for SAVN. Not only did the HCCC investigate: it found against the AVN, saying that the information on its website was misleading. In reaching this conclusion, the HCCC seemed to have taken the government's vaccination policy as unquestionable, thus enabling it to ignore the AVN's response to the complaints.

The HCCC's finding was exactly what SAVN needed to aid its campaign against the AVN. The HCCC demanded that the AVN put a disclaimer on its website, and dictated the exact words to be posted.[9] On the basis of legal advice, the AVN declined to post the HCCC's disclaimer.[10] The HCCC then issued a "public warning" about the AVN. This was the ultimate coup for SAVN. The public warning became a news story in the mainstream media and SAVN quoted the warning repeatedly in its communications, for example when writing to venues to discourage them from hosting AVN talks. SAVN had achieved success with a SCAPP at level three.

The whole basis for the HCCC investigation and warning was dubious. As noted, the HCCC was set up to hear complaints about doctors, nurses and other health

---

9 The AVN already had its own disclaimer on its website, but the HCCC apparently deemed it inadequate.

10 I think this was a major strategic error. See my discussion in "A vaccination struggle," chapter 8 in *Nonviolence Unbound* (Sparsnäs, Sweden: Irene Publishing, 2015), http://www.bmartin.cc/pubs/15nvu/, especially pp. 292–307.

practitioners, and here it was acting on a complaint about the AVN, a group that was not involved in healthcare in the usual sense. The HCCC justified its investigation by classifying the AVN as a healthcare *education* provider, which thus fit within the HCCC's mandate. In my view, this was a sleight of hand, because the AVN was not an education provider in the usual sense, like a school or a company offering short courses. It was a citizens' organisation presenting a point of view about government policy. By the same token, groups campaigning about nuclear power, pesticides and climate change could be considered healthcare education providers, because they provide information relevant to people's health. It is for this reason that I consider the complaints to the HCCC to be SCAPPs. The fact that the HCCC took the complaints seriously, launched an investigation and issued a public warning is compatible with the complaints being SCAPPs, just as SLAPPs are occasionally successful in court.[11]

---

11 Other complaints about the AVN led nowhere. For example, in August 2010, two short complaints were submitted to the HCCC. One complainant said Dorey was providing information about vaccines for payment, and asked that Dorey's lies be stopped. The other complaint was also about Dorey receiving payment, and requested further action against Dorey and the AVN. In November 2011, a complaint was made about the AVN website giving incorrect information about hospital emergency numbers. However, the HCCC, after considering the information provided, decided to take no further action in these cases.

Challenging the HCCC

The AVN took the HCCC to court, arguing that it had exceeded its powers, and won the case. The HCCC immediately withdrew its public warning. It seemed that the AVN, by using the legal system, had won, even though severe damage had been done to its reputation through SAVN's campaigning and media coverage.

But winning in court was not the end of the story. State politicians were encouraged to change the law in a way that would enable the HCCC to investigate the AVN. This meant removing the legal technicality by which the AVN won in its case against the HCCC.

Earlier, I said that the basis for the HCCC's investigation was dubious: it requires public commentary on a contentious issue to conform to the current medical orthodoxy. It is thus a restraint on free speech. Two legal scholars, Tom Vines and Thomas Faunce, examined the AVN's legal action against the HCCC and made these observations:

> In a free society, the views and opinions expressed by Ms Dorey and the AVN should be protected against government interference. Arguments against public immunisation programs are not simply debates over health policy; they are also political discussions. As such, the AVN's website, and Ms Dorey's statements, ought to be protected from interference by Parliament or the Executive by the implied constitutional right of political communication.
>
> Moreover, freedom of expression is an essential human right, protected under international and

domestic human rights instruments, and should not be abridged except in the most limited of circumstances, such as a major pandemic. It would be inappropriate for a government agency to be given a standing mandate to censor debate or force an individual to include a statement on their website with which they do not agree. If the misleading information of the AVN is to be challenged, then it should be through the better dissemination of accurate information and the proper management.[12]

The state parliament ignored such considerations. In a parliamentary session, politicians from all political persuasions thundered against the AVN, as recounted in a newspaper column dealing with state politics:

> Wing-nuts, flat-earthers, weird, wacky and wrong. Wilful manslaughter. Potentially murderous. The language in the NSW Parliament condemning the Australian Vaccination Network and its hijack of the internet to spread an anti-vaccination message couldn't have been stronger. Both sides of politics piled it on.[13]

---

12 Tom Vines and Thomas Faunce, "Civil liberties and the critics of safe vaccination: Australian Vaccination Network Inc v Health Care Complaints Commission [2012] NSWSC 110," *Journal of Law and Medicine,* Vol. 20, 2012, pp. 44–58, at p. 54. Footnotes in the quote omitted.

13 Kirsty Needham, "Jabs fly in fight to raise rates of vaccination," *Sun-Herald,* 5 May 2013, p. 38.

The politicians' condemnation of the AVN illustrates the technique of denigration. Parliament then passed legislation to increase the powers of the HCCC. This enabled it to launch an investigation into the AVN at its own initiative, which it soon did. Furthermore, shortly after the law was changed, the HCCC received additional complaints about the AVN, and decided to investigate.

The OLGR
There was a spinoff benefit for SAVN from the HCCC public warning. SAVNers had made complaints to another government body in New South Wales, the Office of Liquor, Gaming and Racing or OLGR, which was responsible for determining the charitable status of incorporated organisations. Because of the HCCC public warning, the OLGR banned the AVN from taking new members and from fundraising through donations.

The OLGR's conditions created a new vulnerability for the AVN. On 20 March 2012, SAVNer Dan Buzzard showed, on the SAVN Facebook page, a record of a 1-cent donation to the AVN, made by direct deposit. It shows a deposit of $0.01 to the AVN Gift Fund Account with the accompanying description "Happy downfall." Buzzard's idea was that the AVN would be required to return the donation, because otherwise it would be in violation of the OLGR's conditions on fundraising. The following exchange occurred on SAVN's Facebook page:

Dan Buzzard: Such an arse sometimes.
Bill Rodgers: Are u a member? That might need to be refunded. Buthen how can u even make a deposit if you aren't a member.
Dan Buzzard: It's just a normal transfer, you don't need to be a member to do it. If they do need to refund ALL non-member donations then I just found a way to take-up allot of Meryls time.
Bill Rodgers: 1c donated by 100 people would take a long time to refund.

Probably it would have been impossible to refund such donations, because the identity of the donors could not be determined from the bank.

This is an example of the ingenious methods of harassment dreamed up by SAVNers. However, there is no evidence that this became a common technique, nor that the AVN was sanctioned for not returning 1-cent donations. After the HCCC withdrew its public warning, the OLGR removed its ban on the AVN accepting new members and fundraising.

Fair Trading
One of the agencies that received complaints about the AVN was Fair Trading, a state government agency that deals with incorporated bodies. An organisation, to be incorporated, must satisfy various conditions, for example having a constitution and an annual general meeting according to rules laid down by Fair Trading, and paying an annual fee. There is no requirement that organisations be incorporated, and it can be a bother for a small group. It

does provide some protection for members in the face of legal actions: committee members are not liable for the actions of the organisation (though in practice this protection is not ironclad). Incorporation of the AVN meant that Meryl Dorey, as president of the AVN, could not be personally sued for actions by the AVN.

It should be mentioned that SAVN has never been incorporated. It is a network, without a president or other office bearers and without a bank account.

Though being incorporated can provide some protection and legitimacy for an organisation, for the AVN incorporation became a vulnerability due to complaints made to Fair Trading. One of the requirements of Fair Trading is that incorporated bodies, when they use their name, must follow it with "Inc." to indicate that it is incorporated. This is a minor formality, often ignored. But the requirement was used to harass the AVN. Complaints were made to Fair Trading about the AVN not always including "Inc." after its name, for example on its website, and Fair Trading then wrote to the AVN demanding that it comply. Dorey checked the websites of other incorporated bodies and discovered that noncompliance was commonplace. However, this was no help for the AVN. It still had to address the complaint.

This illustrates a typical feature of bodies such as the HCCC, OLGR and Fair Trading: much of their activity is driven by complaints. In the case of the HCCC — the Health Care Complaints Commission — the word "complaints" is part of the agency's name. The significance of being complaint-based is that there is no requirement that rules be applied across the board. So when Fair Trading told the AVN to comply with the rule about putting "Inc." after its name, Fair Trading did not need to monitor the use of names by thousands of other incorporated bodies and tell non-compliant organisations to follow the rule. Fair Trading could just act in response to the complaint about the AVN. Thus the rules governing Fair Trading were susceptible to SAVN's technique of making complaints as a form of harassment. If Fair Trading made across-the-board demands, this could antagonise a wide range of organisations, and the AVN would not have to defend alone.

Fair Trading was in charge of the names of organisations. SAVN started a campaign to force the AVN to change its name. A few complaints to Fair Trading might not have been sufficient. What made the AVN's name a significant issue was public campaigning, which involved media stories and the involvement of politicians and others.

On the surface, SAVN seemed to have a point. The name "Australian Vaccination Network" gives no indication of the AVN's critical stance towards vaccination. However, this focus on the AVN's name reflected SAVN's successful attempt to set the agenda. There was no general expectation for a review of the names of all incorporated bodies in the state. That could have led to calls for wholesale name changes. The Liberal Party might be called upon to change its name to the Conservative Party or perhaps the Neoliberal Party. It is easily imagined that the pushback against any such name-change demands would be enormous. After all, organisations develop a brand identity based on their names, and the literal meaning of the names can become secondary.

The campaign for the AVN to change its name can be seen as harassment because it was targeted at an alleged problem with the AVN, while ignoring comparable or more serious problems with other organisations. Furthermore, it is not hard to find organisations with seriously misleading names. In what is called astroturfing, corporations set up what appear to be grassroots citizens' groups that actually are fronts for corporate lobbying.[14] Given that the phenomenon of astroturfing has been documented for decades, if Fair Trading was seriously concerned about misleading names, it might have searched for cases in the state. However, this would have brought it up against corporate interests. Instead, Fair Trading acquiesced in SAVN's campaign to have the AVN's name changed.

This campaign was effective because many people, hearing about the issue, said "Yes, if the AVN is mainly critical of vaccination, then its name does seem misleading." SAVN had set the agenda, to look just at the AVN, without looking more widely at the names of other organisations.

According to the law governing Fair Trading, demands to change names must satisfy certain criteria.

---

14 Sharon Beder, *Global Spin: The Corporate Assault on Environmentalism*, second edition (Totnes, UK: Green Books, 2002); John Stauber and Sheldon Rampton, *Toxic Sludge is Good for You: Lies, Damn Lies, and the Public Relations Industry* (Monroe, ME: Common Courage Press, 1995).

According to the AVN, the state government minister responsible for Fair Trading

> ... issued a directive ordering us to change our name. It was then discovered that the Act did not give him the power to make this order so the directive was subsequently rescinded. The Minister then issued an amendment regulation to enable the original directive to be reissued which he then did.[15]

Here's the way the Minister explained this to state parliament:

> To address this issue in the public interest, in December last year the O'Farrell-Stoner [NSW state] government introduced the Associations Incorporation Amendment (Unacceptable Names) Regulation 2012. This amendment expanded the classifications of unacceptable names to include any name that is likely to mislead the public in relation to the nature, objects or functions of an association. Following the commencement of this amendment, on 14 January this year Fair Trading issued the Australian Vaccination Network with a direction to change the name of its association.[16]

---

15 AVN, "AVN's new name approved," media release, 10 March 2014, http://myemail.constantcontact.com/Australian-Vaccination-Network-now-has-a-new-name-.html?soid=1101800214009&aid=8KiZOm4KCgg.

16 Australian Vaccination Network Inc v Department of Finance & Services [2013] NSWADT 266, 25 November 2013, para 11.

This was just one of the intricacies involved in the name-change saga, which involved Fair Trading directing the AVN to change its name, a review of the decision, the AVN making an appeal to the Administrative Decisions Tribunal (with all sorts of submissions from different parties, for and against), and the ADT's decision. Along the way, there was considerable comment in the mass and social media.

It is quite clear that the regulation about names was targeted at the AVN. From the point of view of the AVN, Fair Trading was serving as a partisan for the AVN's opponents. In its submission to the ADT, the AVN made the point that some 16 years had elapsed between its name being approved in 1997 and the request that its name be changed, and that there was no precedent for such a lengthy delay in any jurisdiction in any continent. This was one of many arguments that revealed how the state's regulatory apparatus was being mobilised against the AVN.

Humourist Richard Glover, in a column inspired by the AVN case, spelled out the implications of requiring truth in names:

> The nutbags from Australian Vaccination Network will be forced to change their name to something that better reflects their anti-vaccination stance, following a court ruling this week. Fair enough. I'm all for truth in labelling. But once the principle is established, where does it stop?
>
> The Liberal Party, for instance, has never been very liberal; the Labor Party, according to the voters,

doesn't work; and the National Party is anything but national, representing, as it does, the sectional interests of country people. So all three have to go. [...]
 Nescafe makes coffee for home consumption, so really should be Notcafe; Twitter is for twats, so should be Twatter; and on Facebook everyone pretends they are happier and more successful than they are, so really it should be Farcebook.[17]

More name games
Fair Trading demanded that the AVN change its name, but did not say what it should be changed to. The AVN might have been happy to change its name, for example to Vaccination Choice Australia, except that its website was http://avn.org.au/. If the AVN became VCA, SAVNers might have applied to take over the AVN's domain name. So the AVN resisted Fair Trading's demands as long as possible. Without going into details, a game began between the AVN and SAVN.

 In adopting a new name, the AVN needed to reserve it with Fair Trading. Around the same time, there was a frenzy of business-name registrations. The names "Australian Vaccination Sceptics Network," "Australian Vaccination Skeptics," "Vaccination Sceptics Australia" and "Vaccination Sceptics Network of Australia" were registered with the Australian Securities & Investments Commission (ASIC). The AVN requested a review of

---

17 Richard Glover, "How much honesty do we really want?" *The Age* (Melbourne), 30 November 2013.

these registrations, but this was denied by ASIC. These were, presumably, names that SAVNers did not want the AVN to have (they all have "sceptic" or "skeptic" as part of the name), and it is plausible that SAVNers reserved these particular names. In the end, the AVN won this little tussle by changing its name to Australian Vaccination-skeptics Network, thus retaining its abbreviation AVN. It was able to register this business name, as it was just a little bit different from previously registered names.[18]

After changing its name, the AVN continued to use the same abbreviation. This led to a verbal request from a compliance officer at Fair Trading that the AVN change its abbreviation to AVSN. Apparently no written request or justification was ever provided.[19] This is just one of many small challenges for the AVN resulting from an agency taking up SAVN's agenda.

The AVN's new name was intensely annoying to SAVNers.[20] SAVN has affinities with the Australian

---

18 Other machinations may have been involved. See "Did NSW Fair Trading illegally leak private AVN information?" *No Compulsory Vaccination*, 25 June 2014, http://nocompulsoryvaccination.com/2014/06/25/did-nsw-fair-trading-illegally-leak-private-avn-information/.

19 Greg Beattie, "Apparently our acronym is now misleading?" *No Compulsory Vaccination*, 25 March 2014, http://nocompulsoryvaccination.com/2014/03/25/apparently-our-acronym-is-now-misleading/.

20 Rick Morton, "Anti-vaccine group struggling for new ID," *The Australian*, 2 January 2014, p. 3, reported on the rush to register names with the Australian Securities & Investments Commission, and wrote:

Skeptics, an organisation that opposes alternatives to mainstream science and medicine, for example parapsychology and homoeopathy. The Australian Skeptics are part of a larger international network of Skeptics groups, and in Australia the group uses the US spelling "Skeptic" rather than the usual Australian spelling "Sceptic." Whatever the spelling, the Skeptics consider that they should have a monopoly over the use of the term "skeptic" or "sceptic." In other words, they consider themselves the only true sceptics. Others, though, see the Skeptics as one-sided sceptics, in that they almost never apply their scepticism to mainstream science or medicine.[21]

SAVN had previously given its name as Stop the Australian Vaccination Network and needed to change it because the AVN changed its name.[22] Rather than openly repeat the word "skeptics," SAVN changed its name to Stop the Australian (Anti)Vaccination Network, applying the name it wished the AVN had adopted.

> Ken McLeod, one of the leaders of a group called Stop the Anti-Vaccination Network, said any use of the word "sceptics" in the organisation's new name would be dishonest. "We object to them using any variation of the term because sceptics gather evidence to make an informed choice. The AVN does nothing of the sort," he said. "If they went ahead with this, we would consider putting in a complaint to the Fair Trading Minister."

21 See for example Craig Weiler, *Psi Wars: TED, Wikipedia and the Battle for the Internet* (US: Craig Weiler, 2013).

22 If the AVN had changed its name to Vaccination Choice Australia, then logically SAVN should have become Stop Vaccination Choice Australia, not a good label.

The name change drama received considerable mass media coverage, but after the AVN changed its name, the attention died down. Dorey took a lower profile and the AVN seemed to have less energy than before, though this may have been deceptive, because the media had become less willing to provide coverage.

Surviving attacks via complaints
The AVN somehow survived its struggles with government agencies that took action against it: the HCCC, OLGR, Fair Trading and others. But dealing with the complaints, the adverse decisions and the associated adverse publicity was wearing, requiring huge amounts of effort and money, and exhausting Dorey and some other AVN members. Rather than continuing with their usual activities in presenting their viewpoints and serving their members, AVN office-bearers were preoccupied with defending against attacks.

SAVN's complaint strategy thus turned out to be highly effective. It was successful because some government agencies were susceptible to SAVN's method, which basically was to use them as tools of harassment. This strategy can work when used in support of a dominant position against weaker challengers. It is implausible that the AVN could have used complaints effectively against vaccination promoters, because public opinion, including opinion within agencies, was against the AVN.[23]

---

23 Some vaccination critics have used complaint procedures, for example making submissions to the Australian Press Council

SAVN's SCAPP strategy was actually built on more than making complaints. It was accompanied by media campaigning — primarily social media, followed by some mass media — to discredit the AVN and give support for those within agencies who took a strong line against the AVN.

The complaints required a huge amount of time and effort from three groups. Some of those making complaints, wanting them to be taken seriously, put considerable time and effort into preparing them. As noted, Ken McLeod's initial complaint to the HCCC was long and detailed. The AVN felt obliged to respond to many of the complaints with comprehensive rebuttals. Then there is the effort required in the bodies receiving the complaints: each complaint must be read, assessed and responded to. The effort to harass the AVN through complaints was probably requiring thousands of hours of effort (by complainants, respondents and agency staff) and hundreds of thousands of dollars in salaries.

The AVN was not SAVN's only target for making complaints. Individuals critical of vaccination were also in SAVN's sights. As noted previously, the blog Reasonable Hank has included "outings" of nurses, midwives and chiropractors who are critical of vaccination, accompanied by derogatory comments, which is part of the technique of denigration. As well, SAVNers make complaints when they can. For nurses and midwives, a prime candidate is AHPRA, the Australian Health Practitioner Regulation

---

about unbalanced media coverage, but most of these came to naught.

Agency, which receives complaints and conducts investigations.

An organisation of concerned Australian health practitioners was set up called Health Professionals Australia Reform Association or HPARA. At its first national conference in 2016, several speakers told about being targeted by AHPRA or otherwise coming under attack from the medical establishment because they had challenged dominant views or vested interests. These were not vaccine critics, but rather doctors, nurses and health administrators who had, for one reason or another, been targeted. Their stories highlighted the distress caused by being subject to a complaint and a lengthy investigation. Even when the complaints were eventually dismissed, the process served as a form of harassment.

SAVNers and others have made so many complaints to so many agencies that a full analysis would be a major enterprise, even just for those for which public information is available. Table 5.1 summarises several of the agencies and targets involved.[24]

---

24 Table 5.1 is a partial listing. Among items not listed, complaints have been made that the AVN infringed copyright and Dorey breached the privacy act.

Table 5.1 Organisations receiving complaints
about Australian vaccine critics

Acronym	Full name	Function	Main targets	Main issue
HCCC	Health Care Complaints Commission (NSW)	Dealing with complaints about health practitioners	AVN, Meryl Dorey	AVN criticisms of vaccination
OLGR	Office of Liquor, Gaming and Racing (NSW)	Administering charitable status of organisations	AVN	Donations to AVN
Fair Trading	Department of Fair Trading (NSW)	Regulating incorporated associations	AVN	Name of AVN
TGA	Therapeutic Goods Administration	Safety and efficacy of therapeutic goods	Meryl Dorey	Mentioning of black salve
AHPRA	Australian Health Practitioner Regulation Agency	Proper practice by health practitioners	Nurses, doctors	Criticism of vaccination

ACCC	Australian Competition and Consumer Commission	Fair and honest commercial dealings	Fran Sheffield,[25] Homeopathy Plus	Recommendation of homeopathic prevention and treatment of infectious disease
UOW	University of Wollongong[26]	Education and research	Judy Wilyman	Criticism of vaccination policy
ABC	Australian Broadcasting Corporation	News and current affairs reporting	Journalists, editors	Coverage of vaccine criticism[27]
IXWH	IX Web Hosting	Internet Service Provider	AVN	Dangerous information

SCAPPs are made possible by the way problems are supposed to be addressed, namely by having agencies that handle complaints. Watchdog agencies give the appearance that problems, such as miscreant health professionals, dysfunctional organisations and corrupt practices, are be-

---

25 Fran Sheffield has also been the target of complaints to AHPRA and the HCCC.

26 Brian Martin, "Defending university integrity," *International Journal for Educational Integrity*, Vol. 13, No. 1, 2017, pp. 1–14, http://goo.gl/3y4QMH.

27 Other media organisations have also received complaints. Media coverage of the Australian vaccination issue is an important topic of its own, which I only address peripherally.

ing addressed. However, the complaint-based approach is open to abuse, of which SCAPPs are one manifestation.

There is also a much bigger issue: many complaint-based agencies simply do not work very well for the problems they are supposed to address. The HCCC is a prime example, at least according to media stories and investigations. If you encounter a serious problem with a doctor, nurse or other healthcare worker, what do you do? File a complaint with the HCCC. But in lots of cases the HCCC either does not investigate or botches the investigation. A special commission of inquiry looked at 70 complaints to the HCCC and found that not a single one was properly investigated.[28]

A member of the AVN might say, "Why is the HCCC putting so much energy into pursuing us, when we're citizen campaigners and not health practitioners, when it doesn't do its real job properly?" A cynical answer is that the HCCC was set up to give the appearance of regulating medical malpractice, but actually is not the best way to do this, indeed not a very good way at all.[29]

---

28 Paola Totaro and Nick O'Malley, "They entered hospital full of trust. Now they are dead or damaged. And no case was properly investigated. Not one." *Sydney Morning Herald,* 1 April 2004, pp. 1, 9. Of course it is also possible to question the competence of the special commission that examined the HCCC's investigations.

29 Examples of other ways to improve practice include Liadaine Freestone et al., "Voluntary incident reporting by anaesthetic trainees in an Australian hospital," *International Journal for Quality in Health Care,* Vol. 18, No. 6, 2006, pp. 452–457; Atul Gawande, *The Checklist Manifesto: How to Get Things Right*

The HCCC is an example of what in other contexts is called a medical board, a regulator for a profession, and it may be that medical boards have been captured by the profession, and go soft on the more powerful members of the profession, especially doctors. Jo Barber worked for the Queensland Medical Board and became a whistleblower, exposing its shortcomings. She said that on starting work at the board, she found complaints about doctors sitting in boxes, some of which had not been addressed in years.[30]

Toothless regulators have been studied for decades.[31] What happens is that their existence is smoother if they leave alone the more powerful players in the regulated industry and instead target weaker ones. Whether this adequately describes the HCCC or other medical boards is a matter for empirical investigation. Agencies should not be condemned on a basis of a few cases or news stories. What can be said is that SCAPPs may go hand in hand with agencies that are subordinate to the powerful groups they are supposed to be regulating.

SCAPPs are a potent method of harassment mainly available to those with more power. Complainants need

---

(New York: Metropolitan Books, Henry Holt and Company, 2009); Matthew Syed, *Black Box Thinking: Marginal Gains and the Secrets of High Performance* (London: John Murray, 2015).

30 Jo Barber, "Queensland Medical Board allowed dodgy doctors to work," *The Whistle* (Newsletter of Whistleblowers Australia), No. 77, January 2014, http://goo.gl/YRVTGL, pp. 9–10.

31 Ernesto Dal Bó, "Regulatory capture: a review," *Oxford Review of Economic Policy*, Vol. 22, No. 2, 2006, pp. 203–225.

the capacity to research and write convincing complaints. The most important condition for making a SCAPP strategy effective is the willingness of complaint recipients to act. SCAPPs often exploit a vulnerability in complaint-based systems: as noted earlier, agencies respond only to individual complaints and do not apply their sanctions against all violators. This is crucial, because often the complainant may be just as guilty of a technical violation as the target of the complaint.

DOXXING

One of the nastiest online techniques is doxxing: publishing information about a person, for example their name, address, contact details, employers and relatives, in a context that opens them to attack. For example, in some forums, women who join are encouraged to post revealing photos of themselves. Others on the forum then try to identify the newcomer and, if successful, send a deluge of abusive emails, send her photos to her classmates and parents, and engage in other forms of harassment. The attackers justify ruining a young person's life by saying she deserved it for being so foolish.[32]

Putting someone's personal details online can serve as a form of harassment if it makes them vulnerable or feel vulnerable. This is especially so when the posting of details is accompanied by abusive comments or incitement to take hostile action. This is a potent form of harassment.

---

32 Jon Ronson, *So You've Been Publicly Shamed* (London: Picador, 2015).

Separate from SAVN, there was a website under the name Vaccination Awareness and Information Service. It posted a "hall of shame," listing the names and addresses of numerous individuals and businesses because of their connection with the AVN, most of them because they had placed an advertisement in the AVN's magazine *Living Wisdom*.

I have heard a few stories of individuals listed on this "hall of shame" who received harassing communications. Most of them would be reluctant to speak out about being targeted because this might lead to further attention. In any case, the mere fact of having names and addresses posted online in this context can be a source of fear. Meryl Dorey, as editor of *Living Wisdom,* in 2011 decided not to take any new advertisements due to the risk to the advertisers.[33]

Peter Tierney runs a blog called Reasonable Hank.[34] It is one of the more virulent SAVNer blogs, filled with derogatory comments about vaccine critics. Tierney has run a series of lengthy posts under the title "Anti-vaccine nurses and midwives," each post targeting an individual nurse or midwife, exposing them for joining vaccine-

---

33 For an account of one advertiser's experience, see Meryl Dorey, "You can judge an organisation by their actions," *No Compulsory Vaccination,* 15 June 2010, http://nocompulsoryvaccination.com/2010/06/15/you-can-judge-an-organisation-by-their-actions/.

34 https://reasonablehank.com. Whether the reasonable hank blog is written by one person or several has been a matter of speculation.

critical groups or making statements critical of vaccination. Tierney posts their health practitioner information and screenshots of their online comments, sometimes taken from secret Facebook groups to which, presumably, he or someone he knows has access. He suggests making complaints about these nurses and midwives to their regulatory body. By 2017, Tierney had produced more than 40 such posts. Notices about these posts are put on the SAVN Facebook page and then typically followed by numerous hostile and demeaning comments.

In 2016, a website named "Diluted thinking" added a list of homoeopaths who practise homoeoprophylaxis, the homoeopathic analogue of vaccination.[35] This is seen by SAVNers as "anti-vaccination": these homoeopaths are labelled "antivax homeopaths." In a post to the SAVN Facebook page, administrator Ken McLeod announced that

> Among the many quacks and cranks opposed to the science of vaccination, we find so-called "homeopaths." Until now, they have not featured prominently on our radar, but that is about to change. We note that in NSW, for example, there is the "Code of Conduct for unregistered health practitioners," made under the Public Health Regulation 2012, Schedule 3, which requires that [extracts from the Code quoted here]. When we find a homeopath advocating so-called

---

35 Diluted Thinking in Australian Healthcare, "Antivax health practitioners," http://www.dilutedthinking.com/cat_avaxprac.php.

"homeoprophylaxis" or advocating that their clients avoid vaccines, we will bring the matter to the attention of the regulators. It was this Code of Conduct which brought the AVN undone in 2010.[36]

McLeod thus announced that SAVN would be pursuing homoeopaths, and gave a link to the Diluted Thinking site where information about a dozen or so homoeopaths was listed. The threat to target them with complaints is explicit.

The effect of doxxing on individuals can be drastic. Some of them fear that their employers will see the online material, putting their jobs at risk. If their name is uncommon, web searches for it may lead to the damaging online commentary. Because employers often check for information online about prospective employees, doxxing can make it more difficult to find a new job. As SAVN's pursuit of homoeopaths indicates, there is the possibility of having to deal with complaints.

Doxxing involves a combination of technique and context: information is posted in a situation in which harassment is enabled or encouraged. Often it means there is a group ready to pounce on those whose information is posted. Technically, it might be said that posting information about someone is no big deal, especially if it's accurate. What makes it doxxing is the threat or imminence of adverse actions.

---

36 Stop the Australian (Anti)Vaccination Network, 13 August 2016.

The AVN, like most incorporated organisations, has an elected committee. The AVN's committee includes a president, secretary, treasurer and a number of "ordinary members." After SAVN began its campaign against the AVN, a number of committee members became apprehensive about coming under attack. If their identities and personal details became available to SAVN, they were vulnerable to doxxing. This vulnerability led to a complex struggle over information.

According to the rules governing incorporated bodies, the names and addresses of committee members need to be registered with Fair Trading and made available to anyone who asks. So it would seem SAVN could obtain them easily, except for a Fair Trading provision saying names could be withheld if there was a danger of harassment. The AVN withheld the names on these grounds. SAVNer Ken McLeod then put in an application for the names under the state's freedom-of-information legislation.[37] After being denied the names, he then appealed. The struggle over access to the names of the committee members involved submissions and thus was similar in effect to a SCAPP.

What can be done about doxxing? Prevention is usually better than cure, and that means not volunteering information or material that can be used by attackers. In the case of young women, it means not posting revealing images. There are too many stories of vengeful ex-partners or nasty attackers for this ever to be safe. Furthermore, in

---

37 In NSW, this is called the Government Information (Public Access) Act or the GIPA Act.

some situations it may be risky to reveal any personal details. Some women who become prominent on social media become targets of ferocious campaigns, for no other reason than that they are women voicing their opinions online.[38] A possible strategy is to adopt a pseudonym from the beginning and be very careful about revealing personal details.

In Australia, anyone who does not accept vaccination orthodoxy is potentially vulnerable to doxxing. If they have jobs as nurses or homoeopaths, their livelihoods are at risk. For them, prevention means adopting a low profile, not speaking out about vaccination, even not revealing their views to anyone. For nurses, refusing to be vaccinated sometimes cannot be hidden, so keeping a low profile means not riling up co-workers. When doxxing is a possibility, being outed as "antivax" is to be stigmatised and made vulnerable to attack. This stigma is normally invisible. Unlike an ethnic identity or national origin that can be inferred (sometimes incorrectly) from appearance or accent, being a vaccine critic cannot be determined by looking at a person, nor even from susceptibility to infectious diseases, so it is more akin to homosexuality or political opinions that are usually only known if revealed to others.

How can a target of doxxing respond? One option is escape: seeking a new job, a different appearance or even a new name. This might be necessary for women who are subject to major campaigns of mobbing online, including

---

38 Danielle Keats Citron, *Hate Crimes in Cyberspace* (Cambridge, MA: Harvard University Press, 2014).

messages filled with lies and threats sent to classmates, employers, family and friends. So far in the Australian vaccination struggle, only a few individuals, notably Meryl Dorey, have been subject to long-term mobbing. For nurses, the more likely scenario is being subject to one or two posts on the Reasonable Hank blog, with accompanying commentary on the SAVN Facebook page, and possibly complaints to the healthcare regulator. This is distressing enough, but is unlikely to warrant creating a new identity.

A quite different option is to mobilise support. If you decide to do this, how to do this depends sensitively on your personal circumstances. It might involve talking to co-workers and supervisors, calmly explaining your viewpoints and telling about the campaign to attack you. It's often useful to start with those you think will be most sympathetic, telling them about what's happening and seeking their advice about what to do next. Depending on what they say, you can then approach others. You might write a short summary of your views and circulate it. You might enlist sympathisers to speak on your behalf.

To counter negative comments online, you could set up your own website, Facebook page or other profile, fill it with positive text and images, and encourage your friends to link to it. If successful, this can push links to the attackers' posts down lower on web searches.

This strategy is built around making dissenting views about vaccination seem acceptable, indeed normal. Others may not agree with you, but they should respect your right to hold these views, just as they should respect your right to be a member of a religious minority.

A key part of this strategy is to be a good worker, family member, neighbour and friend. If you are courteous, helpful, attentive and reliable, those who know you will respect you and are likely to see the attacks as unfair. The more you are seen as a balanced and productive member of society, the more difficult it will be to discredit you, at least among those who know you.

When you're under attack, though, retaining your good humour can be very difficult. You may be distressed or angry and lash out. It's unfair that you need to be on your best behaviour when you are the one under attack. But that's the way it is. To make the attacks backfire — to make the attackers seem like the bad guys — you need to avoid doing anything that makes you seem like an aggressor.[39]

Behaving well is just one component of the strategy of mobilising support: it is one way to gain supporters and sympathisers. The bigger picture is joining with others who are either similarly targeted or who want to support targets of harassment. With one or two others, or a larger group or network, it is possible to collect information about the patterns of attack, analyse the factors that make attack possible, propose ways to respond, make plans and take action. Rather than assuming that there is a single best way of responding, the idea is to try out methods and see how they work, and learn from the process.

---

39 See "Backfire materials," http://www.bmartin.cc/pubs/backfire.html.

Collecting information
Attackers often seek to gather information that can be used to discredit or expose targets. Some Australian parents who have reservations about vaccination have set up closed Facebook groups so they can share concerns, exchange plans and tell about their difficulties without being disrupted by pro-vaccination campaigners. However, in some cases these groups are infiltrated by individuals who pretend to oppose vaccination and who take screenshots of the conversations and post them on SAVNer blogs. This is a type of doxxing.

This version of doxxing is damaging in two ways. The obvious damage is from exposure of private information — this would be like someone listening in on a private conversation and telling others about it. The other form of damage is to the trust within groups. Rather than feeling secure among friends, members of closed groups may need to fear exposure. Infiltration thus serves as a form of harassment. The doxxing may not matter too much to individuals who do not use their real names.

Another version of this technique is when pro-vaccination campaigners go to a doctor or other health practitioner and pretend to be concerned about vaccination, covertly recording the interaction hoping to collect information that can be used to expose the practitioner as an "anti-vaxxer." The most obvious targets are those who actually do have reservations about vaccination or who propose alternatives, such as homoeopaths who use homoeoprophylaxis. Always being on guard against the risk of being targeted can be emotionally exhausting. Thus this form of duplicity can serve as a form of harassment.

One response to the possibility of surveillance and exposure is to be even more careful about security. In joining a closed Facebook group, for example, you could use a false name and not reveal any details that might enable your identity to be determined by an infiltrator. However, this response can inhibit a full and frank discussion. Part of what makes close personal interaction worthwhile is to be able to express problems, worries, uncertainties, misapprehensions and mistakes. Discussing them enables learning. Remaining guarded all the time is stifling: it is like always being on stage and never able to debrief in a safe situation.

Most people do not think very highly of spies. So another response is to condemn and expose likely infiltrators. However, this also has disadvantages, because it can cause even greater apprehension in discussions, and there is the possibility of blaming the wrong person.

A more balanced approach is to just be careful but not worry too much. In public forums, it's wise to be cautious in what you say. When talking with a trusted friend, you can be more open about your thoughts. You can use one-to-one communication modes, such as email and Skype, and be more cautious with groups. Although infiltration is always a risk, in practice the exposure of confidential comments has seldom been circulated beyond SAVN and related groups. Sometimes paranoia about surveillance and infiltration is more damaging than the risk of candid comments being exposed.

MAKING THREATS, SENDING PORN

Legal threats

Being threatened with legal action is a type of harassment, and it can potentially escalate to actual court cases. Imagine receiving a letter from a lawyer claiming that you have defamed the lawyer's client. The letter documents certain statements that you made and spells out defamatory imputations. At the conclusion of the letter, you are asked to make a public apology and cover the costs of the client — and perhaps a lump sum besides, perhaps $5000 or $50,000.

It sounds heavy-handed, and it is. Lawyer letters are often bluffs. The client — someone who is trying to shut you up or to hamper your activities — may have no intention of launching a formal legal action. The request for a large payment is a form of intimidation. You don't have to respond to the letter. But unless you're familiar with this sort of legal bluff, you might well be frightened.

Because I've written about defamation law and free speech, I am regularly contacted by people who are being threatened with legal action.[40] Many of them are unduly worried. I am also contacted by people who have been defamed and want to sue. Almost always, I say not to do it unless they have lots of money and don't mind losing it. Going to court can cost hundreds of thousands of dollars, with no guarantee of winning, and it may not help your

---

40 "Brian Martin: publications on defamation," http://www.bmartin.cc/pubs/defamation.html.

reputation. The main long-term winners from legal actions are lawyers.

In the Australian vaccination debate, there have been various informal threats to sue for defamation. For example, Dorey was threatened with a defamation action, and paid a lawyer to draft a letter in response. I'm also aware of a few threats that involved letters from lawyers. However, considering the large number of defamatory comments on blogs and Facebook pages by SAVNers as well as vaccine critics, there have been relatively few threats to sue. In practice, nearly all these comments are ignored, at least so far as legal action is concerned.

This is just what happens in everyday life. Every time you engage in gossip with a neighbour or in the workplace over coffee and make negative comments about someone, you are guilty of defamation and, in principle, could be sued. The law is seldom invoked, though when disputes become bitter — such as when parents are disputing custody of their children — one side or the other may threaten legal action. More commonly, though, defamation actions are designed to silence a critic, as when a business takes out a writ against a customer who posted a negative review of a service or product.

In this context, legal threats in the Australian vaccination debate could be called SLAPPs: Strategic Lawsuits Against Public Participation. They would seem to be a natural accompaniment to SCAPPs, the strategic complaints. So why has SAVN relied so heavily on SCAPPs rather than SLAPPs? The obvious explanation is that it requires a lot of money to launch a legal action, but little or none to make a complaint. The struggle has primarily been between citizens' groups, which helps explain why SLAPPs have been uncommon.

To prevent legal action, it is wise to be careful about what you say. Rather than saying someone is corrupt, it is far safer to provide the relevant facts, for example that Smith, a developer, paid $100,000 to Jones, a local government official, who subsequently approved a zoning change giving Smith a profit of $1 million on a property sale. If you give information like this, you don't need to say that Smith and Jones are corrupt, because readers will draw this conclusion themselves. Of course, your statements about the payment and the profit need to be accurate.

If someone threatens to sue, you have various options. One is to do what you are requested to do, such as making an apology and a payment. If you are asked to remove something from the web, taking it down is often enough to avoid legal action: the person making the threat most of all wants removal of information, not a monetary payment. Then there are the plaintiffs who sue as a form of intimidation. Some of them are willing to spend a lot of money to cause you distress and financial pain.

A different sort of option is to publicise the defamation threat, thereby giving the defamatory material greater visibility and painting the plaintiff as a censor. This can be a high-stakes option, but it is potentially very powerful.[41]

---

41 Brian Martin and Truda Gray, "How to make defamation threats and actions backfire," *Australian Journalism Review*, Vol. 27, No. 1, July 2005, pp. 157–166, http://www.bmartin.cc/pubs/05ajr.html.

Porn

Meryl Dorey and at least one other AVN member have received, via email, pornographic images. One of them is sufficiently extreme to be denied classification by Australian authorities.[42] Dorey also received printed pornographic images via the post. The sender in both cases was anonymous. SAVN denied responsibility and condemned any such actions. It is safe to say that even if the sender was a SAVNer, this would have limited formal significance, because all it takes to be what I call a SAVNer is to be one of SAVN's Facebook friends, there being no formal membership process. It is clear from SAVNer Facebook commentary that SAVN administrators oppose sending of pornography and would expel anyone who did.[43]

---

42 I thank a colleague, knowledgeable in this area, for this judgement.

43 In a lengthy SAVN Facebook discussion on 25 September 2012 triggered by Dorey telling about receiving a threat from the group "Anonymous," various viewpoints were expressed: sympathy for Dorey and hope that the perpetrator would be caught; speculation that the perpetrator was a teenager not linked to Anonymous; and speculation that Meryl did it herself. In the course of this discussion, a SAVN administrator made this statement:

> Unfortunately it appears that it is time to reiterate that the admins of this page do not support any acts or threats of violence. That is not our goal. The information the AVN presents is often inaccurate and potentially dangerous. We want to correct this misinformation. Threatening Ms Dorey personally, or any other members of the AVN or those who

On the other hand, SAVN's campaign, with its extensive use of derogatory language and images, could lead some sympathisers to take more extreme measures. The taking of many and varied actions against the AVN runs the risk of inspiring some individuals to take actions that may be seen by others as excessive and hence become counterproductive.

Threats over the phone
While Dorey was away one night in 2012, two voice messages were recorded on her home phone. She had her phone set up so that it recorded the caller's phone number on her computer, as well as the messages themselves. One of the messages was a man saying "Die in a fire" repeated over and over in a threatening voice. The other: "You bitch. Just fucking burn." Dorey traced the caller's phone number to the home of Daniel Raffaele, one of SAVN's founders.

Prior to this, Raffaele had made various derogatory comments about Dorey, some of them shading into threats. For example, one Facebook comment contained these words:

> [...] Whatever end this [SAVN's] campaign comes to, which will include the demise of the AVN, is her decision. She has made the choice to remain arrogant and cruel. If the demise of the AVN brings with it the

like their Fb page, is unacceptable. The admins unanimously agree on this issue. If your opinion differs to ours, maybe this isn't the place for you. ~HW

demise of Meryl Dorey herself, she only has herself to blame for that. [...]
Meryl Dorey is no better, in my mind, than a Nazi who throws a living baby into an incinerator. I shall afford her no more respect than I would afford a parasite that would drain the very blood from a child.[44]

For a SAVNer to be exposed as making threats over the phone was damaging to the image of SAVN. No SAVNer would admit to making such threats and SAVN administrators would condemn them. Dorey, with her recordings, had strong evidence of threats from a leading SAVNer. She took two actions, one ineffective and one effective.

She first took the evidence to the police. They did nothing. Eventually, following Dorey's repeated requests, they went to Raffaele's home and spoke to him. He denied making the calls, and the police did nothing further. For Dorey, going to the police was ineffective.

She then put recordings of the calls on the AVN's website.[45] This was effective: it exposed a sordid attack technique. Raffaele dropped out of SAVN activities, at least under his own name, and henceforth was not mentioned on the SAVN Facebook page.

---

44 Reproduced in AVN, "Daniel Raffaele," 31 August 2012, https://avn.org.au/2012/08/savn_abuse-2/.

45 "Threats to AVN President made from Stop the AVN founder,"
http://nocompulsoryvaccination.com/2012/10/03/threats-to-avn-president-made-from-home-of-stop-the-avn-founder/.

In the context of the Australian vaccination debate, the sending of pornography and making threats over the phone were too extreme: many people, even those supportive of vaccination, would see them as excessive. Such techniques could hurt SAVN by alienating public opinion.

For Dorey and others at the receiving end, the important lessons were to document the attacks and to publicise them — and not to rely on authorities to help. SAVNers responded by condemning these methods, disowning responsibility and distancing themselves from the individuals involved.

EFFECTS ON TARGETS

Being subjected to verbal abuse, complaints and other forms of denigration and harassment is not pleasant. Different people are affected in different ways, but the impact is almost always negative. I've talked to a large number of individuals who have been harassed, including targets of sexual harassment and bullying at work, including many whistleblowers subjected to reprisals. The effects include high levels of stress, leading to adverse physical and psychological consequences, including insomnia, digestive disorders, migraines and heightened alertness. The adverse health effects experienced by whistleblowers have been documented; as well, many suffer financial and relationship problems.[46] Similarly targets of persistent online harassment often experience significant

---

46 K. Jean Lennane, "'Whistleblowing': a health issue," *British Medical Journal*, Vol. 307, 11 September 1993, pp. 667–670.

adverse psychological and physical effects, including fear, panic attacks and nausea.[47]

I've talked to quite a few targets of SAVN attacks. Responses vary. Some adopt pseudonyms to continue with online commentary, while others find it all too distressing and exit from the issue altogether. A few become angry and resolve to continue more forcefully. Those such as nurses who are targeted with complaints to their employer or to a regulatory agency usually find the experience highly distressing.

Unless you have been the target of harassment yourself, or talked with those who have been, it is difficult to appreciate how upsetting it can be. When under attack, maintaining a sense of balance and considered judgement, indeed just to think and behave "normally," becomes a great challenge. Some targets retreat into a shell while others want to lash out against anyone they see as an attacker. Some start seeing threats even when there are none: hyper-vigilance is common, and indeed is a survival mechanism. When there are dangers, it is helpful to be more alert, but this can become damaging to physical and mental health when the alert state is prolonged.

For SAVNers whose aim is to silence vaccination critics, denigration and harassment serve their purpose quite well. Even so, they seem unaware of the damage they cause to individuals, or think it is a price that must be paid, or think their targets deserve everything they get. SAVNers express outrage when vaccine critics lash out at

---

47 Emma A. Jane, *Misogyny Online: A Short (and Brutish) History* (London: Sage, 2017), chapter 3.

them, but they are getting only a taste of what they regularly dish out. This is a typical pattern. When a person hurts someone else, the target is often greatly affected and holds a grievance for a long time while the perpetrator feels justified, does not think it's a big deal and may forget all about it. So, for example, a target of sexual abuse may be scarred for years or decades while the perpetrator hardly remembers being involved.[48]

In the face of SAVN's attacks, only a few hardy vaccine critics are able to remain active. Dorey was subjected to years of verbal abuse and harassment, and remarkably maintained her involvement, but eventually she had to withdraw and reduce her efforts. Few others would have the stamina to continue like her.

When a group like SAVN enters a debate with a goal to shut down opponents, the result is that only the hardiest will continue. The result is that the debate is polarised even more than before, with opportunities for respectful engagement reduced. Those sitting in the middle, who might offer avenues for dialogue, are the most likely to exit, leaving the field to the more aggressive and committed individuals on each side.

CONCLUSION

Harassment can take many forms, ranging from nasty comments to assault. In types of harassment that have been studied extensively — notably sexual harassment and

---

48 Roy F. Baumeister, *Evil: Inside Human Violence and Cruelty* (New York: Freeman, 1997).

bullying — it is generally agreed that harassment involves the exercise of power. The way this plays out can be complex. Most sexual harassment is by men against women, but there is also some same-sex harassment and harassment of men by women. Most bullying in the workplace is by bosses against subordinates, or between co-workers, but there is also some bullying of bosses by subordinates.

In the Australian vaccination debate, I have looked primarily at harassment by the pro-vaccination group SAVN against vaccine critics, especially the AVN. Given that both SAVN and the AVN are citizen groups, it might seem that they have roughly equal power, but there is one vital difference: the wider configuration of forces in Australian society. Vaccination is endorsed by government health departments and the medical profession, and supported by most doctors and parents. As a result, SAVN can draw on resources from the wider society to a much greater extent than vaccine critics, and it has done this in several of its techniques of harassment.

The technique of making complaints, what I call Strategic Complaints Against Public Participation or SCAPPs, only works when agencies are responsive. Many of the complaints against the AVN have been dismissed, but some agencies used them to mount investigations and impose sanctions, with devastating effects. The sanctions were damaging; just as harmful was the diversion of effort to defend against the complaints.

The technique of posting information about individuals on the web, framed negatively, is only likely to be effective if there are groups or individuals who might take action against those named. When the names and contact details of vaccine critics, or even just representatives of companies that advertised in the AVN's magazine, were posted on the web, this invited derision and potential harassment. The existence of SAVN's campaign enabled doxxing: in the context of the vaccination debate, having one's personal details posted online could be a source of fear. Targeted nurses, for example, worry that they could be subject to complaints to their employer or the health practitioner regulator.

Harassment, as the exercise of power, is quite different from persuasion via providing information. Promoting vaccination by presenting information and giving explanations appeals to rationality. Promoting vaccination by harassing critics is a different matter altogether, and may even suggest that rational argument is seen as insufficient.

6
Censorship

Censorship, in a general sense, involves blocking speech or expression. Hearing the word "censorship," people often think of governments restricting the mass media. For example, during wartime, governments seek to control what can be reported about battles, casualties, troop movements and so forth, on the grounds that the information might aid the enemy or cause demoralisation.

Another sort of censorship involves restricting access to information. Governments classify certain information as secret or top secret: it is supposed to be available only to those with appropriate security clearances. Separately from classified information, secrecy may simply be refusing to make certain types of information available. For example, a government might commission a report and, because the findings are unwelcome, not release it to the public.

There can be good reasons for censorship. Aside from wartime controls, other rationales include privacy and confidentiality. Hospitals do not routinely release information about patients and their health conditions. Courts in some countries deny public access to information about some victims of crime because they are too young or because they may be in danger if their identity is revealed.

Governments are not the only group involved in censorship. Corporations keep many of their operations secret. The usual rationale is commercial confidentiality: people are considered not to have any right to obtain inside information about private organisations. But unlike individuals, corporations commonly have social impacts. Hence, the public needs access to some sorts of corporate information to enable good decision-making. For example, when tobacco companies carried out research on the health hazards of smoking, they did not reveal adverse findings. This can be called censorship.

Censorship routinely occurs within organisations, although what counts as censorship can be a matter of definition and interpretation. Employees in hierarchical organisations may have no expectation of free speech.[1] Consider a worker who writes a draft of a financial report. This text is then modified by others and finally approved higher in the organisation. Whether the modifications count as censorship depends on the details, including the expectations and understandings of various groups — the worker, other workers, and outsiders. If the editing of the initial draft involves matters of expression, correcting mistakes or adding new material, then this would be seen by most observers as legitimate, indeed a beneficial process of producing a high quality piece of writing. However, if the financial report misrepresents the organi-

---

1 Bruce Barry, *Speechless: The Erosion of Free Expression in the American Workplace* (San Francisco: Berrett-Koehler, 2007); David W. Ewing, *Freedom Inside the Organization: Bringing Civil Liberties to the Workplace* (New York: Dutton, 1977).

sation's affairs, or systematically excludes valid material in the draft, this might be called censorship.

Censorship is partly judged by expectations of audiences. If readers of a company's financial report expect a fair treatment of all relevant facts because their own investment decisions depend on it, and regulatory agencies demand it, then intentional misrepresentation becomes censorship. On the other hand, if readers assume the report is just a form of advertising and not to be taken seriously, this is a different matter.

In some organisations, workers expect a degree of autonomy and free expression. For example, scientists working for a government agency might expect to be able to publish papers in scientific journals. Commonly there is an internal vetting process: a paper has to be read by others, for example a supervisor, before being allowed to be submitted. This is a process that can be used for quality control but also can be used to control viewpoints expressed. When certain views are disallowed or systematically modified, it is reasonable to talk of censorship.

Determining whether an action constitutes censorship can be difficult. One criterion is the double standard test, which basically relies on seeing whether different people and different views are treated the same way. In the 1970s, Peter Springell was a scientist in the Australian government's major research institution, the CSIRO (Commonwealth Scientific and Industrial Research Organisation). Springell tackled environmental topics when this was considered radical, and he was outspoken about CSIRO not addressing environmental issues. The CSIRO hierarchy refused to approve some of Springell's environmental articles for submission to scientific journals, though he was allowed to publish them using his home address, with no mention of his CSIRO affiliation. Meanwhile, Springell exposed the chief of his division for publishing an article, with his CSIRO affiliation, having nothing to do with his CSIRO duties. The double standard was that Springell was treated differently than his own chief concerning publication, as well as other ways.[2]

The double standard test is a powerful tool, but open to interpretation. Springell could point to his own chief's behaviour, but in many cases there is no obvious comparator. A standard method of suppressing dissidents is to claim they are underperforming and therefore subject to adverse actions such as denial of research grants or punitive transfer. Sometimes the dissident is an outstanding performer — Springell published much more than most of his colleagues — but sometimes there are few objective criteria to measure performance, so applying the double standard test is difficult.

Censorship can happen on a big scale, as when whole topics are forbidden. Under dictatorships, for example, media outlets are forbidden to publish any criticism of the regime. On the other hand, censorship can occur in tiny ways such as when an editor removes a sentence from an article.

---

2 Peter Springell, "For the freedom to comment by scientists," in Brian Martin, C. M. Ann Baker, Clyde Manwell and Cedric Pugh (editors), *Intellectual Suppression: Australian Case Histories, Analysis and Responses* (Sydney: Angus & Robertson, 1986), pp. 74–78, http://www.bmartin.cc/pubs/86is/Springell.html.

A key issue is whether censorship is justified and, if so, how. Then there is the question of whether the justification is legitimate, about which people may differ. A common justification for censorship is national security, the argument being that publication of certain materials may aid enemies and jeopardise public safety. Many people see this as legitimate, but when too many documents are classified as secret, this level of censorship might be claimed to be unnecessary or harmful. In many cases, documents that would merely embarrass a government are prevented from publication on the pretext of national security.

Another justification for censorship is defamation, which refers to speech that damages someone's reputation. If you say Alfred is corrupt or evil or even just overweight, that can hurt Alfred's reputation and he can sue for libel or slander. Libel is written defamation and slander is spoken defamation. If you're sued, you may be able to defend on the basis that what you said is true, though this depends on the jurisdiction.

Defamation law in Australia is harsh on defendants.[3] You can be convicted for even a seemingly trivial statement if it has defamatory imputations, namely if it seems to imply something harmful to a person's reputation. So if you say that Fred behaved unethically, you might have to prove in court that he did. Fred doesn't have to prove

---

3 Robert Pullan, *Guilty Secrets: Free Speech and Defamation in Australia* (Sydney: Pascal Press, 1994); Brian Walters, *Slapping on the Writs: Defamation, Developers and Community Activism* (Sydney: University of New South Wales Press, 2003).

anything, because the onus of proof is on the defendant, a reversal of the usual principle of innocent until proven guilty. If you lose the case, you might have to pay thousands or hundreds of thousands of dollars in compensation for damage to Fred's reputation.

In practice, people say defamatory things all the time, in nearly every office gossip session. Social media are filled with defamatory comments, yet only rarely is someone sued. The main reason is that suing is very expensive. Just to have a lawyer write a letter might cost thousands of dollars and to pursue a case in court could cost hundreds of thousands.

Defamation law is thus ideally designed to serve the rich and powerful — the main ones able to use the law — and to serve as a tool of censorship. Mass media in Australia are very aware of defamation law, and routinely have their lawyers check articles to modify or remove text that might enable a legal action. Even so, mass media are regularly subject to threats to sue and to legal actions, costing them a large amount of money. The effect of all this is that journalists, editors and owners are very careful. They may want to break a story, but not if it is likely to lead to huge legal costs.

The result is what is called the chilling effect of defamation law.[4] If a story poses a significant risk of legal

---

4 Eric Barendt, Laurence Lustgarten, Kenneth Norrie and Hugh Stephenson, *Libel and the Media: The Chilling Effect* (Oxford: Clarendon Press, 1997). See also Fiona J. L. Donson, *Legal Intimidation: A SLAPP in the Face of Democracy* (London: Free Association Books, 2000); David Hooper, *Reputations under*

action, media may be wary and not run it. This is a process of self-censorship.

Active censorship is when some outside person or organisation restricts expression. If active censorship is exercised for a while, it sends a message: your speech will not be allowed, and you may be subject to reprisals. This can lead to self-censorship, to avoid being censored by others and to avoid reprisals. Defamation threats and actions are just one trigger for self-censorship. Another is access to information. Journalists have their sources in government or the corporate sector, but know that if they say the wrong thing, access to their sources may be withdrawn. Entire topic areas — for example tax avoidance by powerful groups — may be off limits in some media. Journalists who have too many of their stories "spiked" by editors may learn to censor themselves.

There are many studies of active censorship.[5] It is much more difficult to investigate self-censorship, the so-called chilly climate for expression, in part because journalists and others may censor themselves unconsciously. Yet it can be argued that self-censorship is a far more serious matter because it is less visible and therefore cannot easily be exposed and opposed.

Fire: Winners and Losers in the Libel Business (Boston: Little, Brown, 2000).

5 Eric Barendt, *Freedom of Speech,* 2nd edition (Oxford: Oxford University Press, 2005); Sue Curry Jansen, *Censorship: The Knot that Binds Power and Knowledge* (New York: Oxford University Press, 1988).

From the point of view of censors, active censorship is both powerful and potentially risky. It can be highly effective if it provides a lesson to others and encourages self-censorship. On the other hand, active censorship can sometimes trigger outrage and opposition and lead to greater interest in the thing censored. A classic example involves the celebrity Barbra Streisand. The California Coastal Records Project involved photographs of the California coastline that were posted online. One of the photos happened to show Streisand's mansion in Malibu. In February 2003, Streisand's lawyers wrote to the photographer, Kenneth Adelman, and Pictopia.com, which hosted the photo, demanding $50 million in compensation for violation of privacy. After this legal threat was publicised, it had the counterproductive effect of increasing interest in the photo. Prior to the threat, few took any notice: the photo had been downloaded just six times. The legal threat, after being publicised, drew attention to the photo and the attempt to suppress the photo increased interest in it, and before long it had been downloaded hundreds of thousands of times. This phenomenon of counterproductive attempts at censorship has now been dubbed the Streisand effect.[6] It is such a striking phenomenon that some wily film producers seek to encourage religious groups to speak out against their films in the hope that this will generate greater interest in them.

However, most attempts at censorship are not counterproductive. Although there are numerous examples of

---

6 Know Your Meme, "Streisand effect," http://knowyourmeme.com/memes/streisand-effect.

the Streisand effect, they nevertheless are exceptions. In the majority of cases, censorship is effective in silencing an individual or viewpoint. Why are some silencing attempts successful and others not? It is useful to look at techniques used by censors to reduce outrage from their actions.[7]

A key technique is cover-up: the act and effect of censorship are hidden. When a newspaper or television editor decides not to run a story, usually there is no announcement. No one outside the media organisation is likely to know about it. In 1974, a committee of the Australian federal parliament released a report about the prices of soap powders, otherwise known as laundry detergents. The report was highly critical of the industry. Though today this might sound like a non-issue, at the time this was a big news story, as it affected people in their daily lives. Derek Maitland was a young yet already highly experienced journalist at Sydney-based commercial television station Channel 9, and prepared a report on the parliamentary report for the evening news. But it never ran.

Most viewers would have never known the difference. People who watch television take note of what is on the news but seldom know about stories that were not run. This was long before the Internet, so mass media had a near monopoly on information about public affairs. As

---

7 Sue Curry Jansen and Brian Martin, "The Streisand effect and censorship backfire," *International Journal of Communication,* Vol. 9, 2015, pp. 656–671, http://www.bmartin.cc/pubs/15ijc.pdf.

long as knowledge about what had happened to the story remained within the station, the censorship was hidden.

However, Maitland was upset by the decision. He knew the story was newsworthy and he also knew the station was in the process of negotiating an advertising deal with the major manufacturers, whose advertisements provided significant revenue to the station. He also learned that other commercial stations, in a similar situation, had decided not to run the story. Only the government-funded Australian Broadcasting Commission (ABC) broadcast the soap-powder story.

Most journalists in Maitland's situation remain silent. When this happens, cover-up of censorship is successful. However, Maitland on this occasion decided to become a whistleblower. He appeared on an ABC programme, and this stimulated the Broadcasting Control Board — the regulatory body for radio and television — to hold an inquiry, involving great publicity. Maitland's decision meant that the cover-up of censorship was broken.

A second technique of reducing concern about censorship is to devalue those involved in raising awareness about it. Maitland was supported in his stand by John Pemberton, his news director at Channel 9 and a highly respected figure. Lawyers for the commercial televisions cross-examined Maitland and Pemberton at the inquiry and did everything possible to discredit them. At one point, one of the lawyers sneakily suggested that Maitland might be having an affair with one of the women at the station.

Another technique of reducing concern is to give different explanations for what happened. This was the key method used at the inquiry. Various individuals lied about their actions and motivations for pulling the soap powder story, saying that the reason for not running it was because it was unbalanced. They also denied that the negotiations with the companies were relevant to decision-making and denied that telephone calls between managers of different stations at the time meant that there was any collusion in not running the story.

The inquiry itself was set up in response to Maitland's claims, but it turned out not to be a threat to the stations. The Broadcasting Control Board had the power to place sanctions against stations, but in the end made only the mildest of findings. The publicity from the inquiry was bad for the stations, but their transgressions led to no serious consequences. The implication was that the stations could continue to censor stories as long as they were careful about how they went about it.

A final and crucial means of reducing concern about censorship is intimidation. Maitland and Pemberton lost their jobs. This was a strong warning to other journalists not to break ranks. Maitland ended up leaving Australia for 25 years and only writing about the whole affair 40 years after it occurred.[8] Although censorship within the mass media is a regular occurrence, it is significant that working journalists rarely speak out about it. Their careers would be in jeopardy.

Censorship is occasionally exposed in a big way, as Barbra Streisand learned, but in many cases it is hidden or

---

8 Derek Maitland, *The Fatal Line* (Australia: Derek Maitland, 2016).

explained away or justified. As in the Channel 9 soap powder saga, five sorts of techniques are regularly used to reduce public concern about censorship: hiding it, devaluing those who expose it or whose work is censored, reinterpreting it through lies, blaming and reframing, using official channels to give the appearance of addressing it, and intimidating those who expose it and rewarding those who maintain it.

WHAT ISN'T CENSORSHIP?

Censorship has a bad reputation. No one wants to be called a censor. It's far better to say you are protecting reputations, privacy, national security, public health or anything else that gives legitimacy to actions that restrict access to information. Because censorship has a bad reputation, accusing others of censorship is a potent attack technique.

There are many ways to think of censorship. It might be said that an individual can exercise censorship of their own speech, not providing information that others need to know. Most commonly, though, censorship usually refers to actions by groups, especially large and powerful groups. Quite a few studies of censorship focus only on governments.[9] Yet this seems an arbitrary restriction, as there are other powerful groups that control and restrict

---

9 Sue Curry Jansen, *Censorship: The Knot that Binds Power and Knowledge* (New York: Oxford University Press, 1988), challenges this emphasis and gives attention to corporate censorship.

access to information, including corporations, churches, the media, professions and even trade unions and environmental organisations.

One definition of censorship is denial of information to an audience when there is a reasonable expectation of access due to formal requirements or a commitment to serving the public interest. For example, a company might be required by law to reveal its earnings statement. If figures are withheld or altered, this is both illegal and censorship. A company might have information about potential shortcomings in one of its products, and withhold it. This might be legal (in some cases) but still be considered censorship.

Consider a printed newspaper with a page of letters to the editor. The normal expectation is that readers can submit letters and the editor (sometimes a special letters editor) will decide which ones to publish. This is considered editorial discretion and is usually unquestioned unless there seems to be a strong bias contrary to the stated policies of the newspaper. If the newspaper presents itself as presenting news and opinion without fear or favour, in which the letters page roughly represents a cross-section of submissions, then a systematic rejection of a particular viewpoint might be called censorship. However, if the newspaper is published by a church or a Marxist organisation, then it would be reasonable to expect that letters would be selected according to the ideological orientation of the editors.

With the rise of social media, there are new considerations. Suppose the newspaper has an online edition that enables readers to post comments on published articles.

This means the constraint of space no longer applies, but there are new challenges for the editors, mainly due to the work of moderating the comments. When editors selected letters for print publication, they could ensure quality — often by editing text for spelling and grammar, and sometimes length — and eliminate abusive language and defamatory comments. With online comments, the work of editing changes. Instead of selecting a few contributions to be published, and making sure they are expressed appropriately, the task becomes one of deciding which contributions need to be removed. In a sense, the job changes from being a chooser of relevance and quality to being a censor of offensive or irrelevant comments. In some newspapers, both these jobs are carried out. The print edition carries a few letters, and perhaps also a selection of online comments.

A newspaper editor might systematically reject contributions presenting a particular viewpoint. Indeed, this happens all the time. Contributions that are too unorthodox have little chance of being published. This might be considered censorship only when the viewpoint has significant support. Although news media often present themselves as being balanced, in practice this balance operates within certain mainstream perspectives. For example, foreign news seldom if ever gives a balanced view of conflicts occurring around the world. A few conflicts are covered whereas others are almost invisible.[10] This is better seen as a process of news values interacting

---

10 Virgil Hawkins, *Stealth Conflicts: How the World's Worst Violence Is Ignored* (Aldershot, UK: Ashgate, 2008).

with the agendas of governments, corporations and other influential groups than of overt censorship.

In science, there is an expectation that scientific journals will make publication decisions on the basis of quality and relevance. If decisions are influenced by extraneous criteria such as the prestige of the author or of the author's institution, this is better called bias rather than censorship, especially because the influence of these factors is unconscious. On the other hand, sometimes there may be a systematic discrimination against certain viewpoints — on the health effects of fluoridation, for example — in which case the label "censorship" could be appropriate.[11] However, because decisions by referees and editors are couched in terms of quality, and because there are seldom any independent authorities to pass judgement on editorial decisions, it is very difficult to prove that censorship has occurred.

In summary, reasonable expectation of access depends quite a lot on the topic and the venue. Those who say the 9/11 attacks were a US government conspiracy, or that Barack Obama was a Muslim, have had no reasonable prospect of being covered in the mass media as reflecting credible views. However, what is credible is always being contested.

News media might be expected to be balanced within certain parameters. For other organisations, there is no such expectation. It is unrealistic to expect the Taxation Department to open its website to comments critical of the

---

11 For many examples, see George L. Waldbott, *A Struggle with Titans* (New York: Carlton Press, 1965).

principle of taxation, and similar considerations apply to just about any organisation, government, corporate or non-profit. Environmental magazines are not likely to publish articles by climate-change sceptics, and few would call this censorship.

CENSORSHIP IN THE AUSTRALIAN VACCINATION DEBATE

My focus here is on the campaign by Australian vaccination advocates against public critics of vaccination. It is useful to look at the key players, the AVN as a citizens' group critical of Australian vaccination policy and SAVN as a citizens' group supportive of government vaccination policy and seeking to shut down the AVN.[12] In the struggle between SAVN and the AVN — which for the most part involves SAVN attacking and the AVN defending — publication venues can usefully be divided into three categories.[13]

1. Venues controlled by the AVN
2. Venues controlled by SAVN
3. Venues controlled by others

For venues controlled by the AVN — its website, magazine and tweets of its members — SAVN has no reasonable prospect of controlling speech. What SAVNers

---

12 See the glossary and chapter 3 for more on the AVN and SAVN.
13 I thank Danny Yee for suggesting these categories.

have done is to post comments on the AVN's blog and then, when these are deleted or individuals are blocked, to allege censorship. On SAVN's Facebook page, numerous SAVNers have claimed they have been censored by Dorey or the AVN, because their posts were deleted or they were blocked from making posts.

However, as described above, the AVN is a private organisation with no mandate for hosting all points of view, and thus it is inappropriate to refer to its editing decisions as censorship. Or, if this is called censorship, then nearly every organisation concerned with vaccination is also involved in censorship, including health departments and pharmaceutical companies. There is no expectation on these organisations to host comments from members of the public, especially comments critical of the organisation's position. SAVN's complaints about AVN censorship can best be understood as a way of justifying SAVN's own attempts at censorship. Their implicit logic is that if the AVN is censoring our speech, then it's okay to censor the AVN's speech. The shortcoming of this logic is that the AVN is controlling comment on its own venues but not trying to control comment on third-party venues such as newspapers or blogs.

SAVN's Facebook page is SAVN's own venue. On the Facebook page, critics of vaccination are allowed to post, at least sometimes. The most common scenario is that someone (usually using a pseudonym) makes a post critical of vaccination and then comes under attack by SAVNers, with a combination of evidence, references, careful arguments, and derogatory language. Sometimes the critic is allowed to post repeatedly on a thread, leading to an extended and often heated set of exchanges. However, critics are seldom allowed to have the last word. SAVNers have greater numbers and can usually overwhelm critics.

What is unclear is how genuinely open SAVN's Facebook page actually is. Several individuals have told me that they were banned from posting. For example, they might make a critical post but not be allowed to respond to comments. If this is so, then SAVN's Facebook page is only partially open. Furthermore, seldom is there any indication on the page that posts have been removed or individuals banned. The page's appearance of being a fully open forum may be misleading.

A similar process occurs on the blogs of individual SAVNers. Some are open to critical comment, others not. In one experience of my own, I was allowed to post several comments but then suddenly blocked from further comment, without any indication that I had been blocked, so it seemed as though I had not offered any additional comment.[14]

The difference between the operation of the AVN's and SAVN's venues can be explained in terms of a difference in capacity and willingness to comment. SAVNers have greater numbers and energy to comment than AVN supporters. Therefore, it is safe for SAVN to allow a certain number of "intruders" onto the SAVN Facebook page, because they are outnumbered. Furthermore, SAVNers have skill and experience in dealing with

---

14 My account: "Caught in the vaccination wars (part 3)," 2012, http://www.bmartin.cc/pubs/12hpi-comments.html.

vaccine critics, using evidence, arguments, claims to authority and verbal abuse, so there is little risk of a new entrant being able to dominate the discussion. If necessary, vaccine critics can be blocked.

The situation is reversed on the AVN's blog. Because SAVNers can muster numerous energetic "intruders," potentially outweighing the capacity of AVN supporters, it is risky for AVN blog administrators to allow SAVNers regular access. There are too few AVN supporters who have the energy and skills to keep the discussion firmly under AVN control.

Another factor involves the tone, style and purpose of the AVN's and SAVN's venues. AVN administrators intend their blog to be a discussion of concerns about vaccination. Some posts are critical of the government, the pharmaceutical industry or particular proponents of vaccination. However, the primary purpose of the AVN is concerns about vaccination. Its tone is relatively calm: there is little verbal abuse. In contrast, SAVN's Facebook page is the central venue for articulating an attack on the AVN and other vaccine critics, and is filled with verbal abuse.

This asymmetry in purpose and tone implies an asymmetry in the impact of interventions by opponents. SAVN interventions on the AVN blog are far more disruptive, because they are designed to change both the style and orientation of the discussion. They change the style towards an attack-counterattack engagement that is typical of SAVN's page.

Because SAVNers regularly denigrate individuals and, if their identities are known, subject them to harassment, there are relatively few AVN supporters who are willing to engage online with SAVNers. Most of those who do use pseudonyms, because revealing their identities would open them to abuse and harassment. Most AVN supporters became involved because of their concerns about vaccination, and that is what they want to discuss. They did not become involved because they wanted to engage in a vendetta against vaccination proponents. This is yet another factor helping to explain differences between the AVN and SAVN venues, in particular their susceptibility to disruption.

Now consider venues controlled by others than the AVN and SAVN. Most of SAVN's efforts at censoring speech by vaccine critics have been aimed at such venues. There have been two main types: the mass media and venues for public talks.

Traditionally, the mass media — newspapers, radio, television, magazines — have had an enormous influence on public perceptions. With the rise of social media, fewer people are direct consumers of the mass media. Even so, the mass media still influence public conversations via what is called "agenda-setting." As a saying in the field puts it, mass media do not tell people *what* to think but what to think *about*.

Newspapers in particular play a powerful agenda-setting role, despite declining circulations. In many cases, radio and television stories are triggered by coverage in newspapers. Likewise, the agenda for quite a lot of social media comment about public affairs is set by mass media coverage. There is also a growing reciprocal influence, with mass media outlets addressing topics trending on social media.

The news media commonly present themselves as non-partisan: they seek to report the news, not to make it. In traditional news coverage, journalists seek to report on stories without inserting their own opinions. When addressing controversial issues, the goal is accuracy and an "appropriate" balance.

Innumerable influences make it difficult for the news media to achieve the public-interest functions of fairness and accuracy.[15] Governments, corporations and other pressure groups seek to shape media coverage through a variety of means, including building relationships with individual journalists, providing information that is easy to turn into stories, offering lucrative advertising contracts, and taking reprisals against journalists and editors who challenge vested interests. For example, a journalist doing crime stories may form relationships with police informants and spokespeople, enabling access to information. However, if the journalist runs stories critical of the

---

15 On problems with the news, see W. Lance Bennett, *News: The Politics of Illusion*, 10th edition (Chicago: University of Chicago Press, 2016); Nick Davies, *Flat Earth News: An Award-winning Reporter Exposes Falsehood, Distortion and Propaganda in the Global Media* (London: Chatto & Windus, 2008); Tom Fenton, *Bad News: The Decline of Reporting, the Business of News, and the Danger to Us All* (New York: ReganBooks, 2005); Alexandra Kitty, *Don't Believe It! How Lies Become News* (New York: Disinformation Company, 2005); Martin A. Lee and Norman Solomon, *Unreliable Sources: A Guide to Detecting Bias in News Media* (New York: Carol, 1990).

police, future access to these sources may be jeopardised. Governments and corporations issue media releases with information easy to turn into stories. Because mass media are being relentlessly squeezed financially, journalists are now expected to produce more stories in less time, thereby limiting time for checking facts and obtaining a variety of perspectives, so it is easy simply to use the material in media releases as the basis for a story. What often happens is that what looks like news is actually public relations material slightly repackaged. This is advantageous to governments and corporations because a news story, seen as independent and objective, is more credible than an advertisement.

Journalists and editors decide on what counts as news according to a set of "news values." These include prominence, locality, topicality and conflict. The actions and statements of prominent individuals are far more likely to be covered than those less well known. If a celebrity slips and falls, it's news; if you are hospitalised, it's not. If local people are travelling abroad and killed in a war, it's news; if a thousand people are killed in a war in Africa, and no outsiders are involved, it's not. If there's a terrorist attack in France, it's news; if there's a peaceful community in France, it's not.

When it comes to reporting on vaccination, usually there is little that is newsworthy. Routine vaccinations are not a news story precisely because they are routine. To be newsworthy, something out of the ordinary has to occur.

If there is a flare-up of an infectious disease, this might warrant a story, especially if local people are affected and health officials or scientists make a statement.

An outbreak of measles or whooping cough is an opportunity for vaccination proponents to get their message to the community.

Adverse reactions to vaccination also have the capacity to trigger news coverage if local people are affected. If there are numerous reports of adverse reactions, health officials might issue a warning about a defective vaccine.

Journalists often seek comment from prominent and powerful individuals and groups, such as leading scientists and health authorities. As noted, when journalists become close to powerful sources, they may be reluctant to criticise them. This is especially true when criticism might jeopardise continued access. Continued access is important for writing more stories, the basis of a journalist's career.

Influencing the media narrative

One of SAVN's key techniques for changing the media narrative is to make complaints to media organisations when a story is run that presents criticisms of vaccination. SAVN is able to mobilise quite a number of individuals who can make their own complaints. For example, when a story quotes Meryl Dorey as having a viewpoint worth reporting, this is a cue for a storm of complaints by SAVNers to the editor or proprietor.

This technique is especially potent for affecting the Australian Broadcasting Corporation. The ABC is continually under close scrutiny by various groups, including politicians, who demand that its coverage of issues be balanced according to their own criteria. A formal complaint to the ABC can lead to an internal inquiry that, even if it clears the journalists and editors involved, is an exhausting process, one preferably avoided. SAVN complaints to the ABC seem to have had the desired effect of deterring most coverage of vaccine critics.

Little of SAVN's activity in making complaints about media coverage is on the public record. Knowledge about SAVN's media campaigning mainly comes from comment on SAVN's Facebook page. However, the basic technique is well known from a number of instances involving topics other than vaccination. For example, Maryanne Demasi, a science journalist, prepared a story about the health effects of microwave radiation that ran in 2016 on the ABC weekly television programme *Catalyst*. There was a storm of protest about the story, some even before it ran. This protest and complaints about previous stories were probably factors in the ABC closing down the regular *Catalyst* programme and its entire team.

Attacks on journalists have a powerful demonstration effect: they serve as a warning to other journalists to avoid a similar treatment, thus encouraging self-censorship. In principle, the mass media subscribe to an ethos of fearless reporting and therefore shouldn't succumb to a partisan campaign designed to suppress certain points of view. In practice, mass media are often quite sensitive to audience response, especially the response of powerful groups. When there is a storm of protest and no countervailing pressure from the other side, the easiest option is to acquiesce.

As well as the negative approach of making complaints about coverage that SAVN deems unwelcome, there was a positive approach of finding sympathetic journalists and feeding them material. As noted, journalists are under increasing pressure to produce more stories in ever shorter periods of time, so it is a great temptation to rely on ready-made information and text from groups with an interest in particular types of coverage.

In relation to vaccination, journalists often use media releases from health departments, for example about a new vaccine or the need to vaccinate, as a basis for stories. There have also been quite a number of stories attacking vaccination critics. Jane Hansen, writing for the *Daily Telegraph*, a Sydney newspaper with a large readership, has written numerous stories attacking Meryl Dorey and the AVN.[16]

The degree to which SAVNers have fed material to journalists that has ended up published cannot be determined directly, for neither SAVNers nor journalists tell about their interactions. Indeed, it is uncommon for this sort of influence to be publicly documented on any issue, though it is sometimes exposed through investigative stories. A connection can be inferred by looking at the agenda of particular groups and the stories published. Sometimes the connection is obvious. When stories are pretty much word-for-word reproductions of media releases, without acknowledging the source, it is apparent a journalist has taken the easy road.

However, SAVN does not issue media releases, at least not publicly, so its influence on journalists is less easy to document. The role of SAVNers can be inferred

---

16 For example, Jane Hansen, "Anti-vax mob full of jabber," *Daily Telegraph,* 8 November 2015.

from particular instances. On 11 January 2016, information that Judy Wilyman had received her PhD from the University of Wollongong was made public, and her thesis was posted on the university's website. Within 24 hours, Kylar Loussikian, a journalist writing for *The Australian,* posed a series of questions to the university. His front-page story about the thesis was published on 13 January. It included several quotations from the thesis, plus much additional specific information.[17]

Are we to suppose that Kylar Loussikian, with no prior history of writing about vaccination or related issues, somehow became aware of Judy's thesis, independently decided it was newsworthy and spent his time going through it choosing quotes for an article as well as contacting various sources? Or is it more plausible that SAVNers keep tabs on anything newly online about Judy (for example using a Google Alert) and immediately sprang into action on the news of her graduation, and fed information to Loussikian?

The efforts of SAVNers and their allies have helped shape the Australian media narrative concerning vaccination.[18] SAVNer complaints may have scared some outlets

---

17 Kylar Loussikian, "Uni accepts thesis on vaccine 'conspiracy'," *The Australian,* 13 January 2016. I undertook a detailed analysis of this article in "News with a negative frame: a vaccination case study," 4 March 2016, http://www.bmartin.cc/pubs/16Loussikian.html.

18 It would be challenging to measure SAVN's impact on media coverage, which needs to be disentangled from other influences such as the denigration of Andrew Wakefield and the personal views of some editors and journalists.

away from coverage presenting criticisms of vaccination sympathetically or even neutrally. Meanwhile, a number of journalists, with or without help from SAVNers, have joined in the attack on the AVN and other vaccine critics. Indeed, often the main story is the AVN itself and its alleged misdemeanours — exactly the narrative of SAVN itself.

SAVN, throughout the years of its existence, has itself remained remarkably free of mass media scrutiny. SAVN spokespeople are sometimes quoted and reference is sometimes made to SAVN efforts, but no journalist has examined SAVN in any depth. There are several possible explanations. One is that most journalists support vaccination and do not want to question pro-vaccination campaigners or their techniques. Another is that any critical scrutiny of SAVN would probably be met by the usual SAVN technique of a barrage of complaints, so it would require considerable courage for any journalist, editor and publisher to publish a critique.[19]

To debate or not to debate?
On quite a number of occasions, Australian vaccine critics have offered to debate proponents. In most cases, proponents have declined. Few of them want to engage in an open debate or discussion with critics. On some occasions,

---

19 Academic journals seem to more open to publishing critiques of SAVN's tactics, especially journals with no stake in vaccination orthodoxy. That has been my experience with most editors of and referees for social science journals.

critics have invited numerous proponents to debate, all of whom have declined.

Why not engage in debate? If all the evidence supports vaccination, a debate might seem like an ideal opportunity to make the case for vaccinating and to demolish the arguments of the critics. However, there are several reasons not to debate. One is that very few proponents — health department officials, doctors and scientists — are on top of the evidence and arguments. They know that vaccination is a good thing but, because it is the dominant view and promoted through government policy, have not taken the time and effort to prepare the case in favour. In contrast, quite a few critics, because they are constantly confronted by proponents in daily conversations, have taken the trouble to acquire information to defend their views, and have practised countering proponent arguments.

There is another important reason why few proponents are willing to debate: unless they can win hands down, it will give more credibility to the critics. Proponents prefer to say that there is no debate, by which they mean that there is no credible reason for opposing vaccination. In this way, they stigmatise critics as irrational, unreasonable and indeed crazy — and who would want to debate someone who's crazy? To engage in a debate is to accept that there is something worthy of debating, and this means giving some recognition to the critics as having a point of view that might be taken seriously.

Proponents seldom articulate their reasons for refusing to debate; they usually just decline. For insight into the reasons, from a strategic point of view, it is useful to look at the public debate over fluoridation of public water supplies as a means to reduce tooth decay.

The fluoridation debate has a number of similarities to the vaccination debate, one of them being that, in countries like Australia and the US, nearly all dental, medical and scientific authorities support fluoridation, just as medical and scientific authorities support vaccination. In the US, fluoridation obtained endorsement in the 1950s by the US Public Health Service and dozens of dental, medical and other bodies. However, citizen opposition soon developed. (There were a few dentists, doctors and scientists opposed as well.) Fluoridation proponents in the 1960s and 1970s pondered whether to engage in debates with opponents, and some of them wrote about the dilemma involved.[20]

Debating had the disadvantage, for proponents, of giving more credibility to opponents by acknowledging that there was something to debate. Furthermore, some anti-fluoridation campaigners were highly knowledgeable and talented speakers, so proponents could not guarantee winning a debate, even though they believed all the arguments were on their side. Some fluoridation advocates therefore advised against engaging in public debates. But they also acknowledged a problem: refusing to debate made proponents seem arrogant. In the US, although many

---

20 Brian Martin, *Scientific Knowledge in Controversy: The Social Dynamics of the Fluoridation Debate* (Albany, NY: State University of New York Press, 1991), pp. 60–64, http://www.bmartin.cc/pubs/91skic.html.

people deferred to authorities, there was also an antiestablishment sentiment to which antifluoridation campaigners could appeal.

Australian vaccination proponents face the same dilemma.[21] Refusing to debate denies vaccine critics a platform. It means fewer people hear the contrary arguments head to head, and fewer people hear views different from vaccination orthodoxy. However, refusing to debate runs the risk of seeming to be arrogant or perhaps of seeming to be afraid of facing the critics. Some members of the public might ask, "Why are they refusing?"

The choice to refuse to debate works best when one side has an overwhelming advantage in terms of credibility, resources and access to mass media. Vaccination proponents in Australia have this advantage. Therefore, when proponents refuse to debate, critics have no easy way to turn this to their advantage. There are no prominent media commentators prepared to call out vaccination proponents for their refusal to debate, asking "If the evidence is overwhelming, why are they afraid of opponents?"

---

21 Brian Martin, "Dealing with dilemmas in health campaigning," *Health Promotion International*, Vol. 28, No. 1, 2013, pp. 43–50, http://www.bmartin.cc/pubs/12hpi.html. This article, which discusses some SAVN techniques, was criticised in blogs by Paul Gallagher and Peter Tierney. For my response, see "Caught in the vaccination wars (part 3)," http://www.bmartin.cc/pubs/12hpi-comments.html. A complaint about this article was made to the editor-in-chief and publisher of *Health Promotion International*. No changes or declarations were required. The editor-in-chief supports well-argued scholarly work.

Refusal to debate is not censorship, at least not in the usual sense. When those with a near-monopoly on credibility and public forums refuse to debate, this operates to reduce the visibility of the minority position, which might be said to be de facto censorship. However, even this judgement needs to be made in context. In some circumstances, a minority position has so little credibility that it seems reasonable to ignore it. For example, consider the people who believe the earth is hollow and we live inside. Hardly anyone takes this view seriously, and therefore scientists can safely ignore requests to debate it. However, vaccination proponents apparently cannot ignore critics, at least in Australia, where there has been a campaign to denigrate and harass them. In this context, refusal to debate is not a matter of simply ignoring a claim with no credibility but of not wanting to enable critics to have a platform.

PUBLIC TALKS

Suppose a group organises a talk. It engages a speaker or perhaps a panel of speakers. It books a venue, for example a church or public library, and advertises the talk to members. Perhaps it is a public talk, so members of the public are invited to attend. There might or might not be an admission fee.

There is a very long tradition of giving talks. It is a mark of a free society that people can meet and discuss issues of concern. In repressive societies, in contrast, meetings — even private meetings — can be risky if they tackle topics considered subversive. Those attending realise the possibility of surveillance and arrest.

In Australia, in most cases giving talks is so routine that no one pays any attention to them, except of course those attending them. Service clubs like Rotary regularly hold meetings with visiting speakers. Universities host all sorts of guests for seminars and conferences. Clergy speak at religious services to which any member of the public can attend. And so on through a wide variety of organisations in a range of areas.

There are a few exceptions. David Irving is a British historian whose views about the Holocaust — the systematic killing of millions of Jews and others by the Nazis during World War II — are non-standard. Irving is often seen as a "Holocaust denier," someone who believes the Holocaust did not happen, though his views are more nuanced than this. Irving had made a couple of visits to Australia in the 1980s, largely unremarked. Subsequently the Australian government refused to grant him entry. This form of censorship turned out to be counterproductive: the government's ban triggered a flurry of media commentary about Irving and free speech, giving his ideas far more visibility than if he had been allowed into the country.

In 2011, Christopher Monckton, also from Britain, visited Australia and was scheduled to give a talk at Notre Dame University in Perth. Monckton is a climate sceptic: he disagrees with the dominant scientific view that global warming is occurring and is largely caused by human activities, especially burning coal and oil. A number of climate scientists were alarmed that Monckton, whom they considered ill-informed and lacking credibility, was being offered a forum at a university. The scientists organised a petition to have Monckton's talk cancelled. However, this censorship attempt failed and, furthermore, was counterproductive. Monckton gave his talk and the furore about it provided more attention to his views than if he had been ignored.[22]

Philip Nitschke is a campaigner for do-it-yourself voluntary euthanasia. Australia's Northern Territory in 1995 passed a law legalising voluntary euthanasia and Nitschke was the only doctor willing to help terminally ill individuals to die. The Northern Territory law was soon overruled by federal parliament and Nitschke began investigating and promoting ways for individuals who were suffering to end their lives peacefully, most commonly by obtaining the drug pentobarbital (commonly called Nembutal) from other countries or by constructing an "exit bag" for breathing in an inert gas.

Nitschke's activities, run through the organisation Exit International, were met by extraordinary censorship from the Australian government. Nitschke's book *The Peaceful Pill Handbook*, co-authored with Fiona Stewart, was banned by the government, the only book banned in the previous 35 years. (It can be legally purchased and owned in all other countries.) A law was passed making it illegal to communicate information about ending one's life, peacefully or otherwise, over the phone or Internet.

---

22 Brian Martin, "Monckton and Notre Dame: a case for free speech?" *The Conversation*, 30 June 2011, https://theconversation.com/monckton-and-notre-dame-a-case-for-free-speech-2104.

The Australian Medical Association moved to deregister Nitschke.[23]

Another group targeted by the Australian government is Islamic radicals who are seen as supporting terrorism. Targeted individuals may be subject to surveillance or arrest. Some, intending to visit Australia, are denied visas.

There are also cases in which protesters attempt to disrupt talks by particular speakers. For example, students might try to shout down a speaker — usually a prominent figure — who is seen as racist or imperialist.

To summarise: in most cases, if someone wants to organise a public talk, usually there are few obstacles. Giving a talk is routine. Overt censorship is unusual — and can be counterproductive.

There is also the question of the venue for a talk. If a Rotary club has a visiting speaker, it is up to the club to decide whom to invite. Free speech does not mean anyone can speak at a Rotary Club function. Likewise, if historians organise a conference and put out a call for papers, only some will be accepted. Free speech does not mean you can present any paper you like at a history conference.

---

23 For my analyses of Australian government efforts to censor Nitschke and others who provide information about peaceful dying, see "Techniques to pass on: technology and euthanasia," *Bulletin of Science, Technology and Society*, Vol. 30, No. 1, February 2010, pp. 54–59, http://www.bmartin.cc/pubs/10bsts.html, and "Euthanasia struggles," chapter 7 in *Nonviolence Unbound* (Sparsnäs, Sweden: Irene Publishing, 2015), pp. 208–258, http://www.bmartin.cc/pubs/15nvu/nvu-7.pdf.

On the other hand, free speech means that any group can organise its own public talk and invite whoever it wants. If the government told a Rotary club or the organisers of a history conference who not to invite, that would be censorship. In Australia, such intervention would be highly unusual. The government, when it intervenes, usually does so at a higher or different level, for example in denying visas or passing laws about what can be said about euthanasia or national security.

Corporations can influence who is invited to give a talk. At their own functions, corporations choose speakers, in the usual fashion. For other venues, corporate influence is usually indirect and sometimes does not involve any action by employees. For example, in a company town — a town dominated by a particular large firm — most venues would be reluctant to organise a talk by someone critical of the company, even without prodding or other intervention by the company. Such an influence can be called non-decisionmaking.[24] This is quite different from overt censorship, but the effect is much the same. Furthermore, the exclusion of particular viewpoints is more effective when it occurs without overt intervention.

Popular viewpoints can also influence who is invited to give a talk. In a religiously-minded community, it is unlikely that schools or local government bodies would host an ardent atheist. In a community put on the alert

---

24 The classic account is Matthew A. Crenson, *The un-politics of air pollution: A study of non-decisionmaking in the cities* (Baltimore: Johns Hopkins University Press, 1971).

over terrorism, hosting an outspoken militant could be risky. And so on through a range of topics.

SAVN censorship of talks
On several occasions when the Australian vaccine critics have been scheduled to speak at public venues, SAVNers have made efforts to have the talk cancelled. The most prominent instance was in 2011. The Woodford Folk Festival is held every year over a number of days in Woodford, a small town in Queensland. As well as folk music, the festival organisers arrange for a number of other events, including talks. Meryl Dorey had been a speaker at several festivals, talking about vaccination. SAVNers mounted a major campaign to stop Dorey's talk. They wrote to the festival organisers, to the media, to the local government and to commercial sponsors of the festival, telling them that Dorey was the purveyor of false and dangerous information and that her talk should be cancelled.

SAVN's censorship campaign is well documented.[25] There was extensive discussion about it on SAVN's Facebook page. As well, at least 17 SAVNers wrote about it on their own blogs. On many of these blogs, Dorey was the target of verbal abuse. For example,

---

25 Brian Martin, "Censorship and free speech in scientific controversies," *Science and Public Policy*, Vol. 42, No. 3, 2015, pp. 377–386, http://www.bmartin.cc/pubs/15spp.html.

> Daniel Raffaele: "They are giving a stage and a microphone to someone who's facile ranting should not be heard outside her own nut farm."[26]
>
> Chrys Stevenson: "rapid-fire, baffle-them-with-bullshit stylings of anti-vaccination virago, Meryl Dorey"
>
> Askegg: "None of this stops Meryl Dorey from spreading her emotive propaganda, however it does force her delusion to evolve into new age conspiracy theories, 'one world governments', the Illuminati, New World Orders, chemtrails, and AIDS denialism. This is the kind of ideology which informs Ms Dorey's creative reinterpretation of the scientific data."

Verbal abuse was addressed in chapter 4. Here we see the use of verbal abuse as part of a censorship campaign. Several of the blogs included revealing descriptions of SAVN's efforts.

> A Drunken Madman: Dorey's appearance at Woodford would have perhaps been her most high-profile unopposed appearance since the emergence of Stop The AVN, whose tireless efforts have led to the media spotlight being turned, with most outlets now rejecting her "expertise" — some spectacularly, such as [radio host] Tracey Spicer hanging up on Meryl mid-sentence. Some hold-outs remain, generally in

---

26 Dorey's husband is a macadamia nut farmer.

conspiracy-mongering talkback jock backwaters, but overall her audience is vastly reduced.

So there was no way Stop The AVN would be letting Dorey have a free kick at Woodford.[27]

Bastard Sheep: StopAVN first approached WoodfordFF [Woodford Folk Festival] to let them know just what/who they were providing a platform to, and they didn't care. If anything, their response yet again showed they supported the unhealthy and dangerous stance Meryl promotes. StopAVN then went to the media contacts. This second approach has proven more successful, with numerous sponsors pulling out due to the misinformation claims not only of Meryl and the AVN, but also of other stalls and speakers at WoodfordFF. Numerous organisations including council/governments who support but don't sponsor the festival requested their names and logos be removed from sponsor lists.

Mooselet: This year Meryl was invited back to the Woodford Folk Festival to spread her anti-vaccine message, claiming the thoroughly debunked myth that vaccines and autism are related. Owing to the wonders of social media, the Festival was inundated with outraged letters, emails, tweets and blogs. The Queensland Health Minister openly referred to Meryl's brand of information as "nonsense." I even wrote to my local councillor to express my concerns,

---

27 A "free kick" here refers to giving a talk without any hindrance.

since the Festival takes place in my council area. Following this much publicised and prolonged criticism of allowing such misleading and potentially dangerous information to be presented from a self-styled expert, the Woodford Folk Festival changed Meryl's presentation from a one woman bullshit band to a forum featuring Immunologist Prof Andreas Suhbier

As indicated in Mooselet's account of SAVN's campaign, the festival organisers responded to the campaign by changing the format from Dorey giving a talk to a debate between her and a pro-vaccination speaker. The campaign to stop Dorey's talk led to greatly increased interest in it: the audience was far larger than in previous years. SAVN hired an aeroplane to fly over the festival with a banner saying "Vaccination saves lives," and in their blogs SAVNers expressed great pride and delight in this intervention.

Several of the SAVN bloggers provided justifications for censorship, which can be classified into four arguments.

1. The AVN provides misleading information dangerous to public health.
2. Dorey lacks expertise.
3. The AVN practises censorship.
4. Dorey can speak somewhere else.

It is revealing that SAVNers feel the need to justify their actions. One reason is censorship's bad reputation: few people want to be seen as censors; they would rather be seen as protectors of the public. Justifications for censorship are an attempt to reframe the discussion.

It is worth noting that there is no law against criticising vaccination. In Australia, some sorts of speech are against the law, for example yelling "fire" in a theatre, urging people to commit crimes, revealing classified information about national security, and letting people know how to die peacefully. Surely if criticising vaccination warranted silencing, there would be attempts to pass laws against it, but there have been no such attempts.

One SAVNer, in an email exchange with me, brought up seatbelt laws. In Australia, there is a law mandating wearing of seatbelts while in a moving car or other motor vehicle. This SAVNer suggested that opposing vaccination was like advocating not wearing a seatbelt. This is not a good analogy. Questioning vaccination is like opposing seatbelt laws, and it is certainly legitimate to oppose these laws.

Argument 1, that the AVN provides misleading information dangerous to public health, assumes that all truths about vaccination have been definitively established. Actually, there continue to be debates within scientific publications. Should the AVN be banned from reporting findings from scientific studies?

Another assumption underlying argument 1 is that vaccination is a unified whole, and the only possible stances are to be for it or against it. As discussed in chapter 2, it is possible to break down the issue and analyse the pros and cons of individual vaccines. Is questioning the HPV vaccine, or suggesting changes to the vaccination schedule, dangerous to public health?

Another assumption is that criticisms of vaccination actually lead to people changing their behaviour. Yet SAVN has never presented good evidence that the AVN's activities have affected vaccination rates in Australia.[28]

Then there is the question of who gets to decide what is considered misleading. Given that scientific papers critical of vaccination continue to be published, surely not *all* the information provided by the AVN is misleading. If only some of it is misleading, is this a good justification for censoring all of its speech?

If argument 1 were applied more generally, the result would be that a large proportion of speech about all manner of scientific controversies would be shut down. There have been fierce debates over climate change, pesticides, forestry, whaling, nuclear power, intersex and genetic engineering, among other issues. For example, climate change campaigners might argue that any public criticism of the view that global warming is real and largely caused by humans should be silenced because it is wrong and is dangerous to the future of the planet. Such a stance would have little prospect of success, though, in part because climate sceptics are supported by some powerful groups, notably the coal and oil industries.[29]

---

28 See chapter 9 for more on this.

29 In Australia, *The Australian* has given prominent coverage to climate sceptics, meanwhile being a leader in attacking vaccination sceptics. These divergent treatments of challenges to scientific orthodoxy are compatible with the newspaper lining up with groups having more money.

Argument 2 is that Dorey lacks expertise. Again, it might be asked, who gets to decide whether a person has expertise? In any case, there is no precedent for barring a person from giving a talk, to a public audience, on the grounds of lack of expertise.

Argument 3 is that the AVN practises censorship, specifically by blocking certain messages and contributors from its blog. As discussed above, it is questionable whether this should be called censorship, given that there is normally no expectation that an organisation's blog should be open to all comers. In any case, even if the AVN practises censorship, so what? This is not a justification for censoring the AVN.

Argument 4 is that Dorey can speak somewhere else — just not at the Woodford Folk Festival. This is not a justification for censorship at all, especially given that SAVN has tried to block Dorey from speaking at other venues.

That SAVNers brought up all these arguments to justify their efforts against Dorey speaking at the festival is testimony to their need for legitimacy, in their own eyes, for censorship.

SAVN's furious campaign had a significant impact. Although the festival organisers stood firm for some time, eventually they agreed to change Dorey's talk to a debate between her and a vaccination supporter. (Ironically, Dorey and others had been offering to debate but, as noted above, most vaccination proponents refused.) The huge publicity about Dorey's talk led to a record crowd for the debate.

The most significant outcome of SAVN's campaign was that the festival organisers did not ask Dorey to speak again. In the short term, SAVN may have sparked greater interest in the vaccination controversy, but the longer-term effect seems to have been to frighten groups that might sponsor a talk.

SAVNers on censorship
Several typical SAVNer views on censorship are revealed in comments on a thread on the SAVN Facebook page, 30 July 2017, concerning media coverage of the AVN. The trigger for the thread was a comment by "Julie Miller": "If vaccines were so safe and effective ex vaxxers and non vaxxers wouldn't be censored!" The responses included the following:

> **Veronique Denyer** They should be censored because they spread ignorance and disinformation. […]
>
> **Jeff Keogh** There is a very real difference between censorship and idiots not being given a platform. No one is censoring antivaxxers. They just aren't putting up with their stupid bullshit any more.
>
> **Lauren Christie** ...they aren't censored. Hence why their websites, facebook groups, public talks, public protests, etc etc still occur. If they were censored, we wouldn't even be hearing what Meryl Dorey has to say.
>
> **Yolanda Bogert** Refusing to legitimise a view with access to public facilities to use as a platform to

spread damaging views is =\= [does not equal] censorship.

Stephen Sherley You'd be confusing "censorship" with "please provide some actual support for your lies before we let you start killing babies." Nearly the same thing, I know.

Kylie Gibson How many of us have been banned from the AVN page? It was in the hundreds, wasn't it? Most were banned for answering questions. No abuse, just answered questions. Ms Dorey is the queen of censorship.[30]

Veronique Denyer says vaccine critics *should be* censored. Others, though, prefer to say critics aren't being censored. Jeff Keogh says not giving "idiots" a platform and not "putting up with their stupid bullshit" isn't censorship. Similarly, Yolanda Bogert says denying access to facilities isn't censorship. Lauren Christie says they "aren't censored" because they are still able to speak elsewhere.

Stephen Sherley's comment is harder to decipher. He seems to imply that SAVNers should be able to demand answers from the AVN and, because the answers are not acceptable, the AVN has no right to speak because its speech amounts to "killing babies."

---

30 For the convenience of my subsequent commentary, I have slightly rearranged the order of these comments, which themselves were interspersed among other Facebook comments not reproduced here.

Kylie Gibson offers a different approach, attacking the AVN for its own censorship. An implicit implication is that the AVN has no business complaining about censorship if it's a censor itself.

When a public talk has to remain a secret
In August 2012, Dorey gave talks at nine towns in New South Wales, usually accompanied by Greg Beattie. Dorey reported that some people were afraid to attend because they feared violence by SAVNers or because their neighbours would find out they had attended and, in a small town, they would be blacklisted or their children penalised. On the other hand, some people drove long distances to attend.[31]

In October 2012, Meryl Dorey wrote this in her blog "No compulsory vaccination":

> A few days ago, the AVN announced that it would be holding a seminar in Canberra on Saturday the 10th of November. For the first time, we have decided not to release the name or location of the venue — only saying that it is centrally located within Canberra so it will be easy for anyone in that area to get to.
>
> The reason we did this is that over the last 3 1/2 years or so, every single time we have held seminars, there have either been threats to the venues, requiring us to hire security guards at our expense – or letters

---

31 Meryl Dorey, "Central NSW seminar tour — first impressions," *No Compulsory Vaccination*, 22 August 2012, http://nocompulsoryvaccination.com/2012/08/22/1937/.

and phone calls to the venue urging them not to allow us to speak. The source of these threats has always been both the hate group, Stop the AVN (SAVN) and their parent group, the Australian Skeptics.[32]

Dorey reproduced a post on SAVN's Facebook page of "Addryanne Adamsyn" (obviously a pseudonym) saying she had made a complaint to Fair Trading in Canberra about the advertising of the event.

The AVN's response to campaigns of complaints to venues in this case was to only tell people who had signed up to attend the location not long before the starting time. This defence against complaint campaigns would become a standard practice for the AVN and other vaccine critics in years to come.

In 2014, the AVN paid for a stall at the Healthy Lifestyles Expo, held on the Sunshine Coast in Queensland. Vaccination proponents were quite open in advocating censorship, and seemingly this came directly from health authorities and parents. The lead sentence in an article in the *Courier-Mail,* Queensland's major newspaper, read:

> The state's top health experts have called for the Australian Vaccination Skeptics Network to be barred from disseminating information at the Healthy

---

32 Meryl Dorey, "Hate, threats and cowardice," *No Compulsory Vaccination,* 24 October 2012, http://nocompulsoryvaccination.com/2012/10/24/hate-threats-and-cowardice/.

Lifestyle Expo, arguing their views were dangerous and inaccurate.[33]

A local newspaper, the *Northern Star,* described actions against the AVN's display:

> An anti-vaccination group exhibiting at a Sunshine Coast Healthy Lifestyle Expo has sparked national outrage.
> An organiser of next weekend's event, Annie Infinite, says the expo has received so much hate mail since allowing the Australian Vaccination-sceptics Network a paid booth at the event, it has had to call police.
> Nearly 500 people have signed a petition for the expo to ban the AVN and its chief proponent, Meryl Dorey.
> Messages to the Expo have included "you should just die for supporting her" and "we are going to take you all down, all you natural therapist c****."
> Despite the barrage of complaints, Ms Infinite said she would not cancel Ms Dorey's stall without an official request in writing from an authority to do so.[34]

---

33 Laura Chalmers, "Health experts call for ban on anti-vaccination campaigner Meryl Dorey at Healthy Lifestyle Expo," *Courier-Mail,* 13 May 2014.

34 Sundstrom, "Outrage against anti-vaccination lobby at health expo," *Northern Star,* 15 May 2014.

In 2014 and 2015, SAVN coordinated a campaign of censorship against a different speaker, Sherri Tenpenny, a vaccination critic based in the US. Tenpenny, an osteopath, is one of the few outspoken critics of vaccination with professional credentials, and therefore is a special threat to the usual hegemony of expert opinion in favour of vaccination. For years, SAVNers had denigrated Tenpenny on any relevant occasion.

Stephanie Messenger, an Australian campaigner against vaccination, had the idea of organising a series of talks about vaccination and related matters, with Tenpenny as a keynote speaker. Anticipating opposition from SAVN, Messenger considered planning the events with a degree of secrecy, for example notifying ticket-holders of the venue the day before. However, this level of secrecy is virtually impossible, given that SAVNers join vaccine-critical groups so they can find out what is happening.

When SAVNers obtained information about the planned public meetings, with Tenpenny a featured speaker along with several others, they mounted a campaign to sabotage the meetings. SAVNers wrote to various groups, most importantly the venues hosting the talks. Under great pressure, most of them withdrew, undermining the viability of the tour. Tenpenny, amazed at the level of antagonism, cancelled her trip to Australia.[35]

---

35 Julia Medew, "US anti-vaccination campaigner Dr Sherri Tenpenny cancels tour of Australia," *Sydney Morning Herald*, 29 January 2015.

On SAVN's Facebook page, the campaign against Tenpenny's speaking tour was touted as a great success:

> Following an announcement by anti-vaccination campaigner Stephanie Messenger that she, or rather her "organisations" the "Get Rid of SIDS Project Inc" and the "GanKinMan Foundation" were about to host an Australian tour of American anti-vaccination campaigner Dr Sheri Tenpenny, SAVN began a national campaign to prevent that. After alerting venue operators to the Messenger's deceit in how she presented the seminars, all bookings were cancelled, and her tour was then cancelled.[36]

It is difficult to judge the overall impact of SAVN's campaign. It demonstrated the power to stop prominent critics of vaccination from giving public talks. It also showed that few venues are willing to stand up to a barrage of complaints. On the other hand, the alarm raised about Tenpenny's proposed visit may have stimulated more interest in her views and her website than if she had visited Australia without any opposition.

AVN campaigners learned from the Tenpenny experience.[37] In July-August 2017, they organised a road trip across Australia with screenings of the film *Vaxxed*, with

---

36 Stop the Australian (Anti)Vaccination Network, "About, " https://www.facebook.com/pg/stopavn/about/?ref=page_internal, accessed 11 July 2017.

37 Some of these lessons were noted years earlier: Meryl Dorey, "Going underground," *No Compulsory Vaccination*, 18 February 2012, http://bit.ly/2E8A2TM.

11 stops in cities in eastern and southern Australia. Tickets could only be obtained online. A notice about upcoming events stated:

> There will be no door sales. Because each venue is secret, only ticket holders will know where they are located and even then, just 2 hours before doors open to the public. Ticket sales cease prior to this so to ensure you are one of the lucky few who will be able to view this amazing documentary in the presence of your own supportive community, don't wait too long to get your tickets![38]

By notifying attendees only slightly in advance, it was difficult for SAVN to put pressure on venues. Furthermore, there was an extra precaution. The text message giving the location led attendees not to the venue but to a gathering point nearby. Shortly before the meeting began, they were taken to the actual venue.

For screenings of *Vaxxed*, AVN organisers did not announce the presence of any international speakers, instead saying they would appear via Skype. But, as it turned out, they were in Australia and available in person for after-screening question-and-answer sessions. The AVN thus anticipated and avoided SAVN pressure to deny visas for the international speakers.

---

38 Katherine Smith, "Australia: Vaxxed tour down under begins Sunday!" *Natural Medicine,* 21 July 2017, http://www.naturalmedicine.net.nz/news/australia-vaxxed-tour-down-under-begins-sunday/.

As indicated in the quote above from the notice about the screenings, the events brought together like-minded individuals in circumstances that were made more dramatic and bonding due to the secrecy. Studies of persuasion show that scarcity makes things more attractive.[39] SAVN's prior attempts at censorship may have enabled the AVN to make the *Vaxxed* tour an experience far more influential for participants than it would have been otherwise.

One of the visiting speakers accompanying the *Vaxxed* tour was Polly Tommey. On leaving Australia, Tommey was informed that she was banned from entering the country for three years because of the danger caused by her views about vaccination.[40]

The ban reveals the influence of SAVN-aligned pressure to censor vaccine critics. It is hard to imagine immigration authorities taking any interest in visitors such as Tommey except for campaigning by SAVN and its allies.

The ban is mainly of symbolic significance, showing the Australian government's commitment to vaccination and intolerance of any questioning of government policy. The ban has limited practical impact because Tommey's

---

39 Robert B. Cialdini, *Influence: How and Why People Agree to Things* (New York: Morrow, 1984).

40 Jon Rappoport, "Lying Australian press and the Vaxxed scandal," *Jon Rappoport's Blog,* 11 August 2017, https://jonrappoport.wordpress.com/2017/08/11/lying-australian-press-and-the-vaxxed-scandal/.

websites and publications are freely available, and she can readily access Australian audiences via Skype.

The potential of using a ban to stimulate greater interest was shown shortly afterwards. Kent Heckenlively announced that he was the "world's number one antivaxxer" and that he was planning a trip to take his message to Australians. His blog, which included a copy of a letter to the prime minister, was obviously satirical.[41] Nonetheless, several media outlets treated it as a serious plan and, not long after, the Immigration Minister, Peter Dutton, announced a ban on Heckenlively visiting the country. Heckenlively's publicity stunt generated more coverage than he could have hoped, inserting his name into the Australian vaccination debate.

The online comments following some of the news stories about the ban on Heckenlively reveal considerable support for censorship of vaccine critics, as well as some support for free speech.[42] It seems that few of those backing the government's ban have any sense of how censorship can be counterproductive.

Using the ban on Tommey to help create interest, in October 2017 the AVN announced a new series of screenings of *Vaxxed*, with Tommey to join the post-

---

41 Kent Heckenlively, "Kent Heckenlively's 'dangerous science' tour heads to Australia?..." *BolenReport,* 15 August 2017, http://bolenreport.com/kent-heckenlivelys-dangerous-science-tour-heads-australia/.

42 For example, Stephanie Peatling, "'World's number 1 anti-vaxxer' Kent Heckenlively denied entry to Australia," *Sydney Morning Herald*, 1 September 2017.

screening discussions via Skype. The AVN's notice featured a picture of Tommey with "Banned!" emblazoned over her face.

CONCLUSION

SAVN set itself the goal of shutting down the AVN and silencing any public criticism of vaccination. Its three main types of methods have been denigration, harassment and censorship. In practice, these often are mixed together. For example, in attempting to have talks by Dorey and Tenpenny cancelled, SAVN wrote numerous letters denigrating these individuals.

Based on its actual practice, it seems that SAVN wants to protect the public by ensuring that people never hear criticisms of vaccination. SAVN sees criticisms from individuals with knowledge and credentials as especially threatening, so much of their efforts are devoted to denigrating and, when possible, silencing Dorey, Tenpenny, Andrew Wakefield, Judy Wilyman and others.

SAVN's censorship efforts are largely waged through electronic means, including comments on SAVN's Facebook page and SAVNer blogs, and complaints made to regulatory bodies, media organisations and venues for talks. SAVNers seldom challenge their targets face-to-face.

Although supporting vaccination, SAVN's major mode of operation is attack on those considered opponents of or threats to vaccination. It labels targets as "anti-vaxxers," in which case SAVNers might be called "anti-anti-vaxxers." For SAVN, censorship is a key goal. It is not really necessary for SAVN to present the pro-vaccination view because it is the dominant one anyway, endorsed by government health departments and medical authorities, who have ample access to public forums.

SAVN's relationship with health authorities is unclear. Some pro-vaccination doctors and health officials may privately support SAVN's efforts, but there have been no official endorsements.

To better understand the dynamics of censorship in this contest between SAVN and its targets, especially the AVN, it is useful to think of venues or forums for speech. In SAVN's own forums — primarily its Facebook page and blogs of individual SAVNers — critics of vaccination are sometimes allowed a voice, but in circumstances in which they are outnumbered and can be blocked at any time. In the AVN's own forums — primarily its blog — critics of the AVN are usually blocked. SAVN calls this censorship, but this is primarily a rhetorical move to justify its own actions, given that organisations normally control speech on their own forums. Government departments, corporations, churches, trade unions and environmental groups, among others, seldom provide open forums, and their restrictions are not normally called censorship.

Then there are public forums where there is an expectation of some openness to different points of view. Among these are mass media, where the criteria for publication include fairness and balance as well as newsworthiness, and venues for public talks. SAVN's censorship efforts have been focused on these public forums, the goal being to ensure that vaccine-critical views are either unheard or stigmatised.

There are numerous other groups, with much more power than SAVN, seeking to censor opponents. Governments censor challengers, for example on national security. Corporations use various means to censor criticism. Religious organisations seek to censor sacrilegious expression. And so on. SAVN's campaigns are only exceptional in being a coordinated citizen campaign directed at other citizens.

Nearly everyone supports free speech in principle, but very few are willing to take any risk to support the free speech of those with whom they disagree. Many venues for public talks succumbed to SAVN-inspired pressures to withdraw invitations to vaccine critics: defending free speech was not a high enough priority in the face of significant costs in terms of reputation or hassles. In the mass media, no mainstream editors or journalists have stood up for free speech by vaccination critics. This suggests that free speech is precarious.

SAVNers do not present their efforts as censorship but rather as protecting the public from ideas that would endanger public health. This reframing has been so effective that the issue has been shifted from free speech to whether vaccine critics are credible, with the assumption that if they are wrong and dangerous, they should not be allowed to speak.

SAVN's censorship campaigns have not entirely prevented the expression of vaccine-critical views. Indeed, in some cases, SAVN's efforts have helped give those views a higher profile. Censorship efforts do not occur in a vacuum: there is resistance, the subject of the next chapter.

7
Defending

After the formation of Stop the Australian Vaccination Network (SAVN) in 2009, Australian vaccine critics faced a difficult challenge.¹ SAVN was dedicated to shutting down public criticism of vaccination, and used methods of denigration, harassment and censorship. Should vaccine critics resist and, if so, how? To appreciate the strengths and weaknesses of various options, it's useful to look at the generic issue of defending against attack.²

It is useful to begin by looking at strategy, in this case strategy for vaccine critics. A strategy is basically a plan for moving from present circumstances to a desired goal. To develop a strategy involves analysis of the present circumstances, articulation of goals and formulation of plans to get to the goals. The plans need to take into account opponents (and their actions), resources, allies and much else. Tactics are methods used along the way.

For Australian vaccine critics, the present circumstances are the dominant vaccination paradigm (a set of beliefs and practices), the commitment to vaccination by the medical profession, health departments, pharmaceuti-

---

1 For information on SAVN and the AVN, see the glossary and chapter 3.

2 Chapters 3 to 5 include some discussion of how to defend against attacks. In this chapter, I look at additional and more general considerations about defending.

cal companies and most of the public and media, the history of continued and expanded use of vaccines, the activities of SAVN, and the limited resources of the vaccine critics themselves.

To develop a strategy means having a goal. However, among vaccine critics there are several goals. One is overthrowing the vaccination paradigm, which would mean discrediting vaccination altogether. This might seem illusory given the growing power of vaccination proponents, so as a goal it is more like a guiding light than a practical proposition. A more limited goal, and more achievable, is facilitating genuine choice concerning vaccines. In Australia, this would mean reinstituting conscientious and religious objections to vaccination and reversing the laws restricting welfare benefits and schooling that discriminate against non-vaccinated children and their parents. This goal is encapsulated in the slogan "No compulsory vaccination." An even more limited goal is to allow vaccine critics, and parents with concerns, to have a fair opportunity to present their views, without denigration, harassment or censorship.

The belief underlying much of the activity of vaccine critics is that if people were presented with unbiased information about both the benefits and risks of vaccination, many would decline. Based on this assumption, their goal then becomes having a fair debate, without extraneous pressures to vaccinate coming from doctors and campaigners.

When different members of a movement have different goals, there can be difficulties due to pulling in different directions. Sometimes a movement has stated goals, yet internally there can be struggles over direction.

My aim here is not to articulate or propose goals for vaccine critics or, as some of them call themselves, the pro-choice movement. Instead, my interest is in a much narrower matter: defending against attack. In the face of the extraordinary campaign launched by SAVN, it is a reasonable goal simply to survive, namely to continue to be able to make public criticisms of vaccination. Given this goal, a strategy is a plan to achieve it. This is of wider interest because other movements are subject to similar attacks. Precisely because the Australian campaign against vaccine critics has been so ferocious, the challenges involved in defending and even surviving are easier to recognise.

The next section presents two options, called exit and voice, for responding to problems. After that is a section describing options for defending against complaints. Then comes a discussion of how an organisation's structure affects its vulnerability to attack. The long final section addresses facets of a process called political jiu-jitsu that offers insights for defending against attack.

EXIT AND VOICE

Albert O. Hirschman in 1970 authored *Exit, Voice, and Loyalty*, a book that has become a classic reference.[3]

---

3 Albert O. Hirschman, *Exit, Voice, and Loyalty: Responses to Decline in Firms, Organizations, and States* (Cambridge, MA: Harvard University Press, 1970).

Hirschman described two options for consumers and workers who are dissatisfied. One option is "exit," namely leaving. If you have been driving a Ford for years but think the quality has declined, you can instead buy a Toyota or some other brand, and likewise for refrigerators and breakfast cereals. For smaller consumer items, it is easy to switch brands, although some people develop a commitment. If you are a worker and don't like your job or are being harassed, you can leave. This is usually a more serious form of exit, not taken lightly if you have years of service. So what makes a consumer or worker stay? The key is loyalty.

Instead of exiting, the alternative is "voice," which means speaking out. If you think the Fords you've been driving are not as good as they should be, you can complain to the company, make suggestions, put comments on social media or otherwise express your opinion. In relation to consumer products, voice usually reflects greater loyalty. When it's easy to exit, expressing your opinion requires more effort, and usually the reason for doing this is that you care. In the workplace, voice means speaking out about problems, and for this you could be targeted with reprisals. In many workplaces, dissent is treated as disloyalty. In Hirschman's picture, however, voice actually reflects greater loyalty, in the sense of caring about making the company a better place, though not in the sense of defending the company even though it is operating badly.

One reason workers stay on the job, despite dissatisfaction, is that they are being paid. Hirschman's important insight is that there is more to loyalty than money. This is clear in voluntary organisations such as religious congregations. In several Christian denominations, there have been struggles over the ordination of women. If advocates of the ordination of women didn't care all that much about their church, they could exit: leave the congregation for another, more hospitable church. But many of them stay and work for many years to bring about change. They are loyal.

Applying Hirschman's picture to the Australian vaccination debate, it is possible to look at parents as consumers with a choice between two products: having their children vaccinated, or not. Most parents are satisfied with the product: they have their children vaccinated and their children seem protected from infectious disease. However, a few become dissatisfied. Perhaps their child suffers an adverse reaction, or they hear about some other child suffering an adverse reaction. Such parents can then choose exit, namely stop vaccinating, or voice, which means expressing their concerns to family, friends or wider audiences.[4]

A few individuals choose voice as a major activity. These are the campaigners, the activists. These are also the ones targeted by SAVN for denigration, harassment and censorship.

For most consumer items, for example products for sale in a supermarket, there is considerable choice, at least in terms of brands. If you don't like one brand of breakfast

---

4 There are also intermediate positions, for example to partially vaccinate or to space out vaccinations. However, these are often treated as opposition to vaccination.

cereal, you can buy another. If you prefer free-range eggs, you can buy them, and there may be several farms supplying them. In a city, usually few will notice or care which brand you buy. Even if you are serving meals to your family, they may not care which brand of soup you use. Governments regulate the quality of products and the claims they make in advertising, but seldom intervene to tell consumers what to buy.

Vaccines are somewhat different. They are not quite like items in a supermarket. Consumers of vaccines can either accept them or refuse them, and seldom given a choice between brands of the same vaccine. More importantly, governments intervene, telling consumers it is their duty to have vaccines.

The categories of exit and voice are too broad to capture the full range of possibilities. Here is a more detailed breakdown.

Exit
Convert
Acquiesce
Self-censor

Voice
Resist openly
Resist covertly
Counterattack

Parents who have concerns about vaccines can exit in several ways. One, the most dramatic, is to change their minds and instead become campaigners in favour of vaccination. A few individuals do this, and some of them become exemplars touted by SAVN.

Far more common is acquiescence. This means going along with the expectations for vaccination, for example by not pursuing doubts and not discussing the issue with friends. Acquiescence is the path of least resistance, in the sense that it usually requires the least emotional energy, though this depends on a person's circle of friends.

Then there are those who exit from the debate — the public debate or discussions with friends and family — while still maintaining their concerns, but keeping them private. This can be called self-censorship, in that beliefs are hidden. The boundary between acquiescence and self-censorship is fuzzy.

The voice option also has several sub-categories. One is to resist openly. This describes members of the AVN and other vaccine-critical groups who campaign for vaccination choice, as well as individuals — not involved in any group — who tell those around them of their sceptical views.

Then there is the option of covert resistance. An individual might speak out critical of vaccination but use a pseudonym. A healthcare worker might leak information to groups like the AVN.

Finally, there is the option of counterattack. Australian vaccine critics are under attack, so some of them decide to use some of SAVN's tactics against SAVNers and other defenders of standard vaccination policy. This can involve verbal abuse and formal complaints. Almost always, this is ill-advised. It is often counterproductive.

Several of these options — acquiescing, self-censoring,

resisting and counterattacking — are worth considering when an attack is mounted by making complaints.

RESPONDING TO SCAPPS

As described in chapter 5, a key technique in SAVN's campaign to destroy the AVN has been submitting complaints about the AVN to regulatory bodies, for example the Health Care Complaints Commission (HCCC) and Fair Trading. These are examples of what I call Strategic Complaints Against Public Participation or SCAPPs. Here I look at several of the matters covered in chapter 5 using the lens of exit and voice.

After receiving complaints from Ken McLeod and the McCafferys, the HCCC began an investigation of the AVN and asked the AVN to respond to the complaints. At this point, the AVN had a few choices, most of them unpalatable. It could respond as requested, as it did, which chewed up considerable time and resources, taking the AVN away from its normal activities. The complaints thus were already effective in hindering the AVN.

Another choice would have been to not respond to the complaints, in which case the HCCC would have proceeded to make a decision. As it turned out the HCCC seemingly ignored all the points made by the AVN in its response, so in retrospect it might have been better not to bother making a detailed response. But initially the AVN did not anticipate that the HCCC seemed to be on a vendetta, taking the side of complainants and moving outside its own mandate to investigate a citizens' organisation that was not a healthcare provider in reality, but treated as one via a slanted interpretation. Years later, the AVN declined to respond to some of the HCCC's requests, having learned that the process of responding only served to give more credibility to the complaint ritual.

Another option for dealing with complaints is to publicise them, pointing out how they are serving as a form of harassment. This is the tactic of exposure. Rather than accepting the process in silence, speaking out about it can potentially generate greater sympathy and support, both by generating anger among supporters at the injustice involved and stimulating concern among some otherwise neutral observers. For this tactic to be effective, it is necessary to frame the complaints as unfair, something that can be done in various ways, for example by demonstrating double standards, namely that complaints are targeted at some individuals or groups but not others.

The AVN used the tactic of exposure on various occasions, for example posting complaints to the HCCC on its website with commentary about the bias involved. Curiously, in many instances SAVN also publicised complaints by its members against the AVN, as part of the tactic of denigration. The two groups were each publicising complaints and interpreting them in their own ways, SAVN as showing what was wrong with the AVN and the AVN as revealing unfair treatment. In these instances, SAVN and the AVN were involved in struggles over the implications of the complaints, each appealing to their own constituencies and wider audiences.

As well as directly responding to complaints, it is also possible to challenge the complaint system. In the long term, this means changing the very basis on which organisations like the HCCC operate, so instead of being complaints-based, they seek systemic change, for example instituting systems for routinely reporting medical error and learning from it. Bringing about a major shift in institutional structures and approaches is a big task, and unlikely to occur in the short term. Nevertheless, raising the possibility of systemic change can be part of a publicity campaign.

The AVN could have mounted a campaign to expose the HCCC's flaws — for example its failure to deal with complaints about rogue doctors — and argue for a different sort of healthcare promotion, based on models in other countries or other industries, such as aviation, in which accidents are carefully analysed and used for learning rather than covered up because they are used to assign blame.[5] However, the AVN is not the best group to pursue such a campaign, because it seems self-interested. It would be far better for the initiative to come from healthcare workers.

Another option is to make counter-complaints. In the legal system, when you are sued for defamation, sometimes it is possible and effective to make a counter-suit for defamation, because some defamation plaintiffs have defamed the parties they are suing. Another possibility is to have someone who frequently sues to be declared a vexatious litigant.

---

5 Matthew Syed, *Black Box Thinking: Marginal Gains and the Secrets of High Performance* (London: John Murray, 2015).

In the case of SAVN complaints against the AVN, these possibilities were limited. The AVN couldn't complain to the HCCC, OLGR or Fair Trading about SAVN, because SAVN wasn't an incorporated body. The AVN could not easily claim that SAVN was a vexatious complainant because the complaints were made by different SAVNers, not on behalf of SAVN. If the HCCC, OLGR and Fair Trading had provisions for declaring individuals to be vexatious complainants, SAVNers could easily sidestep them by having different individuals submit complaints, even when they were written by the same person.

The one thing the AVN did do that could be seen as a sort of counter-complaint was to take the HCCC to court for taking action against the AVN outside its terms of reference. The AVN was successful in court, but this was a pyrrhic victory: it cost the AVN a lot of time, effort and money, and then the government changed the law to enable the HCCC to proceed as it had.

ORGANISATIONAL STRUCTURE

The AVN was vulnerable to SCAPPs in part because it was an incorporated body, namely a formal organisation with a constitution registered as an association with Fair Trading, a government body in New South Wales. Incorporation is commonly seen as a way of giving formal recognition to an organisation, subjecting it to standard protocols and giving legal protection to members should the organisation be sued. This is all reasonable in ordinary times, but with a SCAPP campaign, incorporation becomes a source of vulnerability. Many complaints made by SAVNers relied on the AVN being subject to government scrutiny.

In this circumstance, vaccine critics are less vulnerable if they organise through informal networks rather than incorporated associations. As networks, without registration with any government, they are not subject to the same level of official scrutiny. SAVNers would not be able to complain to the same number of government agencies.

The AVN could have folded up its formal operations and carried out much the same activities by other means. For example, its website could have been assigned to an individual and its list of members used as the basis for an email list run by an individual.

However, for the AVN to do this was more complicated than it might seem. It turns out that closing down an incorporated body requires going through a lot of bureaucratic procedures. In practice, the AVN wound down its operations, in part by design and in part due to SAVN's campaigning, but did not shut down. Complaints were a crucial part of this but certainly not the only harassment technique.

Interestingly, SAVN itself is organised in the form of a network, with its most visible presence being a Facebook page. SAVN apparently has no constitution, no formal financial arrangements, no office bearers and no membership list. This makes it less vulnerable to complaints. Without a constitution, SAVN cannot be held to account for violating its own rules. Without a bank account or other formal way of dealing with money (such as membership fees), it cannot be challenged for financial malfeasance. Without office bearers, there are no individuals with formal responsibilities (for example, written into a constitution or other rules of operation). Without a membership list, SAVNers are less subject to being identified and subject to harassment. Ironically, SAVN's structure is a model for vaccine critics.

SAVN has a few vulnerabilities. Complaints can be made to Facebook about its activities. This actually occurred in 2012, and SAVN's Facebook page was available only for friends, but then it reappeared for open viewing. Complaints can be made about individual SAVNers. But these vulnerabilities are much less serious than the AVN's vulnerabilities through being an incorporated body.

Through reconstituting itself as a network, vaccine critics would become less vulnerable to attack at a collective level. However, individuals could still become targets, and this is an especially serious risk for those working in the health system or who otherwise are subject to professional oversight or employer scrutiny. Doctors and nurses are prime targets. Also vulnerable are chiropractors, homoeopaths and scientists. Such individuals can be targeted through public exposure and complaints to employers and regulators.

As noted in chapter 5, SAVNer Peter Tierney, in a blog called Reasonable Hank, has targeted what he calls "antivax" chiropractors, nurses and midwives. He collects information about criticisms of vaccines by these health workers and presents it on his blog. Reasonable Hank's exposés are highlighted on the SAVN Facebook page, and

SAVNers are encouraged to make complaints to the government regulator and employers.

This form of attack is effective if making criticisms of or deviations from the standard vaccination line is treated as professionally suspect. If employers and regulators said, in response to complaints, "This is not important" or "Stop bothering us," then Reasonable Hank's vendetta would have no effect. However, because SAVN's efforts over several years have stigmatised public dissent from vaccination orthodoxy, complaints have become a potent form of harassment.

When expressing views is risky for some individuals, a general approach for resistance is for public comment to be made by those who are least vulnerable and for those who are most vulnerable to become leakers — allies who are silent in public but provide information confidentially or make public statements using pseudonyms.

On many social issues, ranging from genetic engineering to national security, there are fierce debates, but one side has a monopoly on expert opinion. When dissident experts speak up, they are susceptible to various forms of attack in their workplace. Meanwhile, citizen campaigners, who can become quite knowledgeable about the issues, lack insider information. In such situations, the insider experts, rather than speaking up, can be more effective by keeping a low profile and feeding information to outside activists.[6]

---

6 In my book *Whistleblowing: A Practical Guide* (Sparsnäs, Sweden: Irene Publishing, 2013), this strategy is covered in the chapter on leaking: http://www.bmartin.cc/pubs/13wb.html.

This is very similar to the situation for many whistleblowers. A typical whistleblower is an employee who discovers evidence suggesting corruption, abuse or hazards to the public and who reports the potential problem, most commonly to the boss or others inside the organisation. When the problem implicates higher management, a common response is to target the whistleblower with reprisals, for example ostracism (the cold shoulder), petty harassment, reprimands, referral to psychiatrists, demotion and dismissal. In most cases, whistleblowers are ineffective in bringing about change in the organisation.

It is often far more effective for whistleblowers to remain anonymous and to provide information to journalists or action groups, who can use the information to raise wider awareness. This is the method of leaking. By remaining anonymous, the whistleblower avoids reprisals, can remain on the job and collect additional information.

In the Australian vaccination debate, vaccine critics inside the health system are vulnerable to reprisals even by mentioning their views in forums where Reasonable Hank or others like him can record them. These insider critics are not whistleblowers in the usual sense, but are in a situation similar to that of whistleblowers. To be more effective, such insiders might be better to keep their opinions to themselves while on the job or under their own names on social media, instead confidentially offering information and insights to citizen critics. The citizen critics, such as public figures in the AVN, are less vulnerable to reprisals and can speak out in a more informed and credible way when they have access to insider information.

The information to be provided obviously should not be confidential information about patients, but rather about practices and beliefs at the workplace, perhaps including cases of apparent adverse effects of vaccination that are not reported officially. Insiders also can make statements for publication using a pseudonym, thereby contributing to public debate with less risk of reprisals.

One of the things insiders can tell outside campaigners is how better to pitch arguments and organise actions. Insiders could offer comments on drafts of blog posts, media releases and articles, make suggestions for campaigns and give running feedback on the impact of campaigning efforts. For example, suppose vaccine critics proposed to hand out leaflets to prospective mothers and fathers. Insiders could report on the response to the leaflets by the prospective parents and by hospital workers.

To some extent, this sort of process has been occurring for years. Members of the AVN have been contacted by quite a number of health workers giving their personal observations. As SAVN has increasingly stigmatised criticism of vaccination, insiders are at greater risk when voicing concerns.

In summary, when vaccine critics are under hostile surveillance and harassment via complaints, it makes sense to reduce vulnerabilities in two main ways. First, citizen campaigners are safer to organise as networks rather than as associations subject to government regulations, thereby reducing the number of ways they can be targeted by complaints to authorities. Second, individuals working in the health system or in any other role subject to professional controls may find it safer to keep a low profile publicly and to supply information and advice to citizen campaigners.

Insider critics always have the option of going public, and may decide to do this when they retire, leave for a different career or move to another country, namely when reprisals are less potent. Public expression of dissent is still likely to lead to denigration, so this needs to be taken into account.

POLITICAL JIU-JITSU

Nonviolent action is collective political action that goes beyond routine and accepted methods such as voting and lobbying but does not involve physical violence. Well-known methods of nonviolent action include rallies, boycotts, strikes and sit-ins. Nonviolent action is also known as civil resistance, satyagraha and people power.

Gene Sharp in his pioneering book *The Politics of Nonviolent Action* described a set of elements or stages in a typical nonviolent campaign, such as the movement for Indian independence under Gandhi and the US civil rights movement. One of the elements he called "political jiu-jitsu."[7] If the nonviolent actionists are attacked using violence — this happens most commonly by police or military forces beating or shooting protesters — then the attack can rebound against the attackers, generating more support for the campaigners.

---

7 Gene Sharp, *The Politics of Nonviolent Action* (Boston: Porter Sargent, 1973), pp. 657–701.

There is a crucial prior requirement: the campaigners must maintain nonviolent discipline, in other words they must refrain from using violence themselves. Political jiu-jitsu occurs when the injustice of violence being used against nonviolent protesters is so blatant that it causes outrage among some observers, generating greater support for the protesters.

Shrewd nonviolent campaigners understand this dynamic. US civil rights campaigners, in preparation for sit-ins at Nashville, Tennessee in 1960, spent six months in training to be able to refrain from reacting when they were met with verbal abuse, assault (such as cigarette burns) and arrest when they sat at a lunch counter where previously only whites had been served. With careful preparation, the protesters all refrained from resisting or counter-attacking, and the campaign went on to greater strengths in Nashville and beyond.[8]

In 1975, the Indonesian military conquered East Timor and in the subsequent years perhaps one third of the East Timorese population died in warfare or from starvation. In the late 1980s, the East Timorese resistance changed tactics, emphasising nonviolent protest in urban areas. In 1991, there was a funeral procession in the capital, Dili, which became a protest against the Indone-

---

8 Larry W. Isaac, Daniel B. Cornfield, Dennis C. Dickerson, James M. Lawson Jr. and Jonathan S. Coley, "'Movement schools' and dialogical diffusion of nonviolent praxis: Nashville workshops in the southern civil rights movement," *Research in Social Movements, Conflicts and Change,* Vol. 34, 2012, pp. 155–184.

sian occupation. As the procession entered Santa Cruz cemetery, Indonesian troops opened fire, killing hundreds of the East Timorese. This massacre was witnessed by western journalists and captured on video. When news of the massacre reached outside audiences, it triggered a huge increase in international support for East Timor's independence struggle. The attack on the protesters was counterproductive for the Indonesian government and military. This was a case of political jiu-jitsu.[9]

The Australian vaccination debate does not involve physical violence, but the same dynamic can occur as at Nashville or Dili. If there are attacks, for example verbal abuse, on campaigners, potentially they can be counterproductive — but only if the campaigners do not respond with verbal abuse themselves. Political jiu-jitsu relies on maintaining nonviolent discipline, and likewise a parallel process of backfire relies on refraining from counterattacking.

SAVN and others have specialised in verbal abuse, harassment and censorship. All of these methods have the potential of backfiring if audiences see them as unfair. However, if the targets, namely vaccine critics, counterattack against SAVNers or other supporters of vaccination, this undermines the backfire effect. The implication is that when those in the weaker position counterattack, in other words use the same forceful methods as the attacker, it is likely to be disastrous.

---

9 Brian Martin, *Justice Ignited: The Dynamics of Backfire* (Lanham, MD: Rowman & Littlefield, 2007), http://www.bmartin.cc/pubs/07ji/, chapter 3 (pp. 23–33).

The counterproductive effects of protester violence are behind the use of agents provocateurs by the police and others who deal with protest. An agent provocateur in this case could be a member of the police who pretends to be a protester and who encourages the protesters to use violence. In some cases, the police agent actually initiates action, for example throwing bricks or buying explosives. The point of this devious technique is to discredit the protesters — "they are violent, dangerous and need to be controlled" — and justify the much greater use of violence by the police. Another possibility is for the police to provide inducements to individuals — payments, goods, lodging, job opportunities — to become agents provocateurs. By not being directly involved, the police can more easily deny their involvement.

There are no known cases in which police agents have encouraged protesters to avoid violence but instead to be more effective by using strikes, boycotts, sit-ins, humour and innovative methods of nonviolent action.

In the Australian vaccination debate, the closest parallel to an agent provocateur is a SAVNer who pretends to be an opponent of vaccination and who takes actions that look bad, for example sending abusive messages or making outlandish claims. As recounted earlier,[10] after Victorian health minister Jill Hennessy featured in a video in which she read out abusive tweets allegedly made by "anti-vaxxers," an investigation found it was unlikely any of the comments she read out were actually tweets.

---

10 See appendix to chapter 4.

This episode highlights that when vaccine critics abuse, threaten or harass opponents, it is likely to be counterproductive. Of course SAVNers regularly use these techniques and are seldom held to account. The point is that SAVNers are on the side with much more power and authority, and can take advantage of abusive behaviour by critics much more effectively than the other way around.

Political jiu-jitsu does not happen automatically. Perpetrators of killings and other atrocities regularly use several techniques to reduce the likelihood of outrage. This has been studied in a wide range of areas, from sexual harassment to genocide.[11] Five common methods of reducing outrage are to

- Cover up the action
- Devalue the target
- Reinterpret the events by lying, minimising, blaming and framing
- Use official channels to give an appearance of justice
- Intimidate or reward people involved.

The Indonesian military and government used all five of these methods to reduce outrage over the Dili massacre. Indonesian officials and their allies tried to prevent credible information about the massacre getting outside of East Timor. For example, Max Stahl, a British filmmaker, had taken footage of the killings. When Stahl left East Timor and arrived in Darwin, Australian customs officials

---

11 "Backfire materials," http://www.bmartin.cc/pubs/backfire.html.

— acting on behest of the Indonesian government — searched his luggage to try to find his videotapes.

Indonesian officials made derogatory comments about East Timorese protesters. They initially claimed that 19 people died, later raising the figure to 50. An independent assessment team arrived at a total of 271: Indonesian officials were lying about and/or minimising the scale of the massacre. They blamed the attack on alleged actions by the protesters themselves, claiming they were violent. They framed the event as maintaining security.

There had been previous massacres in East Timor. The Dili massacre was the first one at which western observers had been present. The Indonesian government and military instigated investigations and sentenced a few soldiers to imprisonment. This was a symbolic provision of justice by official channels.

The shooting of protesters in Santa Cruz cemetery could be seen as an attempt at intimidation against support for East Timor's independence. Furthermore, after the massacre, Indonesian troops beat and executed many East Timorese independence supporters.

In summary, the Indonesian government used all five types of methods — cover-up, devaluation, reinterpretation, official channels and intimidation/rewards — to reduce outrage over the Dili massacre. However, in this instance these techniques were insufficient to counter the great increase in outrage, especially internationally. For each of the techniques, there is a counter-technique that can increase outrage.

- Expose the actions
- Validate the targets
- Interpret the events as an injustice
- Avoid or discredit official channels; instead, mobilise support
- Resist intimidation and rewards

The massacre was witnessed by western journalists, who took photos. Filmmaker Max Stahl, who video recorded the killings, hid the videotapes in Santa Cruz cemetery, later returning to collect them. He gave them to someone else to smuggle out of East Timor. The video material was later used in a film by crusading journalist John Pilger that helped publicise the cause of the East Timorese.

Outside of Indonesia, in Portugal, Australia, the US and other places where there were supporters of the East Timorese, it was easy to validate the targets and interpret the killings as an injustice, because the Indonesian government had little influence. The information about the massacre served to mobilise support, and Indonesian official inquiries were not taken seriously. Finally, outside of Indonesia, the Indonesian government had little capacity to intimidate opponents.

This framework can be applied to the Australian vaccination debate, in particular to SAVN's campaign against the AVN and other vaccine critics. The most obvious technique used by SAVNers is devaluation, by continual verbal abuse. However, there is a double process going on here. The purpose of the five methods to reduce outrage is to dampen public concern about what seems to be an injustice. Denigration is part of SAVN's attack repertoire; if it is successful, it also serves to reduce concern about all of SAVN's methods, including harassment and censorship. If vaccine critics are seen as disreputable — as liars, fools, conspiracy theorists or dangers to the public — then harassment and censorship don't seem so bad.

SAVNers are open about many of their methods. Cover-up is mainly used by those (who may not be SAVNers) who make threats and send pornography.

Reinterpretation, in this picture, refers to ways of explaining attacks to make them seem legitimate. It can involve lying, minimising, blaming and framing. SAVNers routinely attribute responsibility for their own campaign to the AVN, saying that vaccine critics are dangerous and need to be stopped. They also justify their actions as the exercise of free speech. These are techniques of blaming and framing.

The technique of official channels is complicated in this case. When a powerful group is exposed for doing something wrong, official channels such as inquiries and courts may be used to give an appearance of justice. This has not been the pattern in the Australian vaccination controversy. SAVNers have used official channels as means of attack, via complaints to various agencies. In this ongoing effort, official channels serve a dual role: they operate as a method of harassment, and they make this harassment seem legitimate because it operates through formal mechanisms set up to deal with problems.

Finally, there is the technique of intimidation. SAVN's attacks on vaccine critics scare many of the targets, some of whom withdraw from the public debate and therefore offer no overt resistance. SAVN's complaints to media outlets, when they run stories that present vaccine critics as having something worthwhile to say, serve to intimidate journalists and editors. Intimidation thus operates to reduce the expression of concern about SAVN's attacks. As in the case of devaluation, intimidation serves a dual function, as a method of attack and as a way of reducing the expression of outrage over the attack.

Overall, SAVN has used all five of the methods commonly used to reduce outrage over an injustice. Unlike many other cases of injustice, such as the Dili massacre, SAVN does not have any significant formal power. It is not a government or professional body. It has exerted influence through denigration and by recruiting others, such as government agencies, to its agenda.

The AVN, to oppose SAVN's techniques for reducing outrage, can use the counter-techniques of exposure, validation, positive interpretation, mobilisation and resistance. It is worth looking at each of these counter-techniques in more detail.

Exposure
Exposure in this context means exposing SAVN's attacks to a wider audience. This may seem obvious and easy, but in practice it can be challenging. Many individuals who are subject to verbal abuse and harassment are traumatised and are reluctant to publicise their treatment. Furthermore, exposing the abuse may lead to an escalation in the attacks (this is the technique of intimidation). For these reasons, many targets do not attempt to expose attacks. In a sense, they acquiesce in the cover-up of abuse.

Meryl Dorey, SAVN's prime target for many years, prepared a web page documenting verbal abuse and threats from SAVNers, listing individual SAVNers and what they had done. This was a potent challenge to SAVN's techniques. However, taking the exposure to wider audiences was difficult because the Australian mass media have not reported on SAVN's campaign.

Validation

Validation is the counter to devaluation. It means creating a positive image for vaccine critics. There are various ways to do this. One is endorsements or recommendations from prestigious members of the community, for example scientists, politicians or clergy. Given that the AVN was subject to relentless denigration for years, few prominent individuals have been willing to associate themselves with the group. As a result, vital sources of validation are the identity and behaviour of vaccine critics themselves. By presenting themselves as typical members of the community, highlighting their roles as parents or concerned citizens, they can counter the SAVN labels of them being crazies or baby-killers. Behaviour is also important. By coming across as calm, serious, sensible, restrained and well-informed, vaccine critics counter the derogatory images purveyed by SAVNers. If SAVNers say "anti-vaxxers" are loopy and dangerous, yet the person you meet seems sane, sensible and concerned about children's health, then SAVN denigration is undermined.

However, when people are under attack, it can be difficult for them to remain calm and behave with restraint. Some become angry and irrational. Some become distressed. Some counter-attack by sending abusive messages to vaccination proponents. This is damaging to the credibility of the critics, who are portrayed as unhinged and dangerous. Of course it is unfair that SAVNers routinely denigrate critics and yet can become outraged when a vaccine critic denigrates one of them or a member of the public. But to complain about double standards is to miss the point. SAVN and other vaccination proponents have far more power than the critics. To try to use SAVN's tactics — in this case denigration — against SAVNers is foolish because it helps legitimate SAVN's tactics, and SAVNers are far better both at using the tactics and at helping raise public concern about them. Periodically, there are media stories about the terrible "anti-vaxxers" who send abusive messages to vaccination proponents, whereas there has never been a single major story (and hardly a mention) of SAVN's regular abusive commentary and personal messages.

To resist SAVN's technique of devaluation, therefore, it is necessary to be far more restrained than SAVN: by behaving with restraint and decorum, SAVN's denigration techniques can become counterproductive, if suitably exposed to wider audiences. I have talked with a number of individuals, not involved in the vaccination debate, who looked at SAVN's Facebook page and who were repulsed by abusive commentary they read on it.

The AVN can refuse to post on its forums any comments that are nasty towards proponents, but it cannot easily control other forums or individuals who decide to send abusive messages to SAVNers, doctors, journalists or politicians. Imagine if the Nashville protesters had behaved with restraint but there were others who joined the sit-ins, shouted abuse at police, fought back, and brought rifles with them.

The AVN might seek to promote what could be called "politeness discipline" — the verbal analogy of "nonviolent discipline" — in several ways. One would be to invite vaccine critics to adhere to a pledge to avoid abusive language, personal attacks and other manifestations of hostility. Another would be to condemn any of these methods when they are used by critics. Yet another would be to run workshops in how to be effective in verbal and written interactions, demonstrating knowledge, concern and a commitment to informed engagement in the face of SAVN's relentless denigration and harassment. Leading figures in the AVN could try to set a good example and praise individuals for particularly effective methods of engagement.

One of the challenging features of the vaccination debate, especially its online dimensions, is the lack of personal accountability, in part due to anonymity. In the Nashville sit-ins, the terrain of the struggle was localised: it involved particular lunch counters. As well, before the sit-ins began, there was considerable training, and those in the trainings learned to recognise each other and to give each other support. Any stranger who joined a sit-in would have been immediately noticed. If the stranger started behaving aggressively towards the police, the activists would have suspected that the stranger was actually an agent of the police. (There is no record of any such strangers in the Nashville story.)

In the Australian vaccination debate, being an agent provocateur is quite easy. It is simple to set up an online account, pretend to be on the other side and behave abominably. Although there is not a lot of evidence about this, the most likely possibility is for SAVNers or other vaccination proponents to pretend to be vaccine critics and to make abusive comments about proponents.[12] They can then trumpet — in social and mass media — the terrible behaviour of the "anti-vaxxers."

In a social movement, agents provocateurs are most readily countered when activists are tightly knit and have a strong sentiment against damaging behaviours. In such circumstances, damaging behaviours can be condemned and those exhibiting them shunned or expelled, and it does not matter greatly whether the perpetrators are sincere or operating as agents. However, very few campaigns have this level of consensus about methods.

Australian critics of vaccination are very far from being a cohesive group with agreements about methods. Those officially speaking on behalf of the AVN can maintain a common stance: it is unlikely that a covert SAVNer could become a spokesperson for the AVN. But the AVN is only one of several groups, and there are many vaccine critics who operate individually. Therefore, Australian vaccine critics are susceptible to agents provocateurs, namely vaccination proponents who pretend to be critics and behave in a way that discredits critics. How

---

12 It would be pointless for vaccine critics to pretend to be proponents and make abusive comments about critics, because SAVN does this openly.

commonly this actually occurs is unknown and probably never will be known. Only occasionally are deceptions of this sort unmasked.

Interpretation
Interpretation of attacks as unfair is the counter to the methods of reinterpretation, which include lying, minimising, blaming and framing. There are two sides to resistance to reinterpretation. The first is exposure and challenge to techniques of reinterpretation, for example exposing lies. The second is highlighting the fundamental injustice of the attacks.

Interpretation and reinterpretation are two sides of what can be called interpretation struggles, namely contests over the meaning of actions. Each side in a struggle explains what is happening in a way favourable to itself. Explanations help campaigners to justify their own actions to themselves. They also can potentially recruit bystanders.

When SAVNers make abusive comments about vaccine critics, subject them to harassment through numerous complaints, and attempt to censor their speech, this potentially can be seen as unfair. To defend, vaccine critics need to explain why these things are wrong. Part of doing this requires the technique of exposure, discussed above. Sometimes exposure is enough on its own, but often some sort of context is needed. One method of doing this is to highlight double standards. For example, SAVN arguments in favour of censorship, or ways of saying that it's not really censorship, can be applied to other public debates — for example on climate change, genetic modification and nuclear power — pointing out that no one is attempting to shut down comment on these topics because it is allegedly false and dangerous.

Much of the commentary about the pros and cons of vaccination involves presenting evidence and arguments to support a position, so the vaccination debate as a whole can be considered to be an interpretation struggle, in particular interpreting scientific studies, or their absence, and drawing implications from them, all within various assumptions about public health, decision-making, economics and other factors. However, this particular interpretation struggle is not my focus here. My focus is on methods of attack and how to counter them. SAVN explains its attack methods in various ways in order to make them seem okay. To oppose this, vaccine critics need to challenge SAVN's explanations and present their own.

Framing is a key interpretation technique. It refers to looking at the world from a particular perspective, called a frame, which is what people do when they use a camera: they frame the shot, which gives a particular perspective on whatever they are photographing. A key frame used by SAVN and other vaccination proponents is that vaccination is a good thing ("Vaccination saves lives") and that publicly criticising vaccination is dangerous, because it might make some people reluctant to vaccinate. Vaccine critics use a different frame: vaccination is not necessarily a good thing (it is not all that effective and can cause harm to some) and people should be able to make their own choice about whether to vaccinate themselves and their children. SAVNers frame their attack on critics as defending the public against a danger; critics frame their position as freedom of choice.

Official channels
Official channels include expert committees, ombudsmen, courts and politicians. Official channels are supposed to provide justice. However, when a powerful group attacks a weaker one, official channels may give only an illusion of justice.

The leaders of the medical profession, government health departments, researchers and nearly all politicians support vaccination. Nearly all parents have their children vaccinated. In this sort of situation, in which one side has overwhelming support, it is likely that official channels will serve the dominant side, even when the weaker side is treated unfairly. The implication is that the weaker side should not expect official channels to offer a means to obtain justice.

Official channels in the Australian vaccination struggle have played several roles. Many of these are in relation to vaccination policy. As noted, the leaders of the medical profession and government health departments endorse and promote vaccination. Another example is legislation remove certain welfare payments from parents whose children are not fully vaccinated.

It is likely to be futile for vaccine critics to challenge these endorsements or laws by appealing to a different official channel. Yet that is what the AVN has attempted to do, in particular by raising a considerable amount of money to obtain legal opinions about appealing the welfare-payment law in the High Court. The AVN's legal advisers recommended against challenging the law. If the AVN had gone ahead with a case, either the High Court would have rejected the appeal or, in the unlikely circumstance that the appeal succeeded, the government might have been able to change the law or to use other methods to get around the legal obstacle.

My focus here is less on vaccination policy than on the efforts by SAVN and other vaccination proponents to discredit and silence vaccine critics. In these efforts, official channels such as the HCCC have also played a crucial role. When the AVN was, in effect, harassed by the HCCC, it sought relief by appealing to a different official channel, the courts. The AVN's court appeal was successful, on a technicality, but the AVN's victory was short-lived, because in response the state government changed the law, giving the HCCC greater powers.

Another example is Meryl Dorey's application to the police for an apprehended violence order (AVO) against three men she claimed were harassing her. One of them went to court to oppose the application. Dorey lost the case and had to pay his court costs, so this attempt at using official channels failed, at least in one out of three instances. Indeed, Dorey's application made things worse, in a couple of ways. First, it took up a fair bit of time and effort as well as money. Second, by not completely succeeding, her application gave greater legitimacy to the men and their activities: it seemed to make their actions more acceptable, as reflected in several comments on the SAVN Facebook page.[13]

On all sorts of issues, from sexual harassment to genocide, official channels regularly fail to provide justice. For effective resistance, then, there are two implications. The first is to not rely on official channels, but instead to ignore or discredit them. The second is to mobilise support.

Rather than expecting some authority to provide protection or restitution, an alternative is to mobilise support. Using official channels means putting trust in someone else. When this is likely to fail, the implication is that trust should instead be put in ordinary people, in non-official capacities, to recognise that an injustice is occurring, and for some of them to provide support.

Mobilising support means getting more people to support vaccine critics and criticism. In a few cases this may mean encouraging more people to become open critics, for example to join the AVN or another such group and participate in its activities. Just as important, though, and more likely, is to encourage more people to see that free speech on vaccination is worth defending, whatever position they themselves take on vaccination. It is to encourage more people to see that many of SAVN's techniques are damaging to the goal of dialogue and

---

13 On the SAVN Facebook page, 17 September 2013, some comments referred to Dorey's legal action as vexatious. Dorey believed she was being harassed. Peter Bowditch, one of the three men — Dorey did not pursue the AVO against him — saw her legal action as an attempt at censoring him.

debate, and perhaps undermining prospects for good public health policy — even policy that involves vaccination as a key component.

Intimidation
To deter resistance, powerful perpetrators of injustice may threaten, harass or assault targets, witnesses, journalists, activists, politicians, bystanders, whoever. Intimidation can serve two roles. It is obviously a means of attack, as in police beatings and massacres of civilians. It can also discourage people from expressing their outrage.

SAVN, in its attacks on vaccine critics, has used several means of intimidation, notably verbal abuse, public attacks on reputations, and complaints to agencies and employers. These serve also to discourage targets from expressing outrage. SAVN also targets others who might speak out. When a journalist does a story that seems too sympathetic to vaccine critics, SAVNers may write letters of complaint to the media outlet. This is a type of intimidation, and serves to discourage further such coverage.

To defend against attacks, it's necessary for some people involved to continue in the face of intimidation. In the Australian vaccination debate, only a few have done this. Key figures in the AVN, notably Meryl Dorey, and as well Greg Beattie and Tasha David and some others, have persisted despite coming under attack. So have some other critics not allied to the AVN, such as Stephanie Messenger. However, many members of the AVN are frightened by SAVN's attacks. They would prefer not to be the subject of abusive comment or complaints, and hence keep a low profile.

Prior to 2009, journalists and editors would run stories about the vaccination issue, quoting Dorey or others the same way they might quote both sides on climate change or nanotechnology. After the formation of SAVN and its strategy of complaining to media proprietors about coverage that SAVNers disliked, few journalists or editors persisted with stories that quoted critics in the same way as before. Journalists are used to being criticised, and any journalist addressing a controversial topic is likely to be condemned by one or both sides. SAVN escalated the level of complaint. Journalists know that vaccination is a trigger topic and that saying anything that seems to give credibility to critics is likely to require much greater effort in preparation or in handling complaints.

Few individuals supportive of vaccination are courageous enough to openly criticise SAVN's techniques, because to do this means becoming a SAVN target. It seems that neither side has a strategy aimed at encouraging the expression of voices that do not conform entirely to either SAVN or AVN positions.

CONCLUSION

For a group espousing an unpopular position, it can be difficult to gain credibility and support at the best of times, with the best of times being when there is tolerance or even support for expressing dissident viewpoints. When such a group comes under sustained attack, defending becomes exceedingly difficult.

After the formation of SAVN in 2009, the AVN attempted for a few years to continue operating the same way it had previously, namely running an organisation, raising funds, producing a magazine, selling merchandise and holding talks. However, being constituted as a formal association, registered with the government, made the AVN vulnerable to harassment via complaints to government agencies. The AVN could have reduced its vulnerability by reconstituting as a network, dispersing its functions and educating its members in effective resistance techniques.

When under personal attack via blogs and complaints, many individuals are embarrassed and humiliated and only want to escape. To turn the attacks against the attackers, though, it is highly effective to expose the attacks to wider audiences.

Becoming angry and counter-attacking is ineffective or worse, because SAVN and its allies have a far greater capacity to expose abuse. Furthermore, counter-attacking legitimises SAVN's methods. To be effective, vaccine critics need to restrain their impulses to respond in kind.

When the attackers have far greater credibility and influence, official channels such as ombudsmen, police and courts may give only an illusion of justice. The AVN sought support from official bodies, mostly to no avail. It would be far more effective to give up on finding a white knight who will slay opponents and instead concentrate on mobilising support. This means concentrating on the issues — concerns about vaccination and compulsion — and avoiding being sucked into either counter-attack or seeking intervention from on high.

8
Contexts

In previous chapters, I examined the campaign by the pro-vaccination citizens' group SAVN against vaccine critics, especially the AVN. I described SAVN's techniques of denigration, harassment and censorship, and outlined ways the AVN could defend.[1]

In this chapter, I turn to some wider perspectives for understanding the SAVN-versus-AVN struggle. Each of these perspectives offers some insight, each from a different angle. There is no single best perspective, because what is best depends on the purpose involved. Each of these perspectives — each context — can be considered in its own terms.

VACCINATION PASSIONS

When I started studying the Australian vaccination controversy several years ago, I was struck by the incredible passions aroused by the issue. It is not a surprise that campaigners are committed and emotional – that was to be expected. In other controversies I've studied, such as nuclear power and fluoridation, leading campaigners are personally invested in the issues. In the 1980s, the

---

1 Information about SAVN and the AVN is available in the glossary and chapter 3.

movement against nuclear war stimulated some fierce emotions: the future of humanity was at stake! (It still is.)

Vaccination is not as earth-shattering as nuclear war, but nonetheless evokes incredibly strong emotions. When acquaintances learn about my studies, many of them have asked me why this is so. I usually say I don't really know, commenting that maybe it has to do with children's health. Both sides in the debate about vaccination put children's health as their number one priority. They just draw different conclusions.

There are other potential threats to children's health, such as pesticides, x-rays, junk food, backyard swimming pools and domestic violence. Nuclear war would harm children, to be sure, and continued global warming would be a major threat to the lives of future generations. However, vaccination is more personal: it involves a tangible intervention. Proponents can point to horror stories of deaths and disabilities from whooping cough, meningococcal and other infectious diseases, while critics can point to horror stories of adverse reactions to vaccines.

Moral foundations[2]

Jonathan Haidt's book *The Righteous Mind* offers insights into why the vaccination issue can be so polarising.[3] Haidt

---

2 This section draws on my blog post "Vaccination passions," http://comments.bmartin.cc/2015/05/12/vaccination-passions/, 12 May 2015.

3 Jonathan Haidt, *The Righteous Mind: Why Good People Are Divided by Politics and Religion* (New York: Pantheon, 2012).

doesn't address vaccination, nor indeed any other such controversial public issue, but his ideas are relevant.

Haidt, like many other psychologists, subscribes to the picture of the human mind as having two aspects or components. One is slow, logical, contemplative and careful. This rational component of the mind Haidt calls the "rider". The other component of the mind is fast, intuitive and judgemental. Haidt calls this component the "elephant". He argues, provocatively, that humans are largely driven by their elephants, namely the intuitive sides to their minds. The primary function of the rider, namely the rational side of the mind, is to provide logical-sounding explanations for the elephant's judgements.

This certainly fits with what I've observed in the vaccination debate. Most people have made up their minds, and seldom does it matter what evidence is provided. They just ignore what is unwelcome and come up with reasons to justify their positions. This helps explain why the debate never seems to progress: the elephants hold sway and the riders are active in justifying the paths chosen by their elephants. Only rarely do I meet someone who is undecided and who wants to hear both sides of the argument and ponder the issue before making a judgement.

Haidt's special contribution concerns the biological foundations of morality. Citing a wide variety of research and ingenious experiments, he identifies six values that seem fundamental to people's views of right and wrong: care, liberty, fairness, authority, loyalty and sanctity.

Haidt is especially interested in how these foundations of morality affect debates over politics and religion in the US. He discovered that US-style libertarians, who oppose government regulations and support a free market, rely mostly on the value of liberty. He says that US liberals (who might be called progressives elsewhere), who support government interventions to assist the poor and disadvantaged, rely especially on the value of care, with liberty and fairness as additional influential values. He finds that US conservatives rely more equally on all six foundations.

This analysis helps explain why US people with different political orientations often seem to be talking past each other. What drives them is different. Their elephants are taking different paths, based on different intuitive moral judgements, and their riders give rational reasons to justify their choices. In this circumstance, rational analysis is, for most people, a sideshow that affects little.

The six foundations of morality have obvious relevance to the vaccination issue. First consider care, something important for both liberals and conservatives. The morality of care derives, in evolutionary terms, from parents caring for their children. Groups of early humans with an innate commitment to protect and care for their own children were more likely to survive. In this sense, care is a fundamental aspect of most people's sense of right and wrong: it is right to protect children and wrong to allow any harm to come to them.

Wanting to protect children is intuitive and doesn't need to be taught. So it is easy to see why vaccination can arouse such passions: it is about care for children.

But the limitation of Haidt's analysis, at least when applied to vaccination, is that it doesn't say how caring can come to be applied in different ways. It is straightforward to feed a hungry child or to protect an infant from a threatening animal. However, vaccination is not such a simple matter.

Supporters of vaccination see children as the prime beneficiaries. Critics see vaccination as a possible danger. They both appeal to care, but reach different conclusions about how to achieve it.

Supporters point to the dangers of infectious diseases such as measles and chickenpox. Critics point to the dangers of adverse reactions to vaccines. Pointing to the role of the morality of care helps explain why the passions around vaccination are so strong, but does not explain differences in attitudes towards it.

In part this can be due to personal experience. Some children contract infectious diseases and suffer seriously from them, or even die. Parents, other relatives and friends see this and may be influenced to support vaccination. Other children suffer adverse reactions to vaccines; their parents, other relatives and friends may be influenced to oppose vaccination.

Other aspects of morality are also relevant. Liberty is a value based around personal autonomy and resistance to overbearing rule. In evolutionary terms, according to Haidt, it derives from the survival value of subordinates being able to gang up on any individual who assumes too much power. When vaccination is pushed on people, for example through mandatory vaccination of soldiers or health workers or through financial penalties for not vaccinating, this may trigger resistance in those for whom liberty is a key moral foundation.

Authority, as a moral value, means accepting the prevailing systems of hierarchy and leadership. When governments, health departments, doctors and nurses support vaccination, this invokes the moral foundation of authority.

Haidt says conservatives are more likely to have authority as a key moral driver. However, this does not seem to fit the pattern for vaccination policy, given that many of the doctors and researchers promoting vaccination are "liberal" in Haidt's sense. Still, it makes sense to say that vaccination gains support through the authority response in those for whom this moral foundation is salient.

Another moral foundation is sanctity. A violation of the sense of sanctity or purity can trigger a feeling of disgust. Many people feel intuitively that certain practices are disgusting, for example incest or eating food that has fallen on the floor — even when the floor is perfectly clean. If that doesn't disgust you, consider eating food that has fallen into a just-cleaned toilet. Sanctity, like the other foundations, is driven by the elephant, and people sometimes cannot give a logical justification for their reactions.

Some critics of vaccination may see the body as a sacred object that, when healthy, should not be assaulted by any medical intervention. If so, this can help explain their conscientious objection to vaccination. However, sanctity has declining relevance in countries like the US and Australia, where attitudes to personal behaviour have changed dramatically over recent decades.

Explaining the other side

From my perspective, both sides in the polarised vaccination debate have the best of intentions: they are concerned about public health, especially children's health. But this seems not to be the way most campaigners think about things. Their usual approach is to assume that "we" — those with similar views — are motivated by high-minded motives whereas "they" — those with contrary views — have less laudable motives.

Some critics point to the manufacturers of vaccines as a driving force behind promotion of vaccination. A few critics believe there is a conspiracy to force dangerous products on an unsuspecting population in the search for profits or even some nefarious scheme of depopulation.

Proponents invariably attribute their own support for vaccination to research showing its benefits. Few of them acknowledge any weaknesses in the science supporting vaccination, and few articulate that vaccination is not just a matter of science, but also involves values, including individual choice. As a result, quite a few proponents have tried to figure out the reasons why some parents refuse vaccinations for their children and others selectively vaccinate or space out vaccinations. A common assumption is that parents who deviate from the vaccination paradigm are ill-informed and need to be educated: if only they knew the facts, they would support vaccination. There are quite a few studies about misinformation on the

Internet as well as studies of the motives for refusing vaccines.[4]

These studies have to address an uncomfortable fact: on average, parents who have concerns about vaccination are more educated than those who do not question it. Many parents with concerns spend considerable time and effort looking at arguments on both sides. They are far from being ignorant.

In the study of scientific controversies, trying to explain the behaviour of those on the other side is called the sociology of error. It is based on the assumption that we are right and they are wrong, and so there must be something wrong with them. This is a one-sided method of social analysis. A different approach is to try to understand both sides of the debate (or multiple sides) without assuming that one side is scientifically correct.[5] There seem to be no studies of the vaccination controversy that use this approach.

In the following sub-sections, I summarise ideas from four books on the vaccination issue, each of them offering

---

4 For example, Anna Kata, "Anti-vaccine activists, Web 2.0, and the postmodern paradigm — an overview of tactics and tropes used online by the anti-vaccination movement," *Vaccine*, Vol. 30, 2012, pp. 3778–3789.

5 For an introduction to four approaches for studying scientific controversies, see Brian Martin and Evelleen Richards, "Scientific knowledge, controversy, and public decision-making," in Sheila Jasanoff, Gerald E. Markle, James C. Petersen and Trevor Pinch (eds.), *Handbook of Science and Technology Studies* (Thousand Oaks, CA: Sage, 1995), pp. 506–526, http://www.bmartin.cc/pubs/95handbook.html.

historical, sociological and/or political perspectives. Each book provides valuable context for helping to understand the ferocious attack on Australian vaccine critics. There are also a number of excellent studies of vaccination hesitancy.[6]

The Vaccine Narrative

Jacob Heller is a sociologist at the State University of New York at Old Westbury. His book *The Vaccine Narrative* appeared in 2008. It is an analysis of the "cultural narrative" of vaccination in the US.[7]

---

[6] Among studies drawing on interviews with parents are Lauren R. Archer, *Validating Vaccines: Understanding the Rhetorical Dynamics of Expertise amid a Manufactured Controversy* (PhD dissertation, University of Washington, 2014); Andrea Kitta, *Vaccinations and Public Concern in History: Legend, Rumor, and Risk Perception* (New York: Routledge, 2012); Melissa Leach and James Fairhead, *Vaccine Anxieties: Global Science, Child Health and Society* (London: Earthscan, 2007); Jennifer A. Reich, *Calling the Shots: Why Parents Reject Vaccines* (New York: New York University Press, 2016); Paul R. Ward, Katie Attwell, Samantha B. Meyer, Philippa Rokkas and Julie Leask, "Understanding the perceived logic of care by vaccine-hesitant and vaccine-refusing parents: a qualitative study in Australia," *PLoS ONE*, Vol. 12, No. 10, 12 October 2017. For the argument that vaccine hesitancy is not based on ignorance but rather on public mistrust of authorities, see Maya J. Goldenberg, "Public misunderstanding of science? Reframing the problem of vaccine hesitancy," *Perspectives on Science*, Vol. 24, No. 5, 2016, pp. 552–581.

[7] Jacob Heller, *The Vaccine Narrative* (Nashville, TN: Vanderbilt University Press, 2008).

A narrative is both a story and a way of making sense of the world. When a story becomes a particularly persuasive way of describing and enforcing expectations, it is called a "master narrative." Heller set out to investigate the master narrative that people use to understand vaccines and vaccination.

On the surface, it might seem that a narrative is just a way of describing the practical reality of disease and vaccination. But narratives are more than descriptions: they affect the way people process information, create meaning and develop values, and this affects reality.

Heller traces the vaccine narrative through four case studies: diphtheria toxin-antitoxin, rubella, pertussis and HIV/AIDS. He examines the history and politics in each case, showing how the vaccine narrative developed and how it impacted on the politics of health. Here is what he identifies as the vaccine master narrative, in its standard form.

> The cultural narrative of vaccines tells the story of a deadly disease that exerts a terrible toll in human suffering and death. Heroic researchers, working altruistically, marshal the forces of modern science to develop a simple intervention to ready the body's own defenses: a vaccine. Properly prepared, we can defend ourselves, just as our science demonstrates human mastery of death. Through the application of a simple, safe, and effective shot, we protect ourselves and set the disease on the road to oblivion. Our compliance with mass vaccination policies is a moral obligation that protects each one of us at the same

time that we contribute to our common goal of eradicating disease. Our compliance is morally right, practically easy, and both scientifically and politically progressive. By explicit extension, those who oppose, refuse, or resist vaccination are ignorant, anti-science, and a threat to the public health. They, too, are part of the story — the "bad guys" who try to subvert our attempts to win the war, but whose plans are doomed to failure.[8]

This narrative has surprising power over thought and behaviour. The trouble with it, according to Heller, is that it distorts history and can lead public health promoters astray.

The classic example of a disease fitting the narrative is polio. It is portrayed as a deadly disease that can affect anyone without warning. Then along came the brilliant and selfless polio pioneers Jonas Salk and Albert Sabin whose vaccines protected the population. However, Heller says, this misrepresents the realities of polio. It did indeed have terrible impacts on many of those afflicted, but most cases were mild, causing no long-lasting disabilities. Other infectious diseases were more deadly and debilitating but did not receive the attention given to polio. Because the polio story, as told following the standard vaccine narrative, is so moving and convincing, it is regularly used to justify vaccines for other diseases.

Heller highlights the vaccine narrative's potential for damaging consequences by analysing the search for a

---

8 Ibid., p. 22.

vaccine against HIV. After AIDS was first recognised in the 1980s, developing a vaccine was a top priority for US medical researchers, public health officials and AIDS activists. This was despite the fact that HIV, unlike infectious agents such as the measles virus, cannot spread through the air. Other methods of controlling transmission, based on modifying sexual and needle-sharing behaviours, should have been more obvious. Yet so persuasive was the narrative that researchers relentlessly pursued the quest for a vaccine to the extent of compromising scientific and ethical principles.

Heller notes that setting up a bacteriological laboratory is relatively cheap and easy compared to bringing about improvements in sanitation and living conditions. The vaccine route serves the interests of the medical profession while leaving social arrangements unaltered and thus can partly undermine non-vaccine public health efforts.

The vaccine narrative is not fixed. With the increasing role of corporations in vaccine development and sales, the profit motive entered the story, somewhat displacing the idea of the heroic researcher. This modification of the narrative may be linked to increasing vaccine hesitancy.

The vaccine narrative continues to have a powerful effect on struggles over vaccination. Part of the narrative is that anyone who contests vaccination is ignorant and dangerous. Those who attack vaccine critics can be understood as narrative enforcers.

The value of understanding narratives is in bringing to light assumptions that otherwise would remain implicit. Heller takes care to explain that his aim is greater understanding, without taking a side in the polarised vaccination controversy. That is a difficult challenge because, as he puts it, "Part of this polarization stems from the continuing strength of the narrative, and the way it frames vaccines and vaccination as purely beneficent, and anyone who questions them as a crackpot."[9]

Vaccine: The Debate in Modern America

Mark Largent's book *Vaccine* was published in 2012.[10] Largent set out to examine the apprehension about vaccination felt by many parents in the United States, drawing on his personal experience as the father of a young child and his professional expertise as an historian of science. In *Vaccine,* Largent gives the background to the debate and then offers detailed treatments of three topics: thimerosal and autism, MMR and autism, and the role of celebrities, especially vaccination proponent Paul Offit and critic Jenny McCarthy.

In a chapter titled "Getting to the source of anxiety," Largent argues that concerns about vaccination are driven by parents' experiences with the medical system. Most understand that vaccination is valuable protection against serious infectious diseases, but the expansion of the vaccination schedule has changed perceptions. Many do not see why it is essential that their children be vaccinated against diseases that are not deadly or to which they are unlikely to be exposed, at least as children. For example,

---

9 Ibid., p. 23.

10 Mark A. Largent, *Vaccine: The Debate in Modern America* (Baltimore, MD: Johns Hopkins University Press, 2012).

hep B is given at birth, though few children will ever be exposed to hepatitis B and for most of those who are, it will be years down the track. Similarly, chickenpox may be seen as usually being a mild disease.

In the US, young children are expected to have regular wellness check-ups (visits to the doctor when they are not ill), for which the main intervention is vaccination. If some visits are missed due to illness or other reasons, then vaccinations are bunched up, causing concern.

Vaccination protocols are applied inflexibly, with no scope for delaying or omitting particular vaccines. Largent understands the reason for this: it is part of the public health effort to maintain maximum coverage. Babies are vaccinated against hepatitis at birth because doing it later is less reliable. Health authorities expect parents to acquiesce, and see any resistance as an indication of being exposed to misleading information.

In this context, Largent argues, the connection between vaccines and autism has become a lightning rod for more generalised anxieties. Parents may find it difficult to explain their diffuse anxieties and latch onto the autism connection. On the other side, authorities find it convenient to continually castigate the autism connection, imagining that scientific refutation is sufficient to quell all concerns about vaccination.

Largent believes vaccines have been responsible for saving millions of lives, yet takes seriously the concerns of parents due to the expansion of the vaccination schedule. He also notes the large number of new vaccines under development, many of which blur the line between protection and enhancement, namely between protection against illness and contributing to health or performance beyond the norm. An example is a vaccine for breast cancer. Largent realises that he finds himself in a middle ground, sitting comfortably with neither the standard health authority line nor the passionate objectors.

Vaccine Nation
Elena Conis is an assistant professor in the University of California, Berkeley's Graduate School of Journalism. Her 2015 book *Vaccine Nation* looks at the history and politics of vaccination in the US.[11] She tells a story more complicated than the usual official story of vaccines triumphing over disease. A fascinating part of her analysis deals with perceptions of disease, namely what people (including doctors and other health professionals) think about it. She shows through several detailed case studies that the development of a vaccine changes the way its target disease is perceived.

One key example is mumps. It first became of concern during World War II, because outbreaks among soldiers hindered military capacity, so effort was put into developing a vaccine. But use of the vaccine was only seen as important in limited circumstances, when national interests were at stake, and the main target for vaccination was selected groups of adults. Amongst the general population in the 1950s and 1960s, childhood mumps was not considered important. For children, it was usually just

---

11 Elena Conis, *Vaccine Nation: America's Changing Relationship with Immunization* (Chicago: University of Chicago Press, 2015).

a mild illness, and was occasionally a matter of humorous commentary.

After a mumps vaccine for general use was developed, the US medical profession was divided about its value. Some argued that without evidence that it provided long-term immunity, giving it to children might lead to more cases in adults, when it was more serious.

Several factors led to a reassessment of mumps. The existence of the vaccine meant increased interest in mumps as a disease, triggering research. Marketing of the vaccine proceeded by emphasising the rare serious adverse effects of mumps, and often the likelihood of complications was exaggerated. For example, the possibility that mumps could lead to diabetes was raised, though there was no good evidence of this. Within a decade, the perception of mumps had changed dramatically. No longer seen as a mild annoyance, it became something to be feared. Furthermore, to enable coverage of the population, the mumps vaccine was promoted for use in childhood even though the primary concern in previous decades had been about the impacts of the disease for adults.

Another aspect of the reassessment of mumps was its place among other infectious diseases. Polio and diphtheria were widely seen as deadly, so vaccines for these diseases were seen as lifesavers. By emphasising the rare cases of severe damage from mumps, it could be put in the same general category as polio and diphtheria. Vaccination proponents often portrayed all infectious diseases as serious, downplaying differences between them in both infectiousness and seriousness. Mumps thus was able to join more deadly diseases as an equal partner, for which vaccination was seen as vital. This became institutionalised when the MMR (measles, mumps and rubella) triple vaccine was developed. It was no longer easy to skip the mumps vaccine while getting the vaccines for the more harmful diseases measles and rubella.

The story of the mumps vaccine in the history of US vaccination policies shows that understanding policies requires understanding attitudes in the medical profession and the wider population. Vaccination policy and practice are not purely a matter of science, but involve a complex array of factors.

Another factor raised by Conis is the gradual change in the way US parents see their children. Increasing affluence and smaller family sizes engendered a more protective attitude. In this context, the possible complications from diseases loomed larger and made parents more receptive to measures such as vaccination to reduce risks to their children. (Later, this also led to more questioning of childhood vaccines.)

Conis' analysis shows that concerns about disease are shaped by commercial, political and social factors. Extrapolating from this, vaccination passions are similarly influenced by such factors.

Immunization: How Vaccines Became Controversial
Stuart Blume is emeritus professor of Science and Technology Studies at the University of Amsterdam. He has a lifetime of experience researching the politics of science and technology, and two decades ago began studying the vaccination issue. His approach can be called social history: a study of history taking into account social

and political dynamics. Blume brings to the issue the perspectives of science and technology studies, seeing science and technology as subject to social processes.

Blume decided to write a book summarising insights from his research, titled *Immunization: How Vaccines Became Controversial*.[12] It does not mesh neatly with the usual positions in the public debate.

Blume tells two stories, one about vaccines and one about vaccination policy, and neither is a just-so story. Many traditional histories present science as a continual upward trajectory of discoveries and the overcoming of misguided beliefs. Blume, though, follows the path of historians of science who report on uncertainties, mistakes and unproductive paths. The implication is that present knowledge may be just as precarious, in its own way, as past knowledge.

Knowledge about vaccines and the immune system developed gradually, and for many decades there was no assumption that vaccination would prove to be a major route to public health. Smallpox was the initial target for vaccination, but there were many other killer diseases, such as diphtheria and tuberculosis, and other ways to address them besides vaccination. Today, with the focus on vaccination, it is sometimes forgotten that infectious disease can also be addressed through quarantine, sanitation, improved diet and general increases in the standard of living.

---

12 Stuart Blume, *Immunization: How Vaccines Became Controversial* (London: Reaktion Books, 2017).

Vaccination campaigns are not always the best strategy to improve health. Blume highlights a problem with the polio eradication campaign. In a number of poor countries, resources for public health interventions were siphoned off to support polio eradication, which meant that impoverished people, needing food and clean water, were instead offered polio vaccinations, something less important for their own health.

A related tension permeated vaccination development beginning in the 1980s, when commercial considerations became paramount. Effort was put into developing vaccines for problems in affluent countries, where money could be made, while major illnesses in impoverished populations were left unaddressed.

Blume notes that vaccination is often treated in isolation, as a special method of promoting public health, and not compared with other methods. To counter this tendency, he presents vaccination as a technology, in the broad sense of a set of techniques and artefacts, that can be compared to other public health technologies such as sanitation. He sees vaccination as a socio-technical issue, as having both scientific and policy dimensions, and as shaped by social, economic and political influences in both these dimensions.

Blume addresses vaccines separately, rather than as a group. As a result, he does not make a universal judgement about vaccination as a good or bad thing. In these ways, Blume offers a different perspective than the one adopted by most vaccination campaigners.

As many infectious-disease killers were brought under control in western countries — while others, notably

HIV, were proving too difficult — vaccine developers turned to other diseases, seeing opportunities for profits. Blume writes that the rise of neoliberalism led to significant shifts in the rationale for new vaccines. Whereas previously companies and scientists had freely shared information and vaccines in a common commitment to public health, from the 1980s onwards the pharmaceutical industry became more dominant and less public-spirited.

Government health departments in different countries responded to industry pressure in different ways. Health departments sometimes approved new vaccines without as much evidence as they would have required earlier. It became more common to use cost-benefit analysis, especially given that many new vaccines were highly expensive. However, cost-benefit analysis is not a good way to promote vaccines to the public.

In several cases, notably measles and mumps, companies adopted a "rebranding" strategy to convince parents that diseases they had known as a routine and unthreatening part of childhood were actually killers to be feared and thus protected against using vaccines. Blume's analysis here meshes with Conis'.

Blume believes that vaccines have saved millions of lives. Yet he is also sceptical of many of the latest vaccines, developed not as part of a public health agenda but by pharmaceutical companies whose primary aim is profit. Furthermore, there are dozens of new vaccines under development, many of them targeted at non-infectious diseases such as breast cancer. Vaccination seems to have become a single-method solution for health problems, overshadowing primary health care that addresses the conditions that cause disease in the first place. Think how much easier it is to sell a vaccine than to address poverty and inequality, or illnesses due to industrial chemicals.

For many readers, the most interesting part of Blume's book will be the final chapter in which he addresses current anxieties about vaccination, especially in the west. He dismisses the idea, common among vaccination promoters, that the source of the anxieties is vaccine-critical groups such as the AVN. Sociologically, this explains neither the existence of the groups nor their alleged influence. It would be like saying the reason why people are concerned about economic inequality is because of protesters.

Blume cites research into the attitudes of parents that suggests something deeper is at play. Rather than dividing people into vaccine-acceptors and vaccine-refusers, Blume addresses a widespread vaccine hesitancy that affects many parents, especially well-educated ones, even when they adopt all the standard vaccinations.

Rather than vaccine-critical groups being the cause of vaccine hesitancy, it is better to understand them as a result of changed perceptions. Blume says that vaccination has, for many people, become symbolic of a more general unease and sceptical attitude about the role of pharmaceutical companies and the medical profession. This is similar to Largent's assessment. Blume notes that the usual survey research carried out by vaccination proponents can pick up demographic variations in parental concerns but does not get to their source.

It is perhaps relevant that citizens have no say in the development of vaccination recommendations, and even politicians are usually left out of the picture, as decisions are influenced by international organisations subject to corporate lobbying. This does not mesh well with people's increasing knowledge about health matters. The experts might be right but nonetheless be distrusted.

Immunization: How Vaccines Became Controversial provides great insight precisely because it avoids the easy generalisations made by vaccination partisans. Vaccine development was not a straightforward linear process, and vaccination policy has been subject to a variety of influences. Vaccination is usefully seen as a technology, as just one of several approaches to promoting health, and thus judged in a wider context than a narrow calculation of benefits and risks. The contemporary vaccination debate is not just a matter of pro and anti, but should be seen in the wider context of attitudes towards social institutions and citizen participation in decision-making.

Blume does not offer easy answers, but more usefully points to the complexities and contradictions in the history and social dynamics of vaccination. It is essential reading for anyone who wants to get beyond the usual partisan positions in the vaccination debate.

Country comparisons
In countries such as Australia, Japan, Sweden and the US, many vaccines are standard, for example those for polio, measles and pertussis. Their governments are usually responsive to advice from the World Health Organisation. However, there are some differences between the recom-

mendations offered by national governments.[13] For example, in the US there are quite a few more vaccinations recommended than in Sweden. The question is, why?

One explanation is that the risk of certain infectious diseases is greater in some countries than others. Another explanation is that the results of cost-benefit calculations are different depending on factors such as the cost of disease and the cost of vaccines. To my knowledge, no one has carried out a comprehensive analysis of the reasons for differences in national vaccination recommendations.

For me, there is a strange pattern in the differences. The number of recommended vaccines tends to be greater in countries with the least government commitment to welfare. The United States is the most striking example, having no national health insurance and a weak and patchy welfare net that leaves many of those who are poor or disadvantaged with little protection. In contrast, Sweden has a longstanding national health insurance scheme, unemployment payments and other welfare features. US opponents of national health insurance have long labelled it "socialised medicine."

Why, then, is there such a strong push for more vaccines, and for more government coercion for taking them, in the US compared to Sweden? This is counterintuitive, given that in other spheres emphasis on individual rights and opposition to government intervention is very strong in the US.

---

13 In some less affluent countries, access to vaccines is restrained by limited health budgets and access to medical care.

In Australia, some media commentators have applied the derogative label "nanny state" to laws they see as curtailing individual freedoms, for example laws against racial vilification that could undermine free speech. But the same commentators never refer to laws providing pressure to vaccinate as manifestations of a nanny-state mentality.

Decades ago, I studied the fluoridation debate: the controversy over whether to add fluorides to public water supplies in order to reduce the incidence of tooth decay in children. I wrote to officials in dozens of countries asking about government policies on fluoridation. At the time, fluoridation was widely used only in a few countries, including Australia, Canada, New Zealand, Singapore and the US. In most of Western Europe, there was little or no fluoridation, though there had been significant debates in many countries, including strong support from most dental professions.[14]

Fluoridation raises some of the same issues as vaccination. It provides a collective benefit — fluoride gets to nearly everyone in the community, regardless of income or access to dental services — but is seen by opponents as a violation of individual rights. Writing about fluoridation, I could only speculate as to why it had become entrenched in only a few countries, and those countries — mostly the

---

14 Brian Martin, *Scientific Knowledge in Controversy: The Social Dynamics of the Fluoridation Debate* (Albany, NY: State University of New York Press, 1991), http://www.bmartin.cc/pubs/91skic.html. The situation today is not all that different than it was decades ago.

English-speaking ones — were where the rhetoric of free choice was greatest and where government welfare systems were least comprehensive. I suggested that fluoridation was advocated more strongly in places where the dental profession was more autonomous of the state.

I do not have an explanation for national differences in vaccination recommendations, but mention this as a possible topic for study that will give greater insight into the dynamics of vaccination debates in different parts of the world. It may help explain the extreme features of the Australian vaccination struggle.

WHAT DRIVES SAVN?

My focus in this book is on the tactics used in the Australian vaccination debate to denigrate, harass and censor vaccine critics. It is possible to document, classify and analyse tactics without probing into the motivations for using these methods. Nevertheless, many targets of these tactics have speculated about the psychology of SAVNers. Some of their labels applied to SAVN, for example "hate group," contain assumptions about what drives the group.

SAVNers themselves undoubtedly see what they are doing in terms of protecting Australians from infectious disease. They subscribe to the standard set of claims about the benefits of vaccination. In particular, herd immunity provides a measure of protection for individuals whose immunity is compromised for some reason, for example babies too young to be vaccinated.

SAVNers, in addition to supporting vaccination, must have an additional rationale in order to justify attacking vaccine critics. This rationale is clearly articulated in SAVN's self-description online as well as many comments by individual SAVNers: the AVN and other public vaccine critics are a danger to public health. Allowing public criticism of vaccination may discourage some parents from having their children fully vaccinated. This endangers these children and also reduces herd immunity, opening the community to outbreaks of infectious disease.

This all makes sense, but it is not enough to explain the ferocious and persistent efforts by SAVNers to silence vaccine critics. There are no groups like SAVN in other Australian public scientific controversies. Imagine the possibility of groups such as Stop Climate Deniers or Stop Genetic Modification Critics that would use denigration, harassment and censorship against anyone who publicly criticises orthodoxy. The absence of groups like this suggests that something special drives SAVN.

I do not propose to provide an explanation here, but only to indicate some possible avenues for investigation should someone decide to explore this topic. To do this might involve textual analysis of SAVNer discourse, interviews with SAVNers, joining SAVN and participating in SAVN Facebook commentary, analysing the activities of the Australian Skeptics, and other methods of linguistic, psychological and ethnographic research.

I have already raised the idea of "moral foundations" for people's judgements about right and wrong, with the care foundation being especially relevant to vaccination passions. SAVN was formed after the death of a child from pertussis, and it is obvious from comments on SAVN's Facebook page that protecting children is of special importance. However, the care foundation on its own does not explain SAVN's antagonism to vaccine critics, because care can be manifested in different ways, for example support for measures to reduce poverty, discrimination and domestic violence. Furthermore, it is worth repeating that vaccine critics are also motivated by caring for the young. They just have a different assessment concerning the role of vaccination in this care.

Another avenue for investigation is the idea of in-groups and out-groups. There is a large amount of psychological research showing that people can quickly and easily identify with a group, seeing themselves as part of the group and everyone else (especially rivals) as not part of the group. In-group identification can even be created by trivial and arbitrary distinctions, such as eye colour.

Members of SAVN very clearly see themselves as an in-group, in explicit rivalry with vaccine critics. As observed from Facebook page commentary, SAVNers nearly always support each other and nearly always exhibit hostility to outsiders.[15] When vaccine critics post on SAVN's Facebook page, SAVNers join forces to contest claims, often denigrating the interloper.

The in-group versus out-group dynamic provides insight into the cohesion of SAVN. However, it does little

---

15 These may be different processes: Marilynn B. Brewer, "The psychology of prejudice: ingroup love or outgroup hate?" *Journal of Social Issues,* Vol. 55, No. 3, 1999, pp. 429–444.

to explain the SAVNers' vehement antagonism towards vaccine critics.

Psychologists Daniel Wegner and Kurt Gray have analysed the way people attribute minds to others, for example to animals, robots and groups.[16] One particular category they examine is especially relevant to understanding SAVN: the enemy. Anything or anyone classified as an enemy is assumed not to have feelings, but only agency, namely the capacity to do harm.

Wegner and Gray say that people intuitively classify minds into "vulnerable feelers" and "thinking doers." Most capable adults are assumed to have both experience and agency — they are both feelers and doers — but others may fall into one category or the other. Babies and puppies are seen as vulnerable feelers. People can become furious when vulnerable feelers are harmed.

Those seen as the enemy are put in the category of thinking doers and not attributed any vulnerabilities. SAVNers, who see vaccine critics as the enemy, seem to have no concern for the feelings of those they attack. This is compatible with SAVNers treating their targets as thinking doers who have no capacity for feeling.

Wegner and Gray provide another idea useful for understanding SAVN: dyadic completion. When something terrible happens, people look for an agent who is deemed responsible. When a child — a vulnerable feeler — suffers and dies from an infectious disease, dyadic completion is

---

16 Daniel M. Wegner and Kurt Gray, *The Mind Club: Who Thinks, What Feels, and Why It Matters* (New York: Viking, 2016).

satisfied by finding someone to blame. It is not psychologically satisfying to attribute a death to chance or to a social condition such as poverty. SAVNers blame vaccine critics.

The ferocity of SAVN's campaign can partly be attributed to rage over harm to children (vulnerable feelers) combined with dyadic completion in which blame is assigned to vaccine critics. Another factor also plays a role: lack of personal contact with these vaccine critics.

When meeting someone face to face, it is far easier to see their humanity. The other person has emotions as well as a point of view. The other person can converse and has concerns. In face-to-face conversations, social norms discourage brutish behaviour. Even a ruthless dictator can be charming in person.

SAVNers, however, almost never meet vaccine critics face to face. SAVNers conduct almost all their operations online: Facebook comments, blogs, complaints to government agencies, complaints to media. They refuse to engage in public debates with vaccine critics. The lack of face-to-face contact makes it easier to dehumanise the critics, to see them as one-dimensional enemies. It enables what is called the "online disinhibition effect"[17]: face-to-face inhibitions against abusive behaviours are removed in online engagements. Basically, when you can see and hear another person interacting with you, this makes them seem human and discourages antisocial behaviour. Online, interaction lacks facial expressions, tone of voice and

---

17 John Suler, "The online disinhibition effect," *CyberPsychology & Behavior*, Vol. 7, No. 3, 2004, pp. 321–326.

other signals that can trigger empathy and mutual recognition. This helps to explain the proliferation of online hate against women, minorities and others. In the next section, I expand on this connection.

Added to online disinhibition is the experience of operating as part of a group. Being in a group enables behaviours that would not be typical for an individual operating alone. In a group, the sense of personal responsibility is reduced, and there is a mimicking effect.

Group bonding and mutual reinforcement can be used for positive or negative purposes. When protesters join together to challenge a dictatorship, there is safety in numbers and courage is contagious. On the other hand, mobs can undertake crimes that few individuals would contemplate. In the US South after the Civil War, lynchings of blacks were carried out by large groups of white men, all wearing masks.

The capacity of groups to target individuals is shown in what is called mobbing, which is collective bullying. In a typical case of mobbing, an employee is targeted with adverse actions carried out by co-workers and bosses. This can involve ostracism, abusive language, interference in work tasks and physical assault.[18]

---

18 Noa Davenport, Ruth Distler Schwartz and Gail Pursell Elliott, *Mobbing: Emotional Abuse in the American Workplace* (Ames, IA: Civil Society Publishing, 1999); Carol Elbing and Alvar Elbing, *Militant Managers: How to Spot ... How to Work with ... How to Manage ... Your Highly Aggressive Boss* (Burr Ridge, IL: Irwin Professional Publishing, 1994); Susan M. Steinman, *Don't Take Shit from Hyenas at Work: Reclaim Your Dignity — Be Hyena-wise!* (Johannesburg, South Africa: The People

SAVN from its inception has operated like a mob. A few individuals take prominent roles, but many activities are undertaken collectively, namely by the combined efforts of many individuals, for example writing complaints to organisations. As a group, SAVNers provide moral support for each other and, just as importantly, offer role models. This is apparent in discussions on the SAVN Facebook page when comments are liked by others, when particular contributions are lauded, and when numerous SAVNers add their comments critical of an interloper. As group members, SAVNers support each other in the overall aim of silencing vaccine critics.

To explain the direction and dynamics of SAVN, there is one other factor worth noting: the connection with the Australian Skeptics, several of whose members have played important roles in SAVN. The Australian Skeptics are part of an international network of Skeptics organisations. They can be likened to partisans for mainstream science. They are antagonistic to various alternative perspectives, including astrology, parapsychology, faith healing and homoeopathy, which seem — according to Skeptics — to involve violations of the laws of science. Criticism of vaccination is seen by Skeptics as a rejection of incontrovertible science, and therefore is condemned.[19]

Bottomline, 2007); Judith Wyatt and Chauncey Hare, *Work Abuse: How to Recognize and Survive It* (Rochester, VT: Schenkman Books, 1997).

19 For critical views about Skeptics, see Skeptical about Skeptics, http://www.skepticalaboutskeptics.org. For a discussion of the psychology of Skeptics, see L. David Leiter, "The pathology of

However, no group quite like SAVN exists in other countries, so something else must be involved. It can be speculated that the rise and persistence of SAVN is in part due to chance. A possible scenario: Dana McCaffery's death from pertussis led a few individuals to found SAVN to go after the AVN, and the group gained momentum with enough successes to maintain and expand interest and participation.

More on SAVN
SAVN allows anyone to comment on its Facebook page. In principle, this enables discussion with individuals disagreeing with SAVN's goals. Periodically, individual vaccine critics post material or make comments on SAVN's page. Almost always, this leads to an exchange, as one or more SAVNers counter the critic, sometimes with evidence about the benefits of vaccination and often with withering commentary and verbal abuse. SAVNers always have the greater numbers, and if necessary a pesky opponent can be blocked from further posting.

Allowing visitors to post comments serves several purposes for SAVN. It makes the page more interesting, providing a motivation for SAVNers to engage in exchanges. It provides a testing ground for SAVNers to practise responding to contrary views, in a safe venue in which the outcome is never in doubt: the critic is always vanquished, either through argument, evidence, abuse or blocking. Exchanges with critics enable SAVNers to

---

organized skepticism," *Journal of Scientific Exploration*, Vol. 16, No. 1, 2002, pp. 125–128.

demonstrate their knowledge and wit to each other, a sort of competition in which skills of repartee, especially put-downs, are developed to a high level. Finally, exchanges with critics build a sense of community and solidarity within SAVN. By supporting each other against a hostile invader on their home turf, the SAVN Facebook page, SAVNers affirm their membership in a community of like-minded campaigners and their difference from their opponents, the alien vaccine critics. The more heated the exchange, the more potent this process can be in solidifying the SAVN in-group and drawing lines against its opponents as an out-group to be treated with contempt.

SAVN can benefit from allowing visitors with contrary views because it has the numbers and the final word. This would not work so well if the critics had comparable numbers and energy, in which case the critics might be able to change the tone of the exchanges or even take over.

Online harassment
SAVN's campaign against vaccine critics has operated almost entirely online. SAVNers post comments on SAVN's Facebook page and on their individual blogs. They attempt to post comments on the AVN's page. They modify Wikipedia entries. They make complaints to media outlets and government agencies. And so forth.

Some SAVNers do things offline, for example speaking to journalists. SAVNers are real people, and some of them meet each other in the flesh. But as a group, SAVN seldom intervenes on a face-to-face level. Although SAVNers campaign to stop the AVN holding public talks or screening films, SAVNers have seldom appeared at the talks or screenings and never been known to disrupt them. Nor does SAVN hold its own public meetings.

Being a decentralised online presence provides several benefits to SAVN. Several of the key methods SAVN uses against its opponents — notably complaints to government agencies — cannot easily be used against SAVN itself. Not being an incorporated association, SAVN is not subject to government regulations. Furthermore, many SAVNers use pseudonyms or do not offer any information about their occupations and residences, thereby protecting themselves from attacks, for example complaints to their employers.

SAVN's operations have commonalities with those of online hate groups, some of which are long-standing while others apparently are spontaneous crowds that target particular individuals. Danielle Keats Citron is an authority on online harassment. In her book *Hate Crimes in Cyberspace,* she describes three case studies in detail.[20] One involved a female law student who, for no apparent reason, became a target of abusive, threatening commentary on blog sites, including lies about her test scores, sexual behaviour and mental problems. What happens in cases like this is that after a public attack begins, lots of people join in, turning individual bullying into collective mobbing.

---

20 Danielle Keats Citron, *Hate Crimes in Cyberspace* (Cambridge, MA: Harvard University Press, 2014). See also Bailey Poland, *Haters: Harassment, Abuse, and Violence Online* (Lincoln, NE: Potomac Press, 2016).

Her employment prospects were diminished because many potential employers look online to check out job applicants; when they see derogatory material, they seldom seek to verify it, instead just passing over the applicant in favour of someone about whom there is no adverse material.

The attackers went beyond abuse, seeking to wreck the student's life and career. They wrote to her employers making all sorts of false, damaging claims, and also made false claims about her husband.

Another one of Citron's case studies involves a woman who became prominent as a blogger, discussing software design. Simply by being a woman commenting in a male-dominated technological field, she became a target of massive abuse, including death threats, rape fantasies and the like.

The third case study is of woman whose ex-partner posted nude photos of her on various websites, plus her contact details. An online profile falsely stated she wanted sex for money. This and other posts led to a barrage of unwelcome attention. Her boss and colleagues received photos by emails that seemed to come from her.

These examples illustrate several features of what Citron calls "hate crimes in cyberspace": abusive online commentary, false claims and discrediting messages to employers and other organisations. SAVNers have used all these techniques. The SAVN Facebook page is filled with derogatory commentary about individuals. The blog Reasonable Hank has posted hostile commentaries about numerous vaccine critics, including chiropractors, nurses and midwives, with encouragement to make complaints to the professional regulator and to employers.

In some respects, however, SAVN is different from typical hate operations. Some hate-crime victims are targets of convenience, for example women who are prominent online. Those who deploy "revenge porn" are usually disgruntled ex-partners. SAVN, in contrast, chooses its targets based primarily on whether they are publicly critical of vaccination. For many years, SAVN's primary target was Meryl Dorey, but when she became less active, SAVN paid less attention to her. This indicates that SAVN is largely driven by its belief system, namely that open criticism of vaccination is dangerous and should be silenced, and not simply because of a personal grudge, because a target is convenient, or because others have launched an attack. Such factors may play a role, but are far less salient for SAVN than in a number of the cases described by Citron, for which factors like misogyny (as when prominent female bloggers are seen as a threat to a male domain) or personal antagonism (as in revenge porn) seem to be crucial.

Anti-female attitudes may play a role in SAVN's campaign. The majority of prominent vaccine critics are women, and Meryl Dorey has long been the target of particularly nasty commentary. In contrast, the majority of prominent SAVNers over the years have been men. However, only a few of the attacks on vaccine critics — notably the sending of pornography, something that SAVN denies being involved with — have an overtly anti-female dimension.

Another difference between SAVN's campaign and many online hate campaigns is the relative lack of death threats and highly abusive posts. There have been some serious-sounding threats against vaccine critics, but not an inundation of threats to rape, dismember or kill individuals, or invitations for them to kill themselves, that seem so common in online hate speech.[21] The relative tameness of SAVN personal attacks can be explained by the need for the group to maintain a level of public credibility as responsible proponents of vaccination and of public health more generally. It is reasonable to hypothesise that verbal abuse by SAVNers can escalate in the absence of resistance. Escalation can occur by SAVNers mimicking each other, including in a sort of competition to see who can produce the most original and humorous put-downs. However, when SAVNer abuse is exposed to wider audiences, this discredits SAVN, and SAVN administrators and opinion leaders put a brake on the more extreme or discreditable sorts of abuse.

Abusive language can proliferate on SAVN's Facebook page, which is mainly populated by SAVNers and a few intrepid vaccine critics. Very few members of the public ever visit the page and spend enough time to fully grasp the style of commentary. Furthermore, with few exceptions, journalists do not report on personal abuse by SAVNers. However, vaccine critics can expose abuse and threats to their own circles, and no doubt this has a moderating effect on SAVN public discourse.

---

21 Emma A. Jane, *Misogyny Online: A Short (and Brutish) History* (London: Sage, 2017).

As recounted in chapter 5, after Dorey publicised receiving threatening phone messages sent from the home of prominent SAVN figure Daniel Raffaele, this caused SAVNers to back away from admitting responsibility. Though Raffaele denied leaving the messages, thereafter he dropped out of sight in SAVN activities.[22] Going too far meant his name became damaging for SAVN's credibility.

So it might be said that SAVN's level of hate speech is a balance or compromise between, on the one hand, what seems to work — or what seems satisfying, or serves to bond SAVNers — in denigrating and harassing targets and, on the other hand, the need to appear responsible to wider audiences. When SAVNers go too far, for example by sending pornography or making death threats, they may be called into line by SAVN administrators, by statements that this sort of behaviour is not appropriate, and perhaps by disowning or banning (from SAVN's Facebook page) individuals.

There may also be another control process within SAVN's ranks that is less visible. Occasionally there are moderating voices: contributors to SAVN's Facebook page who question abusive language, correct false claims made about vaccine critics, or defend critics against unfair allegations. Such voices are scarce. For example, it is very unusual to hear anyone say that censorship of vaccine critics might be counterproductive. This might be because contributors follow everyone else's example or because moderating voices are banned.

---

22 This is discussed in chapter 5.

It seems more common to see Facebook posts by critics than by moderate SAVNers who support vaccination but question some of the hostile rhetoric. This suggests that internal criticism, from within SAVN ranks, might be more threatening to SAVN opinion leaders than comments by vaccine critics.

SOCIAL PROBLEMS AND BOUNDARY WORK

Social construction of social problems
People become concerned about various problems in society: crime, addiction, paedophilia, drink driving, climate change and terrorism, to name a few. These are called social problems. Most people assume they are due to objective conditions, for example that crime is a social problem because there's too much criminal activity.

Sociologists, who study the way society operates, noticed that what are called social problems do not always correspond to objective conditions. For example, smoking is seen an important problem in some countries but not in others. Arsenals of nuclear weapons are sometimes seen as a major problem, triggering massive protest at some times — as in the late 1950s and early 1980s — but seemingly ignored at others, with not much correlation with the size of the arsenals or the risk of nuclear war. A related example is that North Korean nuclear weapons generate enormous concern but far larger arsenals in the US, Russia and other countries do not. The mere possibility of Iraqi or Iranian nuclear weapons was treated as unacceptable.

If social problems do not automatically arise from objective conditions, then what is going on? In a classic book titled *Constructing Social Problems,* the authors argue that social problems are due to the efforts of "claims-makers," namely people who say or imply that something is a problem.[23] Police pay a lot of attention to certain activities and ignore others: for example, they pay more attention to burglary than to fraud in medical insurance, which is far greater in scale. The attention to particular activities as crime is also affected by media coverage. Then there are campaigners, who are concerned about smoking, corruption, Internet addiction or any of a number of issues. When there's lots of concern about an issue, it becomes a social problem.

The key idea here is that social problems are "socially constructed." They are not just sitting there, generating concern solely due to their scale and impact. Someone has to do something to create concern. In the case of whether something is considered right or wrong, these are "moral entrepreneurs."

The idea that social problems are socially constructed has obvious relevance to the vaccination debate. Proponents of vaccination say that infectious diseases are an

---

23 Malcolm Spector and John I. Kitsuse, *Constructing Social Problems* (Menlo Park, CA: Cummings, 1977); see also Joel Best, ed., *Images of Issues: Typifying Contemporary Social Problems* (New York: Aldine de Gruyter, 1989). There is a vast amount of research using these ideas. For a related perspective, also relevant to vaccination struggles, see Armand L. Mauss, *Social Problems as Social Movements* (Philadelphia: Lippincott, 1975).

important danger, and that there is a problem when not enough people are vaccinated. Critics of vaccination say, to the contrary, that vaccination injuries are a problem, and so are coercive measures to promote vaccination. There are claims-makers on each side promoting their viewpoints about the nature of the social problem and what to do about it.

From the perspective of the social construction of social problems, Meryl Dorey and the AVN were claims-makers, raising concerns about vaccination and challenging the dominant social problem construction, namely that infectious diseases are a significant danger. Then along came SAVN, with a variant on the dominant social problem construction: from SAVN's perspective, vaccine critics, in particular the AVN, were a serious danger. In other words, SAVN aimed to turn vaccine criticism into a social problem.

The key point here is that what is thought of as a social problem is due, to a great extent, to the efforts of campaigners, governments, media and others to turn it into one. There are plenty of things happening in the world, and it is possible to become excited and concerned about a few or many of them. The implication, at least for those who study social problems, is that it is important to pay attention to the efforts of claims-makers, namely those who make efforts to draw attention to issues and get people concerned about them.

Boundary-work

There are boundaries between countries and there are also less tangible boundaries between sets of ideas. One special boundary is between science and non-science. This can also be called a difference or distinction or demarcation. It is an important boundary because science has a considerable level of status and credibility, whereas something considered unscientific has far less status and credibility.

It might seem obvious that some fields are scientific and others are not. For example, astronomy is a science whereas astrology is not. But, it may be asked, how does one area of activity become classified as science and another classified as non-science? It might seem that the classifications are obvious or natural, but actually there is something else going on: efforts to encourage or enforce a particular set of categories. These efforts are called "boundary-work." They are statements and actions that help create and maintain boundaries, or occasionally to challenge or change them.

Consider UFOs — Unidentified Flying Objects — which, in the popular mind, are often assumed to be flying saucers or other vehicles or visits from extra-terrestrial beings. Although some scientists have taken UFOs seriously, most have dismissed UFO sightings as simply being human objects (such as high altitude balloons), unusual atmospheric phenomena, or hoaxes. UFOs, as possibly signifying extra-terrestrial beings or something else different from known phenomena, are treated as outside science, as non-science or pseudoscience. To exclude UFOs from mainstream science, several techniques are used: journal editors reject submissions that take UFOs seriously; scientific conference organisers exclude sessions about UFOs; grant bodies do not fund UFO research; and scientists either ignore UFO research or refer to it in a dismissive fashion. Of these techniques, the most obvious are the ways that UFO studies are denigrated; the other techniques are ones of exclusion.

At the same time that UFO research was excised from the scientific mainstream, some scientists promoted the Search for Extraterrestrial Intelligence or SETI, for example by broadcasting messages to outer space signifying human intelligence. These scientists take seriously the possibility of extraterrestrial intelligence, but distance themselves from UFO research. They think that highly intelligent life probably exists in the universe outside Earth, but that almost certainly such life is far away, not visiting Earth now.

In the case of UFO research and SETI, boundary-work is a delicate matter. UFO research needs to be categorised as non-scientific while SETI is categorised as scientific.[24]

The concept of boundary-work in science was developed by Thomas Gieryn, who mainly looked at rhetorical techniques used by scientists to distinguish their activities from those portrayed as non-science.[25] A key idea here is that the boundary between science and non-science is not natural: it is not inherent in the activities themselves, but is socially constructed. SETI and UFO research do not have pre-ordained identities: they have to be labelled as either

---

24 On boundary-work around astronomy, see Graham Howard, *Legitimating Astronomy*, PhD thesis, University of Wollongong, 2004, http://ro.uow.edu.au/theses/333/.

25 Thomas Gieryn, *Cultural Boundaries of Science: Credibility on the Line* (Chicago: University of Chicago Press, 1999).

science or non-science. Other researchers have applied the idea of boundary-work to various topics and fields. The study of boundary-work can be illuminating because it takes something — a boundary, a distinction, a set of categories — that seems natural and shows that actually it results from the efforts of various people.

Boundary-work can help explain what happens in the vaccination debate. First consider the scientific domain, specifically the publication of articles in scientific journals. There are various journals that publish research about vaccination. A prominent one is *Vaccine,* filled with articles about all sorts of technical topics.[26] Most of the articles published in *Vaccine* assume vaccination is a good thing, but some are critical of certain aspects of vaccination. For example, Gary Goldman developed an unorthodox view about chickenpox vaccination, seeing it as contributing to an increase in shingles, with adverse health impacts. Although his employer tried to suppress his work and publications, *Vaccine* published some of his articles.[27] However, the occasional openness of *Vaccine* and some

---

26 For example, "Immunologic evaluation of 10 different adjuvants for use in vaccines for chickens against highly pathogenic avian influenza virus" and "Accelerated mass production of influenza virus seed stocks in HEK-293 suspension cell cultures by reverse genetics."

27 For example, G. S. Goldman and P. G. King, "Review of the United States universal varicella vaccination program: herpes zoster incidence rates, cost-effectiveness, and vaccine efficacy based primarily on the Antelope Valley Varicella Active Surveillance Project data," *Vaccine,* Vol. 31, 2013, pp. 1680–1694.

other scientific journals to critical articles about vaccination is unusual, especially in the Australian context.

Various pro-vaccination groups in the Australian debate — medical profession leaders, health department spokespeople, doctors, scientists, journalists, politicians and members of the public, as well as SAVN — participate in efforts to classify any form of vaccine criticism as both unscientific and also unacceptable more generally. This is boundary-work as an everyday activity, occurring in public announcements, advertisements, media stories, personal conversations and other venues. The general thrust of this boundary-work is to stigmatise vaccine criticism as uninformed, ignorant and dangerous. The result is that some parents who are opposed to vaccination are afraid to let others know about their views, for fear of alienating friends or even jeopardising their jobs. In quite a few circles, expressing reservations about vaccination marks a person as irrational.

This pro-vaccination boundary-work has been quite successful, but some individuals and groups resist. The AVN and other vaccine-sceptical groups and individuals present information and viewpoints in various forums. Some individuals are unafraid to defend their views, and may become articulate in doing so on a regular basis.

Pro-vaccination boundary-work preceded the formation of SAVN. What SAVN brought to the issue was the use of more extreme methods based around denigration, harassment and censorship. SAVN's approach has rubbed off on some other players, notably some journalists and politicians, so that personal abuse and censorship have been normalised. It is worth noting that only a few doctors and scientists have joined in or adopted SAVN-style methods. Some supporters of vaccination see SAVN has performing a valuable function; others see SAVN as going too far and being counterproductive. But few become directly involved themselves.

In many public scientific controversies, one side has the overwhelming advantage in terms of endorsement by technical experts. This is the situation in debates over nuclear power, pesticides, fluoridation and genetic modification, among others. In such debates, the role of dissident experts — scientists, doctors, dentists — is crucial. When technical experts are unanimous in their viewpoint, then anyone who disagrees can be dismissed as uninformed. However, when even just a few experts question the dominant view, the situation is changed from unanimity to a debate. This greatly empowers citizen campaigners, who can point to the dissident experts in their support.

For this reason, dissident experts are often the targets of efforts to discredit them or hinder their research.[28] For example, scientists, doctors and dentists who have done research or spoken out against fluoridation have been censored, defamed and deregistered.

Within Australia, few individuals in the vaccination debate could be called dissident experts, namely individuals with credentials or publications who are in some way critical of the dominant pro-vaccination position. Viera Scheibner, an earth scientist, became a prominent critic of

---

28 Brian Martin, "Suppression of dissent in science," *Research in Social Problems and Public Policy*, Vol. 7, 1999, pp. 105–135, http://www.bmartin.cc/pubs/99rsppp.html.

vaccination and played an important role in encouraging others to speak out.[29] However, she has not been active in recent years.

The best example of the way SAVN responds to dissident experts is Judy Wilyman, who was my PhD student. With a background teaching science in high school, Judy returned to university to do a masters degree and then a PhD, focusing on vaccination. Because she was outspoken about vaccination, she became a target of SAVN's. After she obtained her PhD, there was an extraordinary campaign to discredit her and her thesis, and as well me and the University of Wollongong. This campaign is documented elsewhere.[30] I mention it here to illustrate how SAVN and other pro-vaccination campaigners mount an attack on any critic who has some relevant credentials.

The campaign against Judy served several functions. Most obviously, it was designed to discredit Judy and her research. It also provided a warning to universities about the risks to their reputation should they enrol students critical of vaccination, a warning also relevant to potential research students and their supervisors. It also established the terrain on which the work of critics would be addressed. Rather than engage in a scholarly exchange about

---

29 Viera Scheibner, *Vaccination: 100 Years of Orthodox Research Shows that Vaccines Represent a Medical Assault on the Immune System* (Blackheath, NSW: Viera Scheibner, 1993).

30 "Brian Martin: publications on scientific and technological controversies," section on Judy Wilyman thesis, http://www.bmartin.cc/pubs/controversy.html#Wilyman.

the issues raised in Judy's thesis, SAVNers and their allies mounted an attack in the mass and social media, thus avoiding the possibility of acknowledging that there might be evidence, arguments and perspectives worthy of discussion.

The process of boundary-work in the Australian vaccination debate thus involves several components. The usual pro-vaccination boundary-work is carried out by figures and organisations with the greatest credibility, including government health departments, the Australian Medical Association, and leading doctors and scientists, augmented by the commitment of numerous doctors, nurses and other health professionals. The result of routine endorsement of vaccination was that vaccine critics had little impact on vaccination policy and little credibility for the majority of the population.

The formation of SAVN in 2009 added a dimension to this usual boundary-work. SAVN sought not just to reduce the credibility of vaccine critics but to stigmatise and silence the very expression of vaccine criticism. SAVN's variety of boundary-work aimed to classify vaccine criticism as outside of science, as outside the bounds of preventive health and as outside of acceptable public speech.

EXPERTISE AND OPINIONS

At the heart of SAVN's operations, there is an intriguing question: how do SAVNers justify their actions? At a surface level, it's possible to look at explanations that

SAVNers give themselves. At a deeper level, there's an apparent contradiction.

To examine this issue, it's useful to look at the role of expertise in public scientific controversies. Vaccination proponents sometimes say that in order to have any credibility, it's necessary to have appropriate credentials and expertise, for example in immunology or epidemiology. This sounds plausible but on closer scrutiny does not make sense. Expertise in immunology is relevant to debates about immunology, but it may have only limited relevance to vaccination policy. Within immunology, expertise can be quite narrow. For example, studying the immune system of the frog does not automatically make one an expert on the human immune system. Studying polio immunity does not automatically make one an expert on infectious disease immunity in general. Most scientific research is highly specialised, more so than most people realise.

What happens in public debates is that the transition from specialist knowledge to more general authority is skimmed over, without justification, so that having a PhD or an MD is taken as a proxy for authority on policy-related issues.

The next step is to assert that anyone without specialist scientific knowledge, for example in immunology or epidemiology, or at least a PhD in a scientific field, therefore has no credibility to comment on vaccination. This is another step without a solid logical foundation, because it assumes incorrectly that having specialist knowledge makes a person an authority in related areas and then goes on to assume, again incorrectly, that lack of this specialist knowledge precludes a person from having any credibility.

The shortcoming of these assumptions is most easily seen by rebuttals to the specialist argument, in the form of questions with obvious answers. Does knowledge of tree-ring dating techniques give special authority to comment on climate change policy? Does knowledge of radioisotope scattering cross-sections give special authority to comment about energy policy? Does knowledge about road-building give special authority to comment about transport policy? In every case, it is obvious that specialist knowledge is inadequate for dealing with the wider issues that are typically debated, all of which have to do with policy, namely decisions about social arrangements.

If specialist knowledge is not enough to justify special authority to comment, there are several possible ways to proceed. One is for policy to be developed and implemented by the groups with the most power. This is an authoritarian approach. A different approach is to accept that many people are capable of having an input into decision-making about policy matters, because lots of people are affected and can understand something relevant to the issues. This provides a rationale for involvement in policy-making by a wide range of individuals, representing different demographics and perspectives. This can be accomplished in various ways, for example via referendums or citizens' juries. In a less systematic way, involvement occurs through the efforts of campaigners who try to influence politicians.

In a number of countries, formal citizen participation in decision-making is encouraged, most commonly by local governments, government agencies, private groups and researchers. However, so far the vaccination issue seems to have been exempt from such efforts. It remains an issue in which recruitment of citizens into deliberative mechanisms is off the agenda: decision-making remains dominated by health authorities.[31] Expertise remains the justification for excluding citizens from formal roles even though, on closer examination, typical forms of narrow expertise do not justify having a special authority to pass judgement on policy matters.

The view that expertise is necessary to be involved in decision-making is seldom articulated and systematically defended; it is more commonly simply assumed. In the Australian vaccination debate, though, this view received an eloquent expression.

The undeserved credibility of an anti-anti-vaxxer[32]

Patrick Stokes became well known within the Australian vaccination debate for his 2012 article "No, you're not entitled to your opinion" in *The Conversation,* in which he argued that non-experts do not deserve to have their

---

31 Mark A. Largent, *Vaccine: The Debate in Modern America* (Baltimore, MD: Johns Hopkins University Press, 2012), pp. 155–156, makes the point that vaccination proponents, despite their talk of education and "open dialogue," do not want citizens to participate in decision-making.

32 I thank Lee Basham, Kurtis Hagen and Patrick Stokes for valuable comments on drafts of this section. This does not imply their agreement with my arguments here or elsewhere.

opinions treated seriously.[33] He returned to this theme with "The undeserved doubt of the antivaxxer."[34] His argument is that those who question scientific orthodoxy about vaccination, and who are not scientists or scientific experts themselves, do not deserve to be taken seriously. He defends the Australian government's removal of conscientious and religious exemptions for parents not having their children fully vaccinated.

Stokes' argument hinges on various assumptions, including that the science underpinning vaccination policies is unquestionable (except by suitably credentialed experts) and that debate over scientific matters is a matter only for experts, with citizens in the role of passive consumers of orthodoxy. A key ethical assumption is that herd immunity, created when vaccination rates above a certain threshold prevent infectious diseases from spreading easily, implies that individuals should be pressured to vaccinate for the good of the community. These assumptions are questionable, as is Stokes' authority to make pronouncements on matters outside his own expertise.

To begin, consider the term "anti-vaxxer" that Stokes uses to refer to critics of the vaccination paradigm and campaigners against coercive vaccination policies. "Anti-vaxxer" is not a precise term suitable for a careful analysis, yet Stokes uses it without providing a definition.

---

33 Patrick Stokes, "No, you're not entitled to your opinion," *The Conversation*, 5 October 2012, https://theconversation.com/no-youre-not-entitled-to-your-opinion-9978.

34 Patrick Stokes, "The undeserved doubt of the antivaxxer," *The Ethics Centre*, 17 October 2015, http://bit.ly/2nOIPU5.

Certainly it includes individuals who reject all vaccinations, but does it also include those who accept some vaccinations but not others or who want to space out childhood vaccinations in a non-standard way? This question is important because the argument about herd immunity applies much more strongly to some vaccines than others. If herd immunity is the key argument for conforming to a measure because it protects the community, then "anti-vaxxer" is an inadequate term for ethical evaluation, because it aggregates individuals whose choices have different implications for community-level protection against infectious diseases.[35]

Next consider Stokes' assumption that credible questioning of the science concerning vaccination is the preserve only of certified experts in the field. But why should criticism from outsiders be dismissed?

The history of science is full of examples of standard beliefs being overthrown or modified by new information, such as the discovery of prions and their role in mad cow disease. There is much that remains unknown about immunity and indeed about how vaccines work. Much of mainstream science operates on the basis of paradigms, which are packages of beliefs, frameworks and practices that guide thinking and research. However, paradigms are constantly being modified, and occasionally they are overthrown and replaced by alternatives.

Also relevant is the experience of "citizen scientists": people without formal credentials or institutional affilia-

---

35 I am setting aside the argument made by some vaccine critics that herd immunity is not relevant or important.

tions who undertake research.[36] For example, in the case of Minamata disease in Japan, citizen researchers discovered the cause — mercury pollution in the ocean — while teams of conventional scientists with ample funding, using computer models and sophisticated ocean sampling, did not.[37] Stokes ignores the existence of citizen science.

One of the problems with relying on certified experts is that they are especially susceptible to influence by employers, funders and professional status. Pharmaceutical companies, medical professions and governments are not neutral pursuers of the truth, but have their own interests in profit, status and legitimacy. When vested interests are present, special efforts are needed to scrutinise both research carried out, because it is likely to be affected by various forms of bias and misrepresentation, and research that might be carried out but is not.[38] It is also important to look at how safe it is to voice scientific dissent.

That most vaccination research is carried out or supported by pharmaceutical companies is an important consideration. This doesn't mean the findings are neces-

---

36 For example, Richard Sclove, "Research by the people, for the people," *Futures*, Vol. 29, No. 6, 1997, pp. 541–549; Jonathan Silvertown, "A new dawn for citizen science," *Trends in Ecology and Evolution*, Vol. 24, No. 9, 2009, pp. 467–471.

37 Jun Ui, "The interdisciplinary study of environmental problems," *Kogai—The Newsletter from Polluted Japan*, Vol. 5, No. 2, Spring 1977, pp. 12–24.

38 Sheldon Krimsky, *Science in the Private Interest: Has the Lure of Profits Corrupted Biomedical Research?* (Lanham, MD: Rowman & Littlefield, 2003).

sarily wrong, incomplete or one-sided, but it is important that they be subject to scrutiny by independent experts. However, there are few well-funded independent vaccination specialists. Furthermore, some scientists and doctors critical of vaccines have come under attack in various ways.[39] The result is a large potential for distortion of the research field. Stokes does not raise any of these issues.

There is a considerable body of research about public scientific controversies, namely those directly affecting the public, such as climate change, nuclear power and pesticides.[40] The view of most controversy researchers is that these controversies involve both scientific and social components; many further argue that separating these components is artificial. In practice, disputes over scientific matters are laced with social influences, and vice versa. The implication is that it is legitimate for non-scientists to question scientific orthodoxy. For example, activists have pointed to areas of research that should be studied but are not, thus questioning positions based on research that is carried out.[41]

---

39 Brian Martin, "On the suppression of vaccination dissent," *Science and Engineering Ethics,* Vol. 21, No. 1, 2015, pp. 143–157, http://www.bmartin.cc/pubs/15see.html.

40 I've outlined ideas from this body of research relevant to campaigners in *The Controversy Manual* (Sparsnäs, Sweden: Irene Publishing, 2014), http://www.bmartin.cc/pubs/14cm/.

41 David J. Hess, *Undone Science: Social Movements, Mobilized Publics, and Industrial Transitions* (Cambridge, MA: MIT Press, 2016).

Stokes addresses the psychology of opponents of vaccination, making sweeping generalisations without providing documentation or references. For example, he states that much anti-vax belief comes from a "cultic milieu" "held together by a common rejection of orthodoxy *for the sake of rejecting orthodoxy.*" Where is the evidence for this? He states, "Anti-vaxxers don't like that loss of authority. They want to think for themselves, but they don't accept we can't think in a vacuum."[42] Again, he gives no evidence for his claim. Stokes has not published any refereed articles about the psychology of vaccination critics, and does not cite any either.

It is easy to see that Stokes' claim that vaccine critics reject "orthodoxy *for the sake of rejecting orthodoxy*" is wrong. Most vaccine critics accept conventional medical thinking about numerous topics, such as the symptoms of measles, the existence of multiple strains of pneumococcal disease and the consequences of vitamin C deficiency, not to mention conventional scientific thinking about topics such as evolution and radioactivity. Stokes, by saying vaccine critics are held together by rejecting orthodoxy for the sake of it, has presented a false claim masquerading as an argument. In doing this, he casts aspersions on vaccine critics rather than addressing their arguments.

Stokes says, "In the twenty-first century nobody has the right to believe scientists are wrong about science without having earned that right through actually doing

---

42 Stokes, "The undeserved doubt of the antivaxxer," http://bit.ly/2nOIPU5.

science."[43] But what about when scientists disagree? Some of them are wrong, indeed perhaps most of them are wrong.[44] It is unwise to simply accept the majority view without question, especially when science and politics are intertwined in public controversies. On a topic such as vaccination, there are many different relevant scientific specialties, such as immunology and epidemiology, and no one is expert in all of them. Science does not automatically translate into policy, because various value assumptions are involved.

Furthermore, people do not have to have credentials to acquire knowledge relevant to vaccination. For example, many parents are astute observers of their children, with a practical understanding that needs to be considered alongside expert knowledge rather than dismissed as anecdotal.

To exempt science from public scrutiny and from disbelief goes against a well-established trend in society to bring authorities down from their pedestals, examine the driving forces behind their claims and assess the social implications of their recommendations. This does not necessarily lead to support for vaccination critics, but it

---

43 Ibid.

44 A highly cited article making this point is John P. A. Ioannidis JPA, "Why most published research findings are false," *PLoS Medicine,* Vol. 2, No. 8, 2005, e124. On challenges to vaccination orthodoxy, see the sources in Neil Z. Miller, *Miller's Review of Critical Vaccine Studies: 400 Important Scientific Papers Summarized for Parents and Researchers* (Santa Fe, NM: New Atlantean Press, 2016).

does provide support for allowing their voices to be heard. Countering their views is the way to proceed, not ruling them out of order in advance.

Stokes' idea is that some people, the experts, are entitled to have their opinions treated seriously, while others, the non-experts, are not. This dichotomy is too simple to address the realities of complex public scientific controversies, in which there is a myriad of different issues (benefits, risks, ethics, decision-making) each with intricate byways, and in each of which individuals might have relevant information, perspectives and detailed knowledge. No one's contributions should be rejected out of hand, nor should anyone's contributions be accorded automatic credibility. It is better to understand credibility as the outcome of debates and power struggles than as a pristine input.

Finally, it is intriguing to apply Stokes' arguments about expertise to his own interventions into the vaccination debate. He says he can address logical considerations by virtue of his training as a philosopher. But when addressing the scientific, social and psychological facets of the debate, he has no special training or publications in refereed journals.

By Stokes' line of thinking, should no one except sociologists be taken seriously in a claim that sociologists are wrong about sociology, including about the sociology of the vaccination controversy? By his own criteria, then, shouldn't Stokes' opinions be treated as "undeserved"?

In this regard, Stokes' position is self-refuting. If only those with certified expertise can be taken seriously, then his own pronouncements about vaccination matters should be dismissed. If, on the other hand, his comments about vaccination are legitimate despite his lack of formal expertise in the area — namely because they have argumentative merit — then likewise it should be considered legitimate for others to comment.

SAVNers were delighted by Stokes' article "No, you're not entitled to your opinion."[45] They saw it as vindication of their dismissal of the views of vaccine critics as uninformed. Stokes' article was not the foundation of this dismissal. In SAVN commentary from the beginning, Dorey, the AVN and other vaccine critics were portrayed as ignorant, misinformed, lying and dangerous.

What is curious in SAVNers' rhetoric is how they never apply the same arguments to themselves. Stokes offers a justification for this: he says expertise is required to challenge the dominant scientific view but is not necessary to "assert" this view. However, this view has difficulties. If a person has no understanding of a theory or therapy, why should they have any credibility when asserting the dominant view about it? If you are totally ignorant concerning xylotherapy, why should anyone listen to your views about it, pro or con? What is usually involved in supporting the orthodox view is some personal judgement, whether about the arguments, evidence, authorities or others with the same or different views. Concerning vaccination, this might be a personal assessment of the plausibility of herd immunity, of the integrity

---

45 This is apparent in the comments on Stokes' article in *The Conversation*, as well as comments on SAVN's Facebook page.

of vaccination researchers or the behaviour of vaccine critics.

There are risks in asserting a view solely on the basis that authorities support it. The view might have been imposed, as in the case of Stalin's support for the views of Lysenko about the inheritance of acquired characteristics. The authorities might be influenced by vested interests, or even by going along with the crowd.

If all that is needed to have some credibility in *affirming* the views of authorities is some understanding beyond unthinking adherence to dominant ideas, then it is equally plausible that those who bring personal knowledge and experience to bear in *challenging* such views have some level of credibility. This throws into question Stokes' claim that it is credible for non-experts to assert the dominant scientific view but not to challenge it.

Among SAVNers who dismiss vaccine critics for lacking relevant expertise, few present a justification as nuanced as Stokes'. It is reasonable to ask, how can they glory in Stokes' argument while not applying it to themselves?[46]

Honour by association
One explanation is that SAVNers assume what is called "honour by association": they unconsciously presume that

---

46 Some SAVNers are scientists, doctors or nurses. Few if any are specialists in vaccination policy. I assume that few if any SAVNers claim no understanding at all of the vaccination issue and simply support the dominant view because it is the dominant view. If they did, Stokes' strictures would not apply.

supporting dominant views means acquiring the authority of those associated with these views, namely the authority of health departments, leading medical figures and vaccination researchers.

A more commonly recognised technique is guilt by association: a person is discredited by being linked with a disreputable or discredited figure, such as a criminal or crackpot. If your friend is a terrorist or a paedophile, then some of the negative attitudes about terrorists and paedophile may be applied to you. Guilt by association helps explain why, for example, the children of a man exposed in the media as being a criminal may be bullied at school, though the children have themselves done nothing wrong. Even objects can acquire a sort of guilt by association. For example, some people are reluctant to buy a house where a murder has been committed.

Honour by association is an analogous process, except that positives rub off. The everyday process of name-dropping fits in here. You hear a friend say she met a celebrity or some other prestigious person. Being associated with someone famous has a spin-off personal glory. On the other hand, there is little to be gained by dropping the name of someone who is unknown, in other words a nobody.

Academics, when writing papers, commonly cite the most well-known contributors in their field, and less commonly cite obscure contributors who said the same thing. On evolution, for example, they are more likely to cite Darwin than Wallace. It could be argued that this is merely a matter of citing the most important contributions. However, this ignores what has been called the Matthew effect where those who become recognised receive ever more recognition whereas those who are neglected become even more obscure.[47] In several social science areas, for example, it is common for Michel Foucault's work to be cited and sometimes the absence of a Foucault citation can be seen as a shortcoming.

When academics apply for jobs or promotions, they list references. Who is the best person to be listed: someone who knows your work really well or someone with higher status who knows it less well? Often, the recommended choice is the person with higher status. It is rare for an applicant to list someone as a reference who is lower in formal status, for example a student. Listing a high-status individual seems to involve honour by association outweighing knowledge.

Students, when choosing where to attend university, are often influenced by status. Having a degree from Stanford University is more prestigious than one from Idaho State, even if you are equally capable. Students flock to the big-name universities even when the actual education they obtain is no better than at lesser ranked institutions. This is rational, because others will judge graduates only partly by what they know and can do: having a degree from a well-respected university has spin-off prestige for graduates.

Some organisations have one or more patrons, which are honorific positions. A patron may have little to do with the organisation, just appearing in publicity or perhaps

---

[47] The classic reference is Robert K. Merton, "The Matthew effect in science," *Science*, Vol. 159, 5 January 1968, pp. 56–63.

performing a ritual activity like opening a building or meeting. Usually, the people selected as patrons are highly prestigious. A local club might ask a politician, a prominent author or a monarch to be the club's patron. For example, Prince Philip was the patron for hundreds of organisations.

Some people like to live in a part of town that has a better reputation. In Australia, different suburbs have different statuses. In Sydney, it is more prestigious to live in Potts Point than Wentworthville, and people will pay a premium to have an address in a more salubrious suburb. Having the same house, in the same sort of neighbourhood, is perceived as better if it comes with a more prestigious address.

Honour by association is part of what drives conspicuous consumption: the purchase of expensive cars, clothes, watches and the like. Driving a Porsche gives spin-off prestige to the owner. Underlying conspicuous consumption is a deeper sort of honour by association: having more money is widely assumed to bring some associated virtue.

Being a supporter of a winning sports team brings a certain personal glory, whereas being a die-hard supporter of a notoriously poor team does not. Some sports fans will not change their allegiances, but others will switch their loyalty or attention to teams that are doing well.

It is common to prefer to be seen with someone who is good looking, and if your friends are famous that's even better. For an older man, having a young, attractive woman at his side seems to provide some reflected glory. It is uncommon for a man to dump his younger, popular and beautiful wife in favour of someone older and less attractive.

Honour by association thus seems to play a role in all sorts of domains. It is a non-rational process: judgements are made, often unconsciously, based on associations that have little to do with quality.

In all sorts of scientific controversies, the process of honour by association helps explain how so many people can presume to know what position is correct. For example, soon after fluoridation of public water supplies to reduce tooth decay was endorsed by the United States Public Health Service (USPHS) in 1950, a wide variety of organisations also endorsed fluoridation.[48] Some had relevant expertise, notably the American Medical Association (AMA) and the American Dental Association (ADA). Others endorsers had no particular connection with the issue, such as the American Federation of Labor and Congress of Industrial Organizations (AFL-CIO). Why would members of the AFL-CIO presume to be able to make a pronouncement about fluoridation? Without witnesses to the discussions at the time, or surveys of what officials in the organisation knew, it is impossible to make a definitive assessment. It is reasonable to suppose, though, that AFL-CIO officials trusted the judgement of the USPHS, AMA and ADA and, without any relevant expertise themselves, endorsed fluoridation. This might be

---

48 I discuss endorsements of fluoridation in *Scientific Knowledge in Controversy: The Social Dynamics of the Fluoridation Debate* (Albany, NY: State University of New York Press, 1991), http://www.bmartin.cc/pubs/91skic.html, pp. 56–60.

called "endorsement by association." It then had a snowballing effect, enabling other organisations to make similar endorsements. It is basically a statement saying, "We trust the experts" or "We trust the most authoritative groups."

Honour by association seems also the process by which individuals become self-righteous in their assertion of dominant views. Many SAVNers have no particular claim to relevant expertise, yet they apparently feel entitled to condemn those who disagree with them.

Looking to what authorities say is, for many purposes, a reasonable shortcut. It takes time and effort to study the relative benefits of eating wholegrain or white bread, using a deodorant with or without aluminium, using a mobile phone with or without hands-free, drinking free-trade coffee, and a host of other issues. Only a few people take the effort to investigate such issues in depth.

What is especially significant about SAVN's campaign is that it is based on a presumption of being correct and on intolerance towards those who disagree: intolerance so great that it leads to attempts to silence others. Many SAVNers justify their position by referencing the alleged ignorance and duplicity of vaccine critics, glorying in Stokes' view that people without expertise are not entitled to their opinions. The neat trick is to assume this applies only to the misguided critics and not to the enlightened adherents to orthodoxy.

9
Moral panics

In 1972, sociologist Stanley Cohen's book *Folk Devils and Moral Panics* was published. Cohen wanted to understand a peculiar phenomenon in which particular groups and activities — such as the counter-cultural groups called the Mods and Rockers — came to be seen as threats to the moral order. These groups were seen as outrageous, indeed dangerous. The implication in Cohen's argument was that these groups were not an actual physical threat — they were not dangerous in a real sense — but threatened people's values.

In a famous quote at the very beginning of his book, Cohen stated his perspective:

> Societies appear to be subject, every now and then, to periods of moral panic. A condition, episode, person or group of persons emerges to become defined as a threat to societal values and interests; its nature is presented in a stylized and stereotypical fashion by the mass media; the moral barricades are manned by editors, bishops, politicians and other right-thinking people; socially accredited experts pronounce their diagnoses and solutions; ways of coping are evolved or (more often) resorted to; the condition then disappears, submerges or deteriorates and becomes more visible. Sometimes the object of the panic is quite novel and at other times it is something which

has been in existence long enough, but suddenly appears in the limelight.[1]

In Australia after 2009, there seems to have been a moral panic about public criticism of vaccination. Vaccine critics were defined as a threat to societal values and interests. They were portrayed in a stereotyped way by their opponents, including pro-vaccination campaigners, journalists and politicians. Vaccine critics, the object of the panic, had been around for many years but were suddenly put into the limelight.

Although the Australian case seems to fit Cohen's picture in several ways, it also differs. The "moral barricades" have been primarily manned by the citizen campaigners in Stop the Australian (Anti)Vaccination Network (SAVN).[2] The panic has two elements: firstly, a concern about unvaccinated members of the population and their contribution to the possible resurgence of infectious diseases and, secondly, a concern that public critics of vaccination are contributing to dangerously low levels of immunity. Socially accredited experts — doctors, scientists and health department spokespeople — have pronounced their recommendations about vaccination but have played little role in the promotion of the panic, which has been driven by SAVN, the media and politicians.

---

1 Stanley Cohen, *Folk Devils and Moral Panics* (London: Routledge, 2002, third edition), p. 1.

2 For information about SAVN and the AVN, see the glossary and chapter 3.

Cohen was primarily concerned with the trajectory of moral panics, including the stages through which they went. He focused on moral panics involving challenges to mainstream culture. Other scholars have taken Cohen's ideas, examined and questioned them and applied them to other arenas.

In this chapter, I look at the relevance of ideas about moral panics to the alarm about vaccination criticism since the formation of SAVN in 2009. This is less a matter of trying to establish whether there has been a moral panic about vaccination or about vaccine critics and more a matter of providing insight into the Australian vaccination controversy using the lens of moral panic theory. Calling something a moral panic does not turn it into anything different, but illuminates it in a particular way that may or may not be helpful for understanding.[3]

Kenneth Thompson has written a convenient summary treatment of moral panics, providing an overview, a history of ideas in the field, and case studies of key areas.[4] The topics he discusses, which had become the focus of social concern, are Mods and Rockers, youth, muggings, sex and AIDS, girl gangs, sex on the screen, and families, children and violence. He says moral panics take the form of crusades, appeal to those concerned about moral breakdown, are led by politicians and/or media, and leave

---

3 On approaches to moral panic analysis, see Sarah Wright Monod, *Making Sense of Moral Panics: A Framework for Research* (Cham, Switzerland: Palgrave Macmillan, 2017). My approach in part follows the one she recommends.

4 Kenneth Thompson, *Moral Panics* (London: Routledge, 1998).

unaddressed the underlying causes of the problem. Note that these are primarily social issues, not scientific ones.[5]

Thompson notes that panics about health are not the same as ones involving morals.[6] The panic over vaccination in Australia involves morals in at least two ways. First, not vaccinating has been painted as a moral transgression, due to undermining herd immunity. Especially when there are disease outbreaks, parents are held morally responsible if their children are not fully vaccinated. Second, public criticism of vaccination has been castigated as dangerous to public health. In a sense, openly criticising vaccines and official policy is seen as immoral, as making speakers culpable in the deaths of innocents. The Australian panic about vaccination is not entirely about morals, but I believe the connection is strong enough to make moral panic theory relevant.[7]

Thompson summarises Cohen's elements or stages in a moral panic this way:

1. "Something or someone is defined as a threat to values or interests."

---

5 For Australian case studies, see Scott Poynting and George Morgan (eds.), *Outrageous! Moral Panics in Australia* (Hobart: ACYS Publishing, 2007).

6 Thompson, *Moral Panics*, p. vii: "Sometimes panics about food (e.g. the BSE scare about infected beef) or health have been confused with panics that relate directly to morals."

7 Thompson, in contrast, would prefer to reserve the concept "moral panic" for issues more directly centred on morals and involving an assumption of moral decline.

2. There is convenient media portrayal.
3. Public concern builds rapidly.
4. Authorities or opinion-makers respond.
5. "The panic recedes or results in social changes."[8]

Most of these elements are found in the SAVN-inspired campaign.

1. Yes. Vaccine critics are defined as a threat to public health.
2. Yes. There is a convenient media portrayal.
3. Probably. Has public concern increased rapidly? This is plausible given the media coverage, but there is no systematic evidence.
4. Yes. Government agencies and politicians have responded.
5. Yes. The panic led to restrictions being put on vaccine-critical groups. It has also resulted in changes to welfare policies to financially penalise parents whose children are not fully vaccinated.

To refer to moral panics is to implicitly assume the concern is excessive in relation to the danger. Indicators of this might include exaggeration or fabrication of statistics, or singling out a particular problem when it's no worse than others. However, such indicators may not be present. I return to this issue later in this chapter.

Thompson cites well-known sociologist Howard Becker, who said that moral entrepreneurs seek to define targets as deviants or criminals, stirring up media and

---

8 Ibid., p. 8.

putting pressure on authorities to act.⁹ A moral entrepreneur is like a businessperson — an entrepreneur — but, instead of selling a product or service, is selling a way of thinking about matters of right and wrong, of morality. In the Australian vaccination debate, SAVNers are the key moral entrepreneurs. They have defined their targets — Meryl Dorey, the AVN and other vaccine critics — as both deviant and criminal, have stirred up the media and have put pressure on government authorities to act.

Cohen looked at media treatment of the Mods and Rockers using three categories. The first was exaggeration and distortion, the second was prediction and the third was symbolisation, namely the use of symbols to give meaning to events. The Australian media that have followed SAVN's framing of the issues have used methods falling in each of these categories. The influence of the AVN on the beliefs and behaviour of parents is exaggerated: it is presented as so great that censorship is required. The key prediction is that if the AVN is allowed sympathetic coverage in the media, this will inevitably lead to a decline in community-level immunity and epidemics might result. The key element of symbolisation is turning "Meryl Dorey" and "the AVN" into things to be feared and which therefore should be silenced and destroyed.

Along the way, infectious disease is turned into an ever-present danger. Even a few cases of measles are

---

9 Ibid., pp. 12–13.

reported as a dire threat to the community.[10] As Thompson puts it, "One of the effects of the symbolization contained in the media reports of deviance is that it sensitizes people to signs of a threat. Incidents and events that might otherwise not be regarded as connected come to be seen as symptoms of the same threatening form of deviance."[11]

Another useful source on moral panics is a collection of readings edited by Chas Critcher. The introductions by Critcher provide a valuable overview of several different approaches to moral panics. Critcher says there are the five Ps whose participation can enable moral panics: pressure groups and claims makers, police and law enforcement, press (media), public opinion and politicians.[12]

SAVN's campaign can be interpreted or reconstructed (without assuming a grand plan by SAVNers) as seeking to win allies or tools in each of the five Ps.

P1: SAVN itself is a pressure group.

P1a: other pressure groups and claims makers. Neither the medical profession nor pharmaceutical companies have joined the campaign overtly. The main active groups have been the Australian Skeptics and Friends of Science in Medicine.

---

10 For example, Kate Aubusson, "Health bosses warn of danger as fourth measles case found," *Sydney Morning Herald*, 29 December 2016, p. 10.

11 Thompson, *Moral Panics*, p. 36.

12 Chas Critcher (ed.), *Critical Readings: Moral Panics and the Media* (Maidenhead, Berkshire: Open University Press, 2006), p. 4.

P2: agencies such as the HCCC. These are not in the list of five Ps, but they can be treated as analogous to police and law enforcement. This is a feature different from usual moral panics.
P3: press
P4: public opinion (largely via media)
P5: politicians

What is distinctive about the Australian vaccination panic is that it began with a panic about infectious disease, with the folk devils being the AVN, and then morphed into a panic about any public criticism of vaccination. Concern about such criticism has escalated, reaching new heights in 2017 with immigration authorities banning foreign critics from entering the country and police raiding the offices of a doctor who granted patients medical exemptions from vaccination.

The war on terror as a moral panic
To better understand moral panics, it is useful to look at examples — especially prominent ones. Gershon Shafir and Cynthia Schairer have perceptively analysed the war on terror as a moral panic, in particular as a special type they call a political moral panic.[13] They modify Cohen's formulation to apply to politics, especially noting the role

---

13 Gershon Shafir and Cynthia E. Schairer, "The war on terror as political moral panic," in Gershon Shafir, Everard Meade and William J. Aceves (eds.), *Lessons and Legacies of the War on Terror: From Moral Panics to Permanent War* (London: Taylor and Francis, 2013), pp. 9–46.

of the state, and then apply their model to the war on terror.

Shafir and Schairer identify four features of Cohen's framework that apply to political moral panics:

1. Threat exaggeration
2. Overly broad definition of the threatening group
3. Excessive response to threat
4. Life cycle, with the response to the threat leading to mobilization of resistance and thus continuation of a spiral.[14]

Compared to the moral panics most commonly studied, "Political moral panics are distinct in involving the state and in being catalyzed by political and moral entrepreneurs who seek to attain goals that are out of reach of politics as usual."[15]

A few points from Shafir and Schairer's analysis are relevant to the Australian vaccination debate. One is that a framework that dominates thinking — in this case, the war on terror as a way of thinking about terrorism — can result from the efforts of "entrepreneurs." In other words, the way most people think about terrorism is not natural, namely not inherent in acts of violence, but is sold to audiences as a worldview. There are alternative ways of thinking but they are submerged. Likewise, the vaccination paradigm has been sold to people as a way to think

---

14 Ibid., pp. 10–11.
15 Ibid., p. 12.

about infectious disease. The point is not whether it is right or wrong, but that there are alternatives.

Another important point is that it is worth looking at who benefits from a moral panic. As Shafir and Schairer put it, "The focus in studies of specific moral panics, therefore, should be on the moral entrepreneurs who transform threats into moral panics and the interests that benefit from such panics."[16] I will be doing this later in this chapter.

PROPORTIONALITY AND RISKS

Moral panic theory can be applied to all sorts of topics, but it seems that the preference of most sociologists has been to look at cultural phenomena in which challenges to traditional ways of behaving are seen as threatening to the moral order, or to the political order in the case of terrorism. Conspicuous by their absence from most analyses are scientific issues.

Even a superficial examination of the Australian vaccination debate suggests the role of moral panic ideas. Prior to the emergence of SAVN in 2009, vaccination rates were high and stable, and they remained so during the years of SAVN's campaigns. Furthermore, the rates of infectious disease did not change significantly, and there were few deaths from measles, whooping cough and other killers from decades previously. SAVN portrayed the

---

16 Ibid., p. 10. On how terrorists can benefit by fostering a moral panic, see James P. Walsh, "Moral panics by design: the case of terrorism," *Current Sociology*, Vol. 65, No. 5, 2017, pp. 643–662.

AVN and other public vaccine critics as a serious threat to health, and furthermore placed moral responsibility on them for illnesses and deaths, as indicated by the epithet "baby killer" levelled at Meryl Dorey. The AVN was portrayed by SAVN as so dangerous that it needed to be not just discredited but destroyed. Overall, despite infectious disease not being a particularly large problem compared to other hazards to health, and not being any more serious than in preceding years, SAVN created alarm about the dangers. Moreover, the alarm was not just about the risk of illness and death but also about people criticising vaccination. In essence, SAVN inspired a moral panic about public criticism of vaccination.

SAVN's campaign has similarities with attacks on vaccine critics in some other parts of the world, notably the US. There, and elsewhere, resistance to vaccination is portrayed as irrational and dangerous. The difference in Australia is the scale and duration of SAVN's campaign to destroy an organisation and silence critics.

On a wider scale, it's possible to ask whether concern about infectious disease has elements of a moral panic. To answer this, it is useful to see whether public concerns about infectious diseases correspond to their dangers as assessed by technical experts.

A few preliminary comments are in order. There has been an enormous amount of research on risk perceptions, namely the way that people perceive risks, for example from hazardous chemicals and traffic accidents.[17]

---

17 A classic study is Paul Slovic, "Perception of risk," *Science*, Vol. 236, 17 April 1987, pp. 280–285.

An important finding is that people's concerns about risk seldom correspond closely to a calculation of probabilities and impacts. Most people are willing to accept much higher risks when they taken voluntarily. For example, base-jumping is quite dangerous but no one is forced to do it: base-jumpers accept the risk. However, base-jumpers might well be upset about a much smaller risk from food contamination.

Another finding is that people are more willing to accept risks when they receive corresponding benefits. This seems obvious enough. People drive cars knowing there is a risk of accidents. However, they might be upset about a chemical waste dump near their homes even though, statistically, the risk to their health is tiny and much smaller than being hurt in a traffic accident. The difference: there is no direct benefit from having a waste dump nearby. Maybe it has to go somewhere, but few people are so altruistic as to welcome it in their own neighbourhood without some compensating benefit.

Risks are also perceived differently if they are sudden and grouped together. When a commercial aeroplane crashes killing a hundred passengers, this is international news: there are many deaths at the same time. In comparison, a hundred people dying one by one from traffic accidents is seldom newsworthy beyond a local area. The result is that there is more attention to air disasters despite air travel being far safer, on a passenger-kilometre basis, than driving. Actually, there is a causative process involved. Because air disasters receive so much attention, airlines have been assiduous in reducing the risks.

Another factor in people's perceptions of risk is whether they seem to be in control. When people feel in control of their own health, life and destiny, they are usually willing to accept a greater risk. Drivers of cars thus may tolerate a risk of serious accident that would not be acceptable when they are passengers in a bus or train. This is especially pointed when drivers knowingly increase the risk, for example driving after drinking alcohol, when extremely tired or while using their phones. However, when some other driver contributes to an accident through such behaviours, this is a cause for condemnation. The difference is that drivers feel in control of their own driving and its consequences but cannot control the actions of other drivers.

Yet another factor is the cultural or symbolic significance of certain risks. For example, being attacked by a shark is seen as particularly concerning even though the number of deaths from shark attacks is quite small compared to other dangers such as drowning in a bathtub. Being assaulted by a stranger is commonly seen as more fearsome than being assaulted by family member, even though domestic violence is statistically far more likely. Part of the difference in these and other cases is familiarity. Bathtubs and family members are familiar whereas sharks and strangers are less so. Danger from things or individuals seen as alien may loom larger even though the bigger risks are close at hand.

In summary, there are various ways in which risk perceptions differ from what might be expected by a straightforward calculation of the probability and scale of harm. Risks are usually less acceptable when they are involuntary, come with no associated benefits, are sudden and grouped together, are not under personal control and are unfamiliar.

It can be argued that people should be more rational and use statistics to judge risks, or at least that policy should be constructed around reliable data about hazards rather than subjective perceptions. In practice, people's perceptions of risk are not easily changed, and policy is often influenced by perceptions.

Risk perceptions are at the core of moral panics. In a panic, people become alarmed by something that, according to published findings by experts in the relevant research field, would not be expected to generate great concern. But given that subjective perceptions of risk differ considerably from those of experts, how can it be said that any particular alarm is excessive? One way is to make comparisons with other risks that have similarities. That is how I will proceed here.[18]

---

18 It is a common view that scientific research aims to provide representations of an underlying reality, with ongoing investigations achieving ever better approximations to this reality. From this viewpoint, risk comparisons involve juxtaposing the best available estimates of real risks and people's perceptions of risk.

A different perspective is offered by social constructivists, who think less in terms of achieving the correct picture of an underlying reality and more in terms of differences between how experts and laypeople understand the world. From this perspective, all knowledge — expert and lay — is influenced by social factors, in other words is "socially shaped." A person's social background and role will affect their perception of risk, and this applies to both laypeople and scientists. For sociologists using the principle of symmetry, the same sorts of social explanations should be used to understand beliefs of laypeople and experts.

Note that pointing to social influences on knowledge does not imply that knowledge is necessarily wrong. Constructivists in their studies commonly set aside the issue of truth. Nor does constructivism imply that all knowledge claims are equally valid. Some claims are backed by more convincing evidence and arguments. Constructivists are more likely to examine how lay knowledge can reveal aspects of the world that experts ignore or dismiss.

In making comparisons between risks, I draw on published information about death rates and so forth. From a constructivist position, doing this might seem to assume that this information is "objective" or corresponding to reality rather than being constructed. Certainly, it is uncommon for constructivists to make risk comparisons; they are more likely to subject claims about risks to critique.

A classic exposition of the sociology of knowledge is Peter L. Berger and Thomas Luckmann, *The Social Construction of Reality* (Garden City, NY: Doubleday, 1966). This general approach can be applied to science in what is called the sociology of scientific knowledge. Important treatments include Barry Barnes, *Scientific Knowledge and Sociological Theory* (London: Routledge and Kegan Paul, 1974); David Bloor, *Knowledge and Social Imagery* (London: Routledge and Kegan Paul, 1976); Michael Mulkay, *Science and the Sociology of Knowledge* (London: Allen and Unwin, 1979). For an insightful overview of positivism and constructivism, see David J. Hess, *Science Studies: An Advanced Introduction* (New York: New York University Press, 1997).

There are three elements to consider. One is the actual damage caused by infectious disease, as measured by illnesses and deaths. The second is the role of contagion or, more generally, the collective danger due to the behaviour of individuals. The third is the potential damage that might occur should individual and herd immunity decline. Any one of these three elements can potentially generate legitimate concern about risks. I will examine each one in turn in relation to vaccination in Australia, with different comparisons for each element.

The comparisons here are not definitive. Each of them can be contested. My aim is to illustrate how to proceed in making comparisons that may help inform understanding of risks and responses. Alarm about vaccine-preventable diseases in Australia may or may not be excessive. However, that is not my main focus. Instead, my primary argument is that alarm about public expression of criticism of vaccination is greatly out of proportion when compared to responses to speech on issues that have commonalities with the vaccination issue.

Accordingly, some of the comparisons here are not ones conventionally made in the field of public health. I have chosen comparisons that highlight the role of speech. In doing this, I have adopted the framework of controversy studies, specifically the study of public scientific controversies. The question is why, in Australia, speech critical of vaccination is seen as so threatening compared to speech on other issues where the stakes seem, or can be argued to be, just as great.

It is important to note that serious illnesses can be traumatic and distressing and should not be dismissed lightly. Disabilities and deaths are even more serious. A disability can have lifetime consequences, and each death is a tragedy for family and friends. Making risk comparisons necessarily puts suffering and anguish in the background, recognising that it is associated with many harms. The purpose of risk comparisons is to provide information that can help inform actions and policies that affect suffering and death overall.

Risk comparison 1: deaths
Decades ago, infectious diseases were deadly in Australia, but death rates have declined greatly. According to the Australian Bureau of Statistics:

> The decline in deaths from infectious diseases, particularly in the younger age groups, was the driving force behind the decline in mortality in the first half of the 20th century. In 1920, infectious diseases accounted for approximately 15% of all deaths for both males and females; the death rate for males from infectious diseases was 189 per 100,000 males, and 147 per 100,000 females. Three of the leading causes of death at this time for males aged under 5 years were infectious diseases; diarrhoea and enteritis, diphtheria and measles.[19]

This death rate later declined to less than 10 per 100,000, a reduction by more than a factor of 10. The death rate

---

19 Australian Bureau of Statistics, "Mortality and morbidity: mortality in the 20th century," 4102.0 – Australian Social Trends, 2001.

declined so dramatically that now it can be a news story for a single young individual to die of pertussis, measles, chickenpox or any of the major killers of yesteryear.

Death rates from infectious diseases were at their lowest in the early to mid 1980s, when the death rate for males was less than 6 per 100,000 and the rate for females was less than 4. By 1999, deaths from infectious diseases had increased to 9 males per 100,000 and 6 for females, mainly due to an increase in septicaemia-related deaths. However, infectious diseases still accounted for only 1% of all deaths in the 1990s.[20]

The Australian Bureau of Statistics provides data on the leading causes of death in Australia. The figures for the top 20 causes for the year 2015 are as follows.[21]

Ischaemic heart diseases	19 777
Dementia, including Alzheimer disease	12 625
Cerebrovascular diseases	10 869
Trachea, bronchus and lung cancer	8 466
Chronic lower respiratory diseases	7 991
Diabetes	4 662
Colon, sigmoid, rectum and anus cancer	4 433
Blood and lymph cancer	4 412
Heart failure	3 541

---

20 Ibid.
21 Australian Bureau of Statistics, "Australia's leading causes of death, 2015," 3303.0 — Causes of Death, Australia, 2015.

Diseases of the urinary system	3 433
Prostate cancer	3 195
Influenza and pneumonia	3 042
Intentional self-harm [suicide]	3 027
Breast cancer	2 967
Pancreatic cancer	2 760
Accidental falls	2 474
Cardiac arrhythmias	2 327
Hypertensive diseases	2 285
Skin cancers	2 162
Cirrhosis and other diseases of liver	1 857

Of the top 20 causes, only one category involves infectious disease, "Influenza and pneumonia." Most of those dying from the flu are elderly, their average age being 88.6 years. Flu deaths among the elderly are seldom mentioned in the Australian vaccination debate. The primary focus in the debate is on children.

The numbers of Australian children in New South Wales under the age of five dying of vaccine-preventable diseases for the years 2008–2011 are as follows.[22]

Diphtheria, 0
Invasive haemophilus influenzae disease, 1
Influenza, 3
Measles, 0

---

22 National Centre for Immunisation Research & Surveillance, *Child Deaths from Vaccine Preventable Infectious Diseases, NSW 2005–2014* (2016). New South Wales has nearly one third of the population of Australia, and the figures are for a four-year period, so they provide a rough sense of annual national figures.

Invasive meningococcal disease, 15
Pertussis [whooping cough], 8
Pneumococcal septicaemia, meningitis and pneumonia, 23
Poliomyelitis, 0
Rotavirus, 0
Tetanus, 0
Varicella [chickenpox], 1

Given these figures, it is possible to question whether a huge alarm over infectious diseases is warranted — an alarm so great that silencing public criticism of vaccination is warranted.[23]

There are quite a few contributors to death rates that might be mentioned in comparison to infectious diseases, each of which is potentially relevant to some of the top-20 causes of death in Australia. For example, one study concluded that watching screen-based entertainment — television, video games, etc. — for more than four hours per day increased mortality rates by nearly 50% compared to watching less than two hours per day.[24] However, there has been no campaign to silence advocates of screen-based entertainment.

---

23 Here I focus on death rates. Vaccination proponents usually focus on illness and associated harms and costs, rather than deaths. A separate comparison could be made of the harms due to illness, injury and disability associated with heart disease, dementia and other conditions.

24 Emmanuel Stamatakis, Mark Hamer and David W. Dunstan, "Screen-based entertainment time, all-cause mortality, and cardiovascular events," *Journal of the American College of Cardiology*, Vol. 57, No. 3, 2011, pp. 292–299.

In October 2017, a news story reported, "At least 155,000 premature deaths in Australia could be prevented if the energy content of sugary drinks was slashed by a third, a study has revealed."[25] There are campaigners concerned about obesity-related health problems. Some of them have advocated putting restrictions on the advertising of sugary drinks, but none have sought to shut down the companies selling them.

Risk comparison 2: collective benefits
Measles and pertussis are contagious whereas many other causes of death, for example falls, are not. Vaccination serves two functions: it protects those individuals who develop immunity and it protects others through herd immunity: when enough people are immune, infectious agents cannot easily find hosts and do not spread. Vaccination of individuals thus has a collective benefit.

One analogy to vaccination in this regard is not smoking. By not smoking, an individual reduces their own risk of lung cancer and other diseases, and also reduces the risk to others due to second-hand smoke. For an individual, not smoking is analogous to being vaccinated: in each

---

25 Esther Han, "Cuts to sugar would save 155,000 lives," *Sun-Herald*, 15 October 2017, p. 8. The study cited: Michelle Crino et al., "Modelled cost-effectiveness of a package size cap and a kilojoule reduction intervention to reduce energy intake from sugar-sweetened beverages in Australia," *Nutrients*, Vol. 9: 983, 2017, doi:10.3390/nu9090983. Michelle Crino informed me that the correct figure from the study is 150,000 lives.

case, the individual reduces personal risk of disease and helps to protect others.

Smoking is responsible for a huge level of death and disease, in Australia and worldwide.[26] One estimate is that, by current trends, smoking could be responsible for one billion deaths worldwide in this century. This level of harm would justify extreme preventive measures. In Australia, action against tobacco harms has been far-reaching.[27] For example, advertising of cigarettes is banned and all brands sold are required to be in plain packaging, without logos. Smoking is not permitted on buses or trains or in airports. Some university campuses are smoke-free.

Actions against smoking might even be considered to have elements of a moral panic. At least that is how some smokers might see it when they are treated as pariahs. But anti-smoking campaigners have not launched an effort to shut down tobacco companies. Nor have they set up Facebook pages that ridicule smokers or cigarette retailers or tobacco company executives. Perhaps, given the trail of disease and death due to smoking, such efforts might be seen as justified. (Whether they would be effective is another question.)

---

26 Robert N. Proctor, *Golden Holocaust: Origins of the Cigarette Catastrophe and the Case for Abolition* (Berkeley, CA: University of California Press, 2012). Note that smoking is implicated in many of the major causes of death in Australia.

27 Simon Chapman, *Public Health Advocacy and Tobacco Control: Making Smoking History* (Oxford: Blackwell, 2007).

In a comparison between vaccination and antismoking, there seems to be a far greater alarm about vaccine critics than about purveyors of smoking, even though the health consequences of smoking are much worse in the here and now, and there are collective benefits in reducing smoking due to the effects of secondhand smoke. Although the Australian government has taken many steps to control and reduce smoking, it has not gone so far as to remove welfare benefits from parents who smoke.

A second analogy to vaccination, also involving a collective benefit, is not drinking alcohol. Alcohol consumption in Australia has a huge negative health impact. Drinkers have an increased number of health problems, most notoriously cirrhosis, which causes more deaths than alcoholism.[28] In addition, alcohol consumption indirectly leads to injuries to and deaths of drinkers through traffic accidents, suicides, homicides and falls. As well as the health impacts on drinkers themselves, they pose a serious risk to others, including through traffic accidents, fights and domestic violence.

There are debates about some of the health consequences of drinking. Moderate drinking may have some benefits for the heart. However, ethanol is classified as a carcinogen, so even moderate drinking may be harmful for some people. The key in a comparison with vaccination is

---

28 The classic reference is Mark H. Moore and Dean R. Gerstein (editors), *Alcohol and Public Policy: Beyond the Shadow of Prohibition* (Washington, DC: National Academy Press, 1981). There is a useful table on page 205.

that when individuals do not drink alcohol, or drink less, this brings definite collective benefits, especially for people who might be assaulted by drinkers or injured by inebriated drivers. Reducing the level of alcohol consumption could be thought of as providing a type of herd immunity.

For decades, there have been efforts to reduce the damage due to alcohol. Australian governments introduced random breath testing of drivers, a measure deemed responsible for significant reductions in traffic injuries and fatalities. At pubs, laws require that staff refuse to serve alcohol to customers who are intoxicated, though these laws are widely flouted and seldom enforced. In New South Wales, laws control the opening hours for pubs, and following public outcry over fights and anti-social behaviour — including deaths due to unanticipated assaults on pedestrians — pubs have been required to close earlier.

From some points of view, there has thus been a moral panic about drinking. This could be attributed to the efforts of "wowsers" (individuals who are obnoxiously puritanical), who earlier were prominent in Australian history. However, efforts against excessive consumption of alcohol have been limited. Alcohol advertisements are legal, and many sports clubs receive sponsorship from brewing companies. In many circles, there is no stigma at all for drinking, but instead strong peer pressure to join in: being a teetotaller (non-drinker) makes one an outsider.

Not drinking thus is analogous to vaccination: each one provides collective benefits, namely reducing health risks to others.[29] However, drinking causes vastly more immediate damage than not vaccinating, yet there are few sustained campaigns to ridicule drinkers,[30] make complaints to their employers about their drinking, or to shut down the companies that make and sell alcoholic drinks. It is fanciful to imagine a campaign, analogous to SAVN's, to stigmatise drinking and shut down all public support for it, perhaps under the banner SAPD, Stop Australian Promotion of Drinking. The comparison in Table 9.1 shows that there is a far greater alarm about vaccine critics than about proponents of drinking, though drinking causes far greater harm to non-drinkers than not vaccinating causes to others.

29 Jennifer A. Reich, *Calling the Shots: Why Parents Reject Vaccines* (New York: New York University Press, 2016), p. 238, notes that collective benefits, seen as an aspect of a social contract, are seldom mentioned in the US in relation to other issues, including "school funding, votes on bonds, taxes, traffic safety, public assistance, fracking, social security, or environmental policy." This raises the question of why collective benefits are taken to be such a crucial argument in the promotion of vaccination and the stigmatising of vaccine critics.

30 One campaign of this sort was a series of television ads by the Transport Accident Commission in Victoria with the tagline "Drink drive, bloody idiot": http://www.tac.vic.gov.au/road-safety/tac-campaigns/drink-driving/another-bloody-idiot-tv-ad.

Table 9.1. Comparison of benefits and advocacy in vaccination and not drinking

	Vaccination	Not drinking
Benefits to self	Immunity to vaccine-preventable diseases	Reduction in cirrhosis, alcoholism, traffic accidents, suicides, falls
Benefits to others	Herd immunity	Reduction in assaults and traffic accidents
Key advocates	Health departments, medical profession, pharmaceutical companies, media	Alcoholics Anonymous
Key opponents	Vaccine-critical groups	Alcohol industry, drinkers, advertisers, mass media

A study of preventable causes of death in the US provides context.[31] The researchers concluded that the top causes were smoking, high blood pressure, overweight/obesity and physical inactivity. They rated alcohol use as being among the top 12 preventable causes of death, showing some cardiovascular benefits from drinking outweighed by risks due to cancer, injuries and other noncommunica-

---

31 Goodarz Danaei et al., "The preventable causes of death in the United States: comparative risk assessment of dietary, lifestyle, and metabolic risk factors," *PLoS Medicine,* Vol. 6, No. 4, April 2009, e1000058.

ble diseases. Significantly for a comparison with vaccines, some of the deaths are due to hazards to non-drinkers.

Incidentally, vaccine-preventable diseases did not rate a mention in this article. It could be argued that such diseases are already being prevented, but by the same token the question is why the alarm should be raised about relatively few vaccine-preventable disease deaths when other preventable causes of death loom so much larger.[32]

Another analogy involving individual and collective benefits concerns how young children get to school. In Australia, four main options are walking, riding a bicycle, taking a bus and being driven by their parents. There are health benefits from walking and cycling. Nevertheless, quite a few parents choose to drive their children to school, protecting them from traffic dangers when walking

---

32 Suppose measles again became a commonplace childhood disease, with nearly all children contracting it. This was the situation in the 1950s, before mass vaccination, when about 450 measles deaths were reported in the US every year (Walter A. Orenstein et al., "Measles elimination in the United States," *Journal of Infectious Diseases,* Vol. 189 (Supplement 1), 2004, pp. S1-S3). This can be compared to the figures in the Danaei et al. paper of 467,000 deaths annually from smoking and 64,000 from alcohol. The comparison needs to be adjusted for various factors, including the increase in the US population and the likely reduction since the 1950s in the mortality rate per case of measles. Calculating years of life lost would change the comparison, making measles more consequential. It can still be good public health policy to reduce the incidence of measles, especially considering the cost and morbidity involved. The same applies to other preventable diseases, infectious and noncommunicable.

or cycling. However, by doing this they increase the danger to other children, namely the ones who walk or cycle. Yet there is little public condemnation of parents who drive their children to school, reducing the risk to their own children but increasing it for others. Table 9.2 summarises the analogy.

Table 9.2. Comparison of benefits and advocacy in vaccination and not driving children to school

	Vaccination	Not driving children
Benefits to own children	Immunity to vaccine-preventable diseases	Exercise (for walkers and cyclists)
Benefits to other children	Herd immunity	Reduction in traffic accidents
Key advocates	Health departments, medical profession, pharmaceutical companies, mass media	[Little public debate]
Key opponents	Vaccine-critical groups	[Little public debate]

Risk comparison 3: resurgence
In assessing vaccination in the light of moral panic theory, the third and final element is the possibility of a massive resurgence in infectious diseases should levels of immunity in the population fall too low. The point often expressed is that disease rates are low because of vaccina-

tion, and hence continual efforts are needed to ensure vaccination levels do not drop, and vaccine critics are a serious threat to these efforts.

This argument sounds plausible, but there is inadequate evidence to back it up. As noted in chapter 3, vaccination rates in Australia in recent years have been high and stable. There is no obvious justification for alarm about resurgence of infectious disease. Furthermore, as discussed in chapter 8, there is no strong evidence that public vaccine critics are a serious threat to current levels of vaccination.

There is yet another issue here. There is indeed the potential for an infectious disease to sweep the country, killing large numbers of people. This would indeed justify raising the alarm. However, this scenario almost invariably involves a new disease such as AIDS, ebola or swine flu.[33] The possibility of such an epidemic does not provide a justification for alarm about a decline in immunity to diseases such as mumps and chickenpox, which are unlikely to ever sweep the country causing thousands of deaths.

It is implausible that a disease like measles could re-emerge in a major way, causing hundreds or thousands of annual deaths in Australia, because if the mortality rate increased, this would provide a strong incentive for more

---

33 On the role of the mass media in both raising the alarm and offering comfort in relation to emerging diseases, see Sheldon Ungar, "Global bird flu communication: hot crisis and media reassurance," *Science Communication*, Vol. 29, No. 4, June 2008, pp. 472–497.

people to be vaccinated. Therefore, as long as current vaccines are effective for most of the population, it should be straightforward to counter a resurgence of currently known vaccine-preventable diseases.

It is important to remember that vaccination is not a single procedure but rather the administration of vaccines for many different diseases. The Australian government mandates that children be fully vaccinated: they must have had all the vaccines in the schedule by specified ages. The possibility of a massive outbreak in one particular disease does not translate into a justification for raising the alarm about less-than-ideal coverage for other diseases. Hepatitis and meningococcal-A were not big killers even before vaccination was introduced.

Note that the point here is that there is no justification for a panic. Each of the diseases causes harm, and a cost-benefit analysis can be used to justify encouraging widespread vaccination. But a cost-benefit calculation is not a rationale for a campaign to censor criticism of vaccination.

For the sake of argument, it is informative to set these qualifications aside and consider analogies to other areas where there are currently few or no deaths but there is a possibility of mass death. One case is nuclear war. Since the bombings of Hiroshima and Nagasaki in 1945, nuclear weapons have not been used in warfare, but the risk remains. A major nuclear war could kill hundreds of millions of people and have major environmental consequences. Yet since the end of the cold war in 1989, there has been relatively little public protest against nuclear weapons, at least compared to the major mobilisations in the late 1950s and the early 1980s. Australia, because it hosts US spy bases that are key components in the US nuclear war-fighting system, is a potential target for nuclear attack. Australia would also experience numerous secondary harms from a nuclear war in the northern hemisphere. Yet so far in this century there has been no major campaign to reduce the risk to Australians from nuclear war. (Through the 1980s, US bases in Australia were a prime focus of the peace movement.)

Another case is human-induced global warming. The impacts today, though small, are statistically significant, and include increased mortality from heat waves, wildfires and floods, and possibly from strong hurricanes. According to most scientists in the field, future generations will experience vastly greater impacts, possibly including mass deaths in parts of the world. Because of possible future risks, global warming is analogous to the possibility of a disease epidemic. Within Australia and globally, there is a great deal of climate activism aimed at reducing emissions of carbon dioxide and other greenhouse gases.

Both nuclear war and global warming hold the potential for massive death, and campaigners have mobilised against each one. Pro-vaccination campaigners also warn about the risk to the population of a resurgence of infectious disease, and in this way there is an analogy to campaigns against nuclear weapons and global warming. On the other hand, there are two distinct differences. One concerns power. There are extremely powerful forces implicated in the risks of nuclear war and global warming: military-industrial systems and the fossil fuel industry. Critics of vaccination are, by comparison, extremely weak, lacking any institutional leverage. The second difference is that campaigners against the dangers of nuclear war and global warming have not tried to silence the speech of their opponents.

The campaign against vaccination critics in Australia is dramatically different from campaigns against nuclear war and global warming — and against the tobacco industry. There are much greater potential dangers to the health of Australians than a resurgence of the diseases now controlled by vaccination, but addressing these dangers — smoking, alcohol, nuclear war, global warming — involves confronting powerful groups. It is far easier to attack and attempt to silence those who are weak.

Rick comparisons: summary
To assess whether the alarm about Australian vaccine critics can be labelled a moral panic rather than a realistic response to a problem, it is useful to examine three areas, making comparisons with other issues. The first is the absolute number of people harmed, the second is the possibility of contagion and the third is the possibility of future catastrophe. For each area, the alarm over vaccine critics in Australia since 2009 seems to fit the moral panic category.

Firstly, the number of deaths due to infectious diseases in Australia is low compared to many other dangers. Secondly, other well-known dangers to individuals, due to smoking and drinking, also create dangers to others — collective benefits from individual restraint are analogous to herd immunity from vaccination — without the same level of alarm. Thirdly, there are other dangers, most dramatically nuclear war and global warming, that cause few deaths today but could be catastrophic in the future, over which concerns have not led to calls for censorship.

I have felt it necessary to belabour the points about death rates, collective benefits and future dangers because, in the vaccination debate, these sorts of comparisons are seldom made. SAVN has mounted its campaign, and others have joined in, without providing a justification for why a special concern about vaccination, and in particular about vaccine critics, is warranted. SAVNers simply assume the existence of risk and collective harm is sufficient to justify their campaign.

The vaccination panic in Australia is largely manufactured. Unlike the Mods and Rockers studied by Cohen and unlike many apparently spontaneously generated panics about threats to moral codes, exaggerated concern about vaccination required a moral entrepreneur, the role played by SAVN. This is obvious enough by observing SAVN's numerous efforts and by noticing that prior to the emergence of SAVN, public discussions about vaccination proceeded much like most discussions in other countries, without a special alarm about the danger allegedly caused by allowing dominant views to be publicly questioned.

Manufactured panics are nothing special. It is routine for governments and advertisers to raise concerns that happen to serve their purposes. Governments raise the alarm about terrorism and advertisers raise the alarm about germs in the household. These are self-interested alarms in that the group raising the alarm benefits. In contrast, SAVN obtains no obvious material benefits from its efforts, such as jobs, profits or bureaucratic empires. To reiterate a point I have made before, undoubtedly nearly all those involved in SAVN and in related efforts are entirely sincere. They are concerned about children's health and are doing what they believe will help prevent disease and death.

The most striking aspect of the Australian vaccination panic lies in its connection with free speech. On the one hand, there is a concern about the dangers of infectious disease due to inadequate levels of individual and herd immunity. What SAVN added to this was an alarm about anyone speaking out in public critical of standard vaccination policy. The danger morphed from low vaccination rates to speech that might encourage people to avoid vaccination.

PANIC AND POLICY

The alarm raised about vaccine critics seems to have been instrumental in encouraging politicians to support coercive measures to promote vaccination. This was manifested, most dramatically, in federal legislation to deny certain child welfare payments to parents whose children are not fully vaccinated. This legislation, called No Jab No Pay, took effect in 2016. The financial loss to parents depended on their income, with some on low incomes losing up to $8000 per year in benefits. However, better-off parents were not affected, though legislative changes may target them in future.

As well, federal parliament changed the law on exemptions from vaccination. Previously, children could be exempt from vaccination on three grounds: medical, religious and conscientious. Medical exemptions are available when a doctor states that a child might be adversely affected by vaccines, for example due to having a compromised immune system. Medical exemptions are granted only in narrowly defined circumstances. For example, if a child has had a mild adverse reaction to a vaccine, this is not considered medical grounds against receiving other vaccines; if a child has had a serious adverse reaction to a vaccine, this is not considered medical grounds for the child's siblings to not receive all vaccines.

In Australia, objections to vaccination on religious grounds seem to be rare, because no mainstream religions oppose vaccinations. Most exemptions have been on conscientious grounds, namely a parent's personal belief. As described later, the number of conscientious objections gradually increased from about the year 2000, until these objections were ruled out by parliament.

In some states, there is related legislation called No Jab No Play, requiring that children be fully vaccinated or on a catch-up programme in order to attend child care.[34] No Jab No Pay and No Jab No Play can be called coercive because they involve financial penalties or service denial.

In Australia, children who are HIV positive or hepatitis B positive can attend school. This leads to the strange situation in which discrimination is possible against a

---

34 The actual policies are more diverse and complex than outlined here. For practical guidance, see National Centre for Immunisation Research & Surveillance, "No Jab No Play, No Jab No Pay policies," http://www.ncirs.edu.au/consumer-resources/no-jab-no-play-no-jab-no-pay-policies/.

child who is healthy but has not received hep B vaccination but not against a child who actually has hepatitis B.

In some occupations, notably in health and the military, there are requirements or expectations for being vaccinated against particular diseases. So far, there have been no requirements that others who work with children, such as teachers, be fully vaccinated. Nor are parents and other relatives required to be vaccinated.

It is plausible that SAVN's campaign and the moral panic it has fostered are at least partly responsible for the measures penalising parents whose children are not fully vaccinated. Some indicators are the mass media stories attacking the AVN and other vaccine critics, and stories supporting coercive legislation. Other indicators include the bipartisan support in the NSW Parliament to give the HCCC greater powers against the AVN, and the praise given to SAVN by Richard de Natale, leader of the Australian Greens.

Although it is plausible that SAVN's campaign has helped enable measures to promote vaccination, a full examination of the factors and players involved remains to be undertaken. This would involve looking at the role of direct contact between SAVNers and journalists, editors, doctors, politicians and others, the influence of media stories on politicians and on public opinion, the influence of individuals (journalists, doctors and others) who joined in raising the alarm about unvaccinated children, and other sorts of influences on politicians.

SAVN and public health

SAVN commentators claim they have been effective in that their activities have curtailed the influence of the AVN by reducing its income and its credibility in media stories.[35] However, SAVN, despite a massive investment of effort in its campaign against the AVN, has never presented any good evidence that its campaign has increased vaccination rates or reduced the incidence or impact of vaccine-preventable illness.

SAVN's campaigning has been based on the assumption that the AVN's activities had negatively affected vaccination rates and that discrediting and silencing the AVN would lead to increased rates. A contrary view is that vaccine-critical groups have little effect on vaccination rates, but rather are a response to concerns that arise for other reasons, such as perceived adverse reactions of children to vaccinations and the low chance that children will ever be exposed to some diseases against which they

---

35 For example, Peter Bowditch, "A TKO for anti-vax network" *Australasian Science,* Vol. 35, No. 4, 2014, p. 45; Rachael Dunlop, "Balance returning to vaccination information," *Australasian Science,* Vol. 35, No. 4, 2014, p. 44; Tracey McDermott, Alison Gaylard, David Hawkes, Anne Coady, Cate Ryan and Rachael A. Dunlop, "Quantitative analysis of the impact of the Stop the Australian Vaccination Network campaign on the public profile and finances of the Australian (anti) Vaccination Network," Poster 8, Public Health Association of Australia, 14th National Immunisation Conference, Melbourne, 17–19 June 2014.

are vaccinated.[36] This is compatible with the findings of a survey of AVN members showing that very few started to question vaccination initially as a direct result of the AVN; more commonly, members had concerns about vaccination and were attracted to the AVN because it provided a forum for these concerns.[37] From this perspective, trying to stifle critics is unlikely to have any impact on vaccination rates.

A possible proxy for the effectiveness of SAVN, in terms of its goal of promoting vaccination by discrediting and silencing critics, is the level of conscientious objection to vaccination. According to government figures,[38] the percentage of children whose parents sought conscientious objection increased every year from 2000 to 2014. The decrease in 2015 is presumably due to the removal of the option of conscientious objection that took effect on 1 January 2016.

---

36 See the discussion in chapter 8 of books by Mark Largent and Stuart Blume.

37 Trevor Wilson, *A Profile of the Australian Vaccination Network 2012* (Bangalow, NSW: Australian Vaccination Network, 2013).

38 Immunise Australia Program, "AIR — National Vaccine Objection (Conscientious Objection) Data," 2017, https://tinyurl.com/ycqcye2k.

Table 9.3. Percentage of Australian children with conscientious objection to vaccination recorded at the end of calendar years

Year	Percentage of children
1999	0.23
2000	0.41
2001	0.55
2002	0.67
2003	0.77
2004	0.86
2005	0.94
2006	1.03
2007	1.10
2008	1.20
2009	1.30
2010	1.36
2011	1.41
2012	1.46
2013	1.61
2014	1.77
2015	1.34

The increases shown in the table for the years 2000–2014 may reflect in part parents' increased awareness of the provision for conscientious objection.[39] The point here is

---

39 Australian Medical Association, "Submission 544 to the Senate Community Affairs Legislation Committee regarding the Social Services Legislation Amendment (No Jab, No Pay) Bill

that this trend predated the formation of SAVN and the furious struggle between SAVN and AVN; the rate of increase, in percentage points per year from 2000–2014, seems not to have changed substantially after SAVN became active beginning in 2009. Although this does not prove that SAVN has been ineffective, it is compatible with the view that vaccine-critical groups are more a product of parental concerns than a cause.

In the short term, SAVN has been effective in hindering AVN operations — for example, it ceased publishing its magazine — but it remains to be seen whether this is effective one or two decades hence. SAVN can point to changes in media coverage, with the AVN being given fewer favourable treatments, but whether this correlates with higher vaccination rates or lower disease rates is another question. Surrogate outcomes might be misleading if campaigning does not improve health.

SAVN has been quick to claim success for its approaches, and health departments simply assume their policies are effective. However, there seem to be no independent studies of policies and approaches.

The targets of campaigning are active agents and may contest or resist efforts to change their behaviour. Though the AVN has come under sustained attack from SAVN and several government departments, it has continued to operate. Some parents may resent pressure to vaccinate, especially when doctors are arrogant or condemnatory.

2015," p. 2; Julie Leask and Kerrie Wiley, "Submission 327," p. 5. Submissions: https://tinyurl.com/y99udkgm.

This is a key argument against coercive measures: they may trigger greater resistance.

It is also possible that SAVN's campaign can sometimes generate greater interest in vaccine criticism. There is a well-documented phenomenon in which scarcity generates greater interest: when a shop advertises a sale that lasts just 24 hours, shoppers are more likely to be attracted than to an ongoing sale. Censorship can stimulate greater interest in the thing censored. So, ironically, SAVN's attacks can potentially trigger greater interest in the targets of the attack.

The PhD theses of students I've supervised are publicly available on the University of Wollongong's online repository,[40] which gives figures for the number of downloads of each thesis. Most of my students' theses have been downloaded between 100 and 1000 times in total. Judy Wilyman's thesis, a critique of the Australian government's rationale for its vaccination policy, came under furious attack beginning in January 2016. It was downloaded 5000 times in the first month alone.[41]

Memes, inoculation and resistance
A meme is an idea or cultural practice. The word "meme" is used by analogy with gene to suggest that ideas are involved in an evolutionary process of natural selection in which some memes survive and thrive while others die

---

40 Research Online, University of Wollongong, http://ro.uow.edu.au.

41 My writings on the attack on Judy's thesis are at http://www.bmartin.cc/pubs/controversy.html#Wilyman.

out, resulting in adaptation to the environment. Examples of Internet memes are lolcats and the flying spaghetti monster.

It's possible to apply the concept of meme to the vaccination struggle in Australia. In the conceptual landscape, vaccination is the dominant belief system. Within this system, vaccine criticism can be thought of as a meme. Perhaps more usefully, some elements of vaccine criticism, such as the alleged link between vaccines and autism, could be thought of as memes.

In this picture, SAVN is engaged in an effort to stamp out dangerous memes, using methods of denigration, harassment and censorship against these memes and those who propagate them. From SAVN's point of view, vaccine criticisms are analogous to disease-causing microbes that need to be killed lest they cause an epidemic. Pursuing the analogy, the trouble with SAVN's approach is that it runs the risk of stimulating the development of resistance. The AVN and other vaccine critics learn what approaches can survive in the face of SAVN's attacks, and adapt, just as selection pressures cause microbes to adapt to be able to survive against antibiotics.

Some other supporters of vaccination do not attack critics but instead respectfully engage with parents, encouraging them to understand the benefits and risks of vaccination. This approach might be thought of as incorporating inoculation against criticisms of the dominant pro-vaccination belief system.[42]

---

42 On inoculation against arguments, see Michael Pfau, Michel M. Haigh, Jeanetta Sims and Shelley Wigley, "The influence of

Ironically, SAVN, in treating vaccine criticism as heresy and trying to stamp it out, may be contributing to making it a more potent threat. At the same time, SAVN's efforts undermine the efforts of those in the pro-vaccination mainstream who favour an inoculation approach to vaccine criticism.

The SAVN-inspired moral panic about vaccine critics is in some respects a self-fulfilling prophecy. As with other moral panics, when groups portrayed as deviant are isolated, stigmatised and subject to harsh measures, this can foster resistance and increased solidarity in the deviant group. Polarisation is increased and the perceived threat looms larger, with no end in sight.

Immunity by other means

Vaccination is a method of stimulating the body's immunity to particular diseases, but it is not the only way that immunity can be boosted. Studies exist showing that immunity can be increased through a good diet, moderate exercise, adequate sleep, control of excess stress, and mindfulness. The improved immune response from such measures provides increased protection against a range of diseases and moderates their effect if contracted.[43]

corporate front-group stealth campaigns," *Communication Research,* Vol. 34, No. 1, February 2007, pp. 73–99 and studies cited therein.

43 In this context, it is worth mentioning Thomas McKeown, *The Role of Medicine: Dream, Mirage or Nemesis?* (Oxford: Blackwell, 1979). In this classic book, McKeown argued that most of the improvements in health in the past three centuries in England were due to improvements in nutrition and hygiene, with

The medical profession's focus on vaccination as the preferred or even sole road to immunity leaves other methods off the public agenda. There is a plausible reason for this. Vaccination is an intervention that puts the medical profession in a central role: only health professionals can prescribe and provide vaccines. Furthermore, the main resistance to this intervention is a small minority of concerned parents.

Other methods of boosting immunity do not put the medical profession in such a special role. They fit into the category of preventive medicine via social change, which is a marginalised area in health policy. Consider for example the role of sleep in immunity.[44] In industrialised societies, there are many obstacles to adequate sleep, including noise, lighting, work pressures, social media and even the status associated with being busy.[45] All of these encourage the development of bad sleep habits. Despite the advice regularly provided about what to do to overcome insomnia and have a more restful sleep, the combined influence of several factors has deprived many people of adequate sleep.

---

vaccination playing a lesser role in the long-term decline in mortality from infectious diseases.

44 For example, Charlene E. Gamaldo, Annum K. Shaikh and Justin C. McArthur, "The sleep-immunity relationship," *Neurologic Clinics*, Vol. 30, No. 4, November 2012, pp. 1313–1343.

45 Judy Wajcman, *Pressed for Time: The Acceleration of Life in Digital Capitalism* (Chicago: University of Chicago Press, 2015).

There are also associated social benefits from improved sleep. People, when well rested, are usually nicer to each other and are less likely to be involved in traffic accidents. Improvements in sleep patterns thus have both an individual and collective benefit, analogous to herd immunity.

In tackling sleep deprivation as a health issue, there is no obvious enemy. Problems arising from inadequate sleep cannot be easily blamed on a few individuals who are encouraging people to burn the midnight oil. It is implausible to imagine the creation of a group called Stop the Sleep Deprivers.

Similar considerations apply to other methods of improving immunity such as good diet,[46] vitamin D supplementation,[47] moderate exercise[48] and mindfulness.[49]

---

46 Peter Katona and Judit Katona-Apte, "The interaction between nutrition and infection," *Clinical Infectious Diseases*, Vol. 46, No. 10, 15 May 2008, pp. 1582–1588 ("Malnutrition is the primary cause of immunodeficiency worldwide," p. 1582); Nevin S. Scrimshaw and John Paul SanGiovanni, "Synergism of nutrition, infection, and immunity: an overview," *American Journal of Clinical Nutrition*, Vol. 66, 1997, pp. 464S-477S.

47 Adrian R. Martineau et al., "Vitamin D supplementation to prevent acute respiratory tract infections: systematic review and meta-analysis of individual participant data," *BMJ*, 2017:356, https://doi.org/10.1136/bmj.i6583.

48 Neil P. Walsh et al., "Position statement. Part one: immune function and exercise," *Exercise Immunology Review*, Vol. 17, 2011, pp. 6–63.

In relation to health more generally, it has been argued that it would be enhanced by greater economic equality.[50] To address these methods of improving health, the medical profession is not in such a special role and there are powerful forces operating against change. Hence, these methods are largely off the agenda so far as health policy is concerned, which affects the amount of research addressed to them. Research on vaccination is a huge enterprise compared to research on sleep and immunity.

Any improvements to immunity and better health from these methods may not be directly comparable to the immunity conferred by vaccines. The point here is that excessive attention, in research and public discourse, is placed on a single route, vaccination. The moral panic over vaccine criticism diverts attention from other roads to improved immunity and health.

Diversion of attention
As already noted, there are several risks to health in Australia, including tobacco and alcohol, that seem far more serious than infectious disease yet have not generated the same public alarm. In this context, the SAVN-inspired panic serves to both exaggerate concern over infectious disease and to divert attention away from larger problems.

---

49 Richard J. Davidson et al., "Alterations in brain and immune function produced by mindfulness meditation," *Psychosomatic Medicine,* Vol. 65, 2003, pp. 564–570.

50 Richard Wilkinson and Kate Pickett, *The Spirit Level: Why More Equal Societies Almost Always Do* Better (London: Allen Lane, 2009).

Vaccination is a health intervention controlled by health authorities and health professionals. The goal of SAVN has been to stigmatise and silence anyone who publicly questions this intervention, and thus SAVN operates to defend and advance medical orthodoxy. Yet looming in the background is a much larger danger to health: the medical system itself. In hospitals across Australia, patients regularly die from mistakes by doctors and nurses, for example from administering incorrect drugs. Then there are the deaths due to pharmaceutical drugs themselves, many of which are marketed based on company research that has shortcomings. So-called iatrogenic (doctor-caused) disease is a major cause of death. Some estimates are that it is the third biggest killer, after heart disease and cancer.[51]

Nearly all doctors and nurses are doing as well as they can, and mistakes can never be entirely eliminated. Nevertheless, there are ways to reduce the number of medical errors, for example by introducing systems to encourage honest reporting of errors and near misses, thereby enabling revision of procedures to improve care.

It is possible to imagine a citizens' group like SAVN that, instead of combatting critics of medical orthodoxy, instead concentrates its efforts on reforming practice within the health system to overcome resistance to better reporting of medical errors. However, there is no such group, and the very existence of medical error as a major

---

51 For a forceful account of problems in medicine, see Peter C. Gøtzsche, *Deadly Medicines and Organised Crime: How Big Pharma Has Corrupted Healthcare* (London: Radcliffe, 2013).

danger to health is not all that well known among the general public.

Some Australian vaccine critics have a broader view of the issues. They adopt a holistic picture in which conventional medicine, alternative medicine and public health interventions are complementary. They turn to conventional medicine for acute care, to alternative medicine for some chronic conditions, and support measures for organic food, cleaner air and safer transport. Likewise, there are some campaigners within the health system who are concerned about iatrogenic illness and who believe much more emphasis should be placed on preventive health measures, for example limiting chemical exposures and encouraging better diet and exercise, and addressing poverty. There is thus a potential synergy between some of those in the sectors commonly called "alternative" and "conventional."

The possibilities of working together for collective welfare are undermined by the us-versus-them mentality fostered by SAVN. The Australian vaccination panic can be seen as a giant diversion from addressing more serious health issues. Significant progress in health and welfare is unlikely to occur by winning the battle over vaccination, whatever winning might entail. Instead, progress may depend on somehow seeing beyond vaccination to bigger issues.

10
Conclusion

Since 2009 in Australia, there has been an extraordinary struggle over vaccination. It has pitted a pro-vaccination group, SAVN, against public vaccine critics, especially the AVN (Australian Vaccination-skeptics Network).[1]

The struggle is about vaccination, but that is not unusual. In many countries there are debates over vaccination, sometimes quite bitter. What is extraordinary about the Australian struggle is that SAVN set out to destroy the AVN and to silence any public criticism of vaccination. In this, it has had a considerable degree of success: the AVN is a shadow of its former self. Australian mass media have mostly avoided reporting criticisms of vaccination, and some are ardent proponents, attacking critics. Politicians have joined the bandwagon, passing laws to enable harassing investigations into the AVN and laws to coerce parents to have their children fully vaccinated according to the government's schedule.

My interest is less in the debate over vaccination policy and practice than in the dynamics of the struggle itself, especially in SAVN's efforts to denigrate, harass and censor vaccine critics. This is basically an issue of free speech. SAVNers oppose free speech by vaccine critics on the grounds that what they say is wrong and

---

1 See the glossary and chapter 3 for information about SAVN and the AVN.

dangerous. However, this restriction on speech is not applied in other public scientific controversies, for example over climate change, genetic modification or chemical sensitivities.

The struggle over free speech for Australian vaccine critics has relevance far beyond the vaccination issue. SAVN's campaign is a rich source of examples of how speech can be curtailed and how targets can respond. In chapters 4 to 6, I looked at SAVN's techniques of denigration, harassment and censorship. This is an especially valuable case study because most of the methods have been deployed openly, and often the perpetrators in SAVN discuss their operations on a public Facebook page or in individual blogs.

If SAVN's campaign is successful, it could provide a template for others elsewhere. Being able to defend free speech against such campaigns is crucially important.

My stake in undertaking this study is not in the vaccination issue itself, because I do not have strong views about it. My personal preference is that vaccination policy be influenced by deliberations of randomly selected citizens, in what are called citizens' juries.[2] However, this is not on the agenda. A second best option is increased understanding and skills useful for defending free speech.

It is important to note that in the vaccination struggle nearly everyone is sincere and committed to improved health, in particular children's health. Although partisans

---

2 Lyn Carson and Brian Martin, *Random Selection in Politics* (Westport, CT: Praeger, 1999), http://www.bmartin.cc/pubs/99rsip.pdf.

on each side attribute bad motives to their opponents, there is little evidence that anyone involved is uncaring. Campaigners care about children's health, passionately, but differ about the best way to promote it.

To help understand the dynamics of the Australian struggle, I introduced the idea of a moral panic, which is a heightened alarm about something seen as a threat to the moral order. Most studies of moral panics look at cultural phenomena, such as clothing and youth behaviour. However, it is also possible to understand the alarm over vaccine criticism as a moral panic, given that the danger to the community from infectious disease is far less than other dangers that do not generate the same level of alarm. For example, drinking alcohol is associated with a considerable rate of death and disease. Furthermore, individuals who drink pose a danger to non-drinkers, for example through drink driving and domestic violence. Yet in Australia there is no group analogous to SAVN that seeks to silence anyone who speaks publicly in favour of drinking. Indeed, that would be almost unthinkable, given the alcohol industry's massive advertising, sponsorship of sport, and influence on ideas about relaxation.

Seeing the alarm about vaccine critics as a moral panic leads to a question: what purposes does this panic serve? One result is to marginalise consideration of other ways to build immunity, for example promoting good diet and alleviating poverty. Such options could complement vaccination, but in practice they are off the agenda.

The medical establishment has become attached to vaccination as *the* solution to the problem of infectious diseases. This can be seen as a path of least resistance, in the context of industrial influences. The pharmaceutical industry obviously has a stake in expanding use of vaccines, especially ones like the flu vaccine that are repeated regularly. But this may not be the largest influence. Other avenues for improving population health would involve confronting powerful groups and entrenched habits. For example, improving diet is very hard in a free market in which unhealthy foods can be advertised and promoted with little restriction. Reducing poverty would improve individual and population health, but it is a massive task that involves confronting powerful and wealthy groups. The moral panic about vaccine criticism obscures these possibilities.

The vaccination struggle thus has several dimensions or levels, each of them important. At the immediate level, the struggle is about vaccination, either applying incentives to accept the full child vaccination schedule or allowing unconstrained parental choice. Another level is free speech: regardless of beliefs about vaccination, it is possible to argue that each side should be able to express its views and, beyond this, that the debate should be conducted in a fair and respectful manner. SAVN's campaign seems to have made this prospect remote. A third level is agendas for public health. The moral panic about vaccine criticism has diverted attention from other possible routes to individual and population health. This might be considered the most damaging consequence of the Australian vaccination struggle.

It is notoriously difficult to predict the future, but one thing seems certain: the vaccination debate in Australia is unlikely to be resolved in the near future. It is daunting to imagine it continuing 20 or 30 years from now, yet this is the most likely possibility, considering that vaccination has been contested, on and off, since its development centuries ago. Some campaigners seem to think victory is around the corner, for example due to some new research finding, but science is only part of what drives scientific controversies. There are conflicting beliefs and agendas that will continue to ensure disagreement.

Although the vaccination debate will almost certainly continue, the continuation of SAVN and its campaign to silence vaccine critics is less certain. The biggest potential challenge to SAVN is not from its targets, vaccine critics, but rather from pro-vaccination figures within the mainstream of medicine who decide that SAVN and the coercive measures it has inspired are counterproductive.

Whatever the future for SAVN and vaccine critics, the Australian vaccination struggle offers many lessons for anyone interested in health, free speech and social change.

Index

ABC, 128, 161, 174–75
absent viewpoints, 15–24, 27, 29–30, 259
ACCC, 128
agenda-setting, 171
agents provocateurs, 227, 236
AHPRA, 125–28
AIDS, 25, 256
alcohol, 332–36, 360
anonymity, 222, 235
antibody testing, 18–19
anti-vaxxer, 25, 68–70, 205, 296–97. *See also* AVN; vaccine-critical groups; vaccine critics
ASIC, 121–22
astroturfing, 118
Australia, 16–17, 31–34, 105, 191, 268, 307; deaths in, 325–32; defamation law in, 156–57; government of, 31; moral panic in, 311–13, 320; as nuclear target, 339–40; *Vaxxed* tour in, 200–1; visits to, 183–85, 199–200, 202–4. *See also* Australian Skeptics; AVN; country differences; SAVN
The Australian, 89, 177, 192n29
Australian Broadcasting Corporation. *See* ABC
Australian Skeptics, 122–23, 197, 275, 316
Australian Vaccination Network. *See* AVN
Australian Vaccination-skeptics Network. *See* AVN

autism, 14, 21, 189, 257–58, 351
AVN, v, 1, 3–5, 34–45, 244, 285, 358; censorship of, 167–171, 176, 178, 190–98, 200–6; defending, 208, 214–20, 222–23, 230–36, 239–44; denigration of, 51–61, 64–65, 73–81, 84, 93, 95; harassment of, 101–2, 107–29, 132–35, 144–46, 150–51; income, 73; and moral panic, 315, 317, 320; name of, 117–24; and Web of Trust, 77–78. *See also* Dorey, Meryl; SAVN; vaccine-critical groups; vaccine critics
AVO, 240–241

backfire, 99, 138, 160n7, 143n41, 226, 228. *See also* censorship, counterproductive; counterproductive attacks
bans, 169, 183–84, 195, 198, 202–4, 317
Barber, Jo, 130
Bari, Judi, 3
Beattie, Greg, 53, 196, 242
Becker, Howard, 314
black backfire, 99. *See also* backfire
blaming, 49, 73–74, 92, 163, 228, 231
blogs, 39, 81, 132, 139, 168–70, 187–90, 193, 206. *See also* Reasonable Hank
Blume, Stuart, 261–66
boundary-work, 285–92
Bowditch, Peter, 55, 241n13

bullying, 147, 150, 274–75, 278. See also harassment; mobbing
Buzzard, Dan, 114–15
bystanders, 81–82

Canan, Penelope, 102–4
censorship, 152–207; active, 158–59; counterproductive, 5, 159, 183–85, 203, 282, 350; justifications for, 190–96; self-, 158–59, 175, 214. See also Streisand effect
Channel 9, 160–63. See also mass media
chickenpox, 258, 288, 329
citizens' juries, 294, 359
Citron, Danielle Keats, 278–80
climate change, 2, 26, 167, 183, 192, 246, 340–41. See also controversies, scientific
Cohen, Stanley, 310–13, 315, 317–18, 342
collective benefits, 27, 268, 330–37, 341–42, 354. See also herd immunity
complaints, 41–42, 73–75, 101–31, 133–34, 150–51, 174–75, 177–78, 197, 200, 231–32; defending against, 215–21, 223. See also SCAPPs
Conis, Elena, 259–61, 264
conscientious objection, 343–44, 347–49
conspiracy theories, 57–62, 84–85, 166, 188–89, 251
constructivism, 284–85, 323n18
controversies, scientific 1–5, 15, 26–27, 192, 252, 290, 293, 299, 302, 308, 325, 359, 362. See also climate change; fluoridation; vaccination

correspondence bias, 28–29
counterattack, 86–88, 92, 213–15, 226, 234
counterproductive attacks, 5, 90, 99, 145, 159, 183–85, 203, 214, 226–228, 234, 282, 290, 362. See also backfire
country differences, 12, 266–69
cover-up, 160–61, 228–29, 231–32
Critcher, Chas, 316
CSIRO, 154–55

David, Tasha, 242
death, 13, 74, 254, 319–22, 325–36, 338–42, 356. See also euthanasia
debate, 88, 106, 178–82, 273, 290. See also controversies, scientific; vaccination
Deer, Brian, 22–23
defamation, 102–3, 105–6, 141–43, 156–58, 217. See also SLAPPs
defending, 84–86, 208–244
Demasi, Maryanne, 175
denier: Holocaust, 183; vaccination, 26
denigration, 46–100; effects of, 79–82; by exposing and hiding information, 49–52; by labelling, 67–72; by pictures, 64–67; responses to, 82–93
devaluing, 48–49, 52–72, 161, 228–34
Di Natale, Richard, 75–76, 345
diet, 262, 352, 354, 361
Dili, 225–26
dissent, 2, 211. See also free speech
diversion of attention, 355–57
Dorey, Meryl, v, 1, 3, 36–39, 41–43, 51–54, 59–61, 64–66, 71–74, 84–85, 91–92, 111n11, 116, 124, 127, 132, 137, 142, 144–47, 149, 168, 187–90, 193–98, 233, 240–43, 280, 315,

320; and conspiracy theories, 59–61.
See also AVN
double standards, 154–55, 216, 237
doxxing, 131–40, 151
drinking, 332–35, 360
driving, 321–22, 336–37
Dunlop, Rachael, 40

East Timor, 225–26, 228–30
emotions. See motivations;
    vaccination, passions
endorsements, 49, 74–79, 93, 180, 206,
    233, 239, 308–9. See also honour by
    association
equality, 355
ethics, 14, 16, 27, 296. See also
    collective benefits; herd immunity;
    moral panics
euthanasia, 184–85
exercise, 337, 354
exit, 210–14
expertise, 3, 190, 193, 292–309
explanation, 73–74, 161–62. See also
    interpretation
exposing information, 48–49, 90–93,
    216, 230–33, 237, 281
exposure to viruses, 6–9, 14n6, 257–58

Facebook, 39, 42, 52–54, 57, 88, 92,
    98–99, 101n1, 133, 139–40, 144,
    168–69, 220, 271, 276–77, 279,
    281–83. See also social media
Fair Trading, v, 115–23, 127, 135, 197.
    See also official channels
Faunce, Thomas, 112–13
flu, 10, 328
fluoridation, 180–81, 268–69, 290,
    308. See also controversies,
    scientific

Folk Devils and Moral Panics, 310
forums. *See* venues
framing, 207, 237–39. *See also*
    agenda-setting; interpretation
free speech, 4–6, 44–45, 69, 102–3,
    105, 112, 153, 185–86, 207, 231,
    241, 343, 358–59, 361. *See also*
    censorship; dissent; SLAPPs

General Medical Council, 22–23
Gieryn, Thomas, 287
global warming. *See* climate change
Glover, Richard, 120–21
goals, 27–29, 208–10
Goldman, Gary, 288
Gray, Kurt, 272
group identification, 80, 271
guilt by association, 61–64, 75, 94,
    305. *See also* honour by association

Haidt, Jonathan, 246–50
hall of shame, 132
Hancock, Bronwyn, 37n11
Hansen, Jane, 39n14, 176
harassment, 41, 101–51, 231, 277–82;
    effects of, 147–49; sexual, 149–50
hate speech, 278–82
HCCC, v, 42, 75, 108–16, 127, 129–
    30, 215–18, 240. *See also* official
    channels
Health Care Complaints Commission.
    See HCCC
Health Promotion International,
    181n21
Healthy Lifestyles Expo, 197–98
Heckenlively, Kent, 203
Heller, Jacob, 24n21, 253–57
Hennessy, Jill, 96–99, 227
Hentoff, Nat, 45

herd immunity, 8–10, 14, 16–17, 27, 269–70, 296–97, 330–33, 335, 337, 341. *See also* collective benefits; ethics
Hirschman, Albert, 210–12
HIV, 256
Hobson-West, Pru, 3n5, 35n9
Holocaust, 26, 183
homoeopaths, 133–34
honour by association, 304–9. *See also* endorsements; guilt by association
HPARA, 126
Hunt, Mina, 54–55, 71

Icke, David, 59–61
Ieraci, Sue, 40, 70
immunisation, 24. *See also* immunity; vaccination
immunity, 6–10, 18–19, 24, 337–38, 352–55, 360. *See also* herd immunity
Immunization: How Vaccines Became Controversial, 261–66
infectious disease, 6–11, 25, 260, 325–30, 355; resurgence of, 337–41. *See also* herd immunity; vaccine-preventable disease
in-group, 80, 94, 271, 277. *See also* identification
inoculation, 351–52
interpretation, 230, 237–39. *See also* explanation; reinterpretation
intimidation, 103–5, 141, 143, 162, 228–32, 242–43
Irvine, William, 83
Irving, David, 183

journalists, 128, 158, 162, 172–78, 207, 230, 242–43. *See also* Deer, Brian; Maitland, Derek; mass media; newspapers

labelling, 67–72
The Lancet, 21–22
Largent, Mark, 21n13–14, 257–59, 265, 295n31
leaking, 221–23
legal action. *See* defamation
liar label, 71–72, 84
Living Wisdom, 36–37, 41, 43, 132
Loussikian, Kylar, 89, 177
loyalty, 210–12, 247

Maitland, Derek, 160–62
mass media, 43, 124, 157, 160, 162, 166, 171–75, 178, 206–7, 233, 338n33, 358. *See also* censorship; journalists; newspapers
McCaffery, Dana, 39n14, 109, 276
McCaffery, David, 109, 215
McCaffery, Toni, 39n14, 109, 215
McLeod, Ken, 40, 54, 56, 71–72, 75, 108–9, 123n20, 125, 133–35, 215
measles, 8, 17, 22, 264, 315–16, 328, 336n32. *See also* MMR
Medical Veritas, 62–64
meetings. *See* talks
memes, 350–52
Messenger, Stephanie, 37n11, 40, 199–200, 242
mindfulness, 352, 354
minds, 247, 272–73
misogyny, 280
MMR, 18, 22–23, 33, 257, 261. *See also* measles; mumps
mobbing, 136–37, 274–75, 278. *See also* bullying; doxxing; harassment
Monckton, Christopher, 183–84

moral foundations, 246–50, 270–71
moral panics, 310–57, 360–61;
  political, 317–19
motivations, 27–29, 251, 269–83
mumps, 259–61, 264. See also MMR

names, 1n1, 37n11, 117–24, 132, 135.
  See also anonymity; hall of shame
narrative, 174, 177–78, 253–57
Nashville, 225–26, 235
networks, 219–20, 223
news media. See mass media
news values, 165, 173
newspapers, 101n1, 164–65, 171–72.
  See also mass media
Nitschke, Philip, 184–85
No Jab No Pay, 34n7, 343–44
No Jab No Play, 344
nuclear war, 246, 283, 339–41

Obukhanych, Tetyana, 14
official channels, 162–63, 228–31,
  239–42, 244. See also Fair Trading;
  HCCC; OLGR
Offit, Paul, 7n1, 20, 257
OLGR, v, 114–15, 127
online disinhibition, 273–74
online harassment, 147–48, 277–83.
  See also harassment
organisational structure, 218–20
orthodoxy, rejecting, 300
out-group, 80, 94, 271, 277. See also
  identification
outrage 160, 225, 228–32, 242. See
  also political jiu-jitsu

paradigms, 11–13, 208–9, 297
parents, 14–15, 17–20, 22, 33–34, 139,
  212–13, 239, 251–52, 253n6, 257–
58, 261, 265, 289, 301, 313–14,
336–37, 343, 345. See also
conscientious objection; vaccine
hesitancy
Pemberton, John, 161–62
pesticides, 2. See also controversies,
  scientific
pharmaceutical companies, 11, 28,
  264–65, 298–99, 337, 356, 361
pictures, 64–67
polarisation, 15, 21n14, 24n21, 27, 29,
  82, 149, 246, 251–52, 257, 352. See
  also absent viewpoints
polio, 6–8, 255, 263
political jiu-jitsu, 224–28. See also
  counterproductive attacks
porn, 76, 144–45, 280
Primero, Michael, 62–63
Pring, George, 102–4
projection, 51
proportionality, 319–43
psychology. See motivations;
  projection
public meetings. See talks

Raffaele, Daniel, 54, 145–46, 188, 282
Reasonable Hank, vi, 39–40, 55–56,
  59–61, 98–99, 125, 132, 137, 220–
  22, 279–80
Reich, Jennifer, 21n13, 253n6, 334n29
reinterpretation, 163, 228–31, 237. See
  also explanation
resurgence, 311, 337–41
risks, 6, 13–16, 319–43

Sabin, Albert, 7, 255
Salk, Jonas, 7, 255
SAVN, vi, 1, 4–5, 38–46, 244, 285,
  358–62; boundary-work by, 289–92;

censorship by, 167–71, 174–78, 187–207; defending against, 208–10, 212, 214–21, 223, 226–28, 230–44; denigration techniques, 51–61, 64–82, 84–93, 95–96, 99; expertise and, 292–93, 303–4, 309; harassment techniques, 101–2, 105–29, 132–35, 137, 139, 142, 144–51; and moral panic, 311–16, 319–20, 342–43, 345–52, 355–57; motivations, 269–83. See also AVN; Stokes, Patrick
SCAPPs, 105–8, 110–11, 125, 128–29, 130–31, 135, 142, 150; responding to, 215–18
Scarborough, Kathy, 37n11
Schairer, Cynthia, 317–19
Scheibner, Viera, 54, 71, 290–91
school, 336–37. See also No Jab No Play
scientific controversies. See controversies, scientific
screen-based entertainment, 329
Sears, Robert, 19–21
seatbelts, 191
SETI, 287
sexual harassment, 149–50. See also harassment
Shafir, Gershon, 317–19
Sharp, Gene, 224
Sheffield, Fran, 128
Skeptics, 121–23, 275, 316
SLAPPs, 102–6, 111, 142–43. See also defamation
sleep, 352–55
smoking, 153, 330–32, 335, 336n32
social media, 164–65, 171–72. See also Facebook
social problems, 283–85

Springell, Peter, 154–55
Stoics, 83
Stokes, Patrick, 295–304, 309
Stop the Australian (Anti-)Vaccination Network. See SAVN
Stop the Australian Vaccination Network. See SAVN
strategy 208–10
Streisand, Barbra, 159, 162; effect, 159–60
sugary drinks, 330
suppression of dissent, 2. See also free speech

talks, 182–202, 207, 277–78
Tenpenny, Sherri, 199–200, 205
terrorism, 29, 185, 187, 317–19
TGA, 127
Thompson, Kenneth, 312–14, 316
threats, 43, 141–48, 196–97; to moral order, 310–18. See also defamation; harassment
Tierney, Peter, vi, 39–40, 52, 54, 71, 132–33, 181n21, 220
Tomljenovic, Lucija, 69–70
Tommey, Polly, 202–4
Truth Library, 97–99

UFOs, 286–87
United States, 103, 105, 180, 225, 248, 253, 256, 258–61, 267, 274, 208, 320, 335, 340. See also country differences
University of Wollongong, 62, 128, 177, 291, 350; see also Wilyman, Judy

V for Vendetta, 65

vaccination, 6–30; absent viewpoints, 15–24; contexts, 245–309; criticism, 13–15; debate in Australia, 31–46; denier, 26; narrative, 253–57; passions, 245–50; and public health, 346–50; rates in Australia, 32; rhetoric, 24–27. *See also* AVN; country differences; herd immunity; measles; mumps; parents; polio; SAVN
Vaccination Awareness and Information Service, 132
Vaccine (journal), 288
vaccine-critical groups, 3, 34–38, 265, 346, 349. *See also* AVN; vaccine critics
vaccine critics, 3n5, 15, 35n9, 51, 99, 127–28, 209–10, 233, 311, 357. *See also* anti-vaxxer; AVN; Dorey, Meryl; vaccine-critical groups
vaccine hesitancy, 33–34, 253, 365
The Vaccine Narrative, 253–57
Vaccine Nation, 259–61
vaccine-preventable disease, 17, 25, 328–29, 335–37, 339. *See also* infectious disease
vaccine refusers, 33–34, 265
Vaccine: The Debate in Modern America, 257–59
validation, 230, 232–37
Vaxxed, 200–4
venues, 167–71, 187, 199–201, 206–7. *See also* talks
vexatious litigant, 217–18, 241n13
Vines, Tom, 112–13
visits to Australia, 183–85, 199–200, 202–4
vitamin D, 354
voice, 210–14

Wakefield, Andrew, 21–23, 70, 177n18, 205
Web of Trust, 76–79
Wegner, Daniel, 272
whistleblowing, 130, 147, 161, 222
Wikipedia, 23n19, 69, 78–79
Wilyman, Judy, 62–63, 89, 128, 177, 205, 291–92, 350
windowlickers, 66–67
Woodford Folk Festival, 187–90, 193–94

Other books by Brian Martin from Irene Publishing:

DOING GOOD THINGS BETTER

This is a book about how to improve what you are already doing well. How to improve your writings as an academic, playingskills as a musician, jogging as a runner or honour codes as a good citizen and friend.

WHISTLEBLOWING: A PRACTICAL GUIDE

You discover some wrongdoing, such as corruption, injustice or danger to the public. What should you do? If you do nothing, the problem will continue. If you speak out, you become a target for attack — and the problem may still continue. Whistleblowing: A Practical Guide tells how to assess your options, prepare for action, use low-profile operations, negotiate official channels, leak, build support and survive the experience. It is filled with sample cases that show what can happen when you make incorrect assumptions or fall into common traps. The advice in this guidebook is based on the author's contact with hundreds of whistleblowers and dissidents, plus consultation with others experienced in the area. Although there are no guarantees of success, Whistleblowing: A Practical Guide can improve your odds of making a difference. Even if you never expect to challenge the system yourself, it will give you valuable insight into the dynamics of individual struggles and what is happening to others.

BACKFIRE MANUAL

In 1991, protesters in Dili, East Timor were massacred by Indonesian troops. This turned out to be a political disaster for the Indonesian government, greatly increasing international support for the East Timorese independence struggle. The massacre backfired on the Indonesian government. The Backfire Manual explains why. Imagine you're planning an action and think you might come under attack. Maybe it's a rally and there's a risk of police brutality. Maybe you're exposing government corruption and there could be reprisals against your group. To be prepared, you need to understand the tactics likely to be used by your opponent, for example covering up the action and trying to discredit you and your group. The Backfire Manual provides guidance for this sort of planning. It outlines the backfire model and gives examples and exercises for using it. This is a practical handbook for being more effective whenever you face a powerful, dangerous opponent.

NONVIOLENCE UNBOUND

Methods of nonviolent action can be used to bring down dictators. Nonviolence Unbound shows how insights into what makes nonviolent action eff ective can be applied to four completely diff erent arenas: defending against verbal abuse, responding to online defamatory pictures, and engaging in the struggles over euthanasia and vaccination. This investigation shows how to analyse options for opposing injustice.

THE CONTROVERSY MANUAL

Climate change, psychiatric drugs, genetically modified organisms, nuclear power, fluoridation, stem cell research — these are just a few of the hundreds of issues involving science and technology that are vigorously debated. If you care about an issue, how can you be more effective in arguing for your viewpoint and campaigning in support of it? The Controversy Manual offers practical advice for campaigners as well as plenty of information for people who want to better understand what's happening and to be able to discuss the issues with friends. The Controversy Manual provides information for understanding controversies, arguing against opponents, getting your message out, and defending against attack. Whether experts are on your side or mostly on the side of opponents, you'll find advice for being more effective. While not taking sides on individual controversies, the emphasis is on fostering fair and open debate and opposing those who use power and manipulation to get their way.

RULING TACTICS

Most people think of the world as divided into countries, and many people identify with their "own" country. Because there's nothing natural in this, governments and others need to continually encourage identification with the nation. This serves those with power and wealth. Ruling Tactics outlines the methods commonly used to foster everyday nationalism and how they can be countered. These methods are described in a range of areas, including crime, sport, language, economics, terrorism and war. Ruling Tactics can serve as a practical manual for recognising how thinking is oriented towards the state, and how this sort of thinking can be changed.

THE DECEPTIVE ACTIVIST

The Deceptive Activist introduces key ideas about lying and deception and then provides a series of case studies in which activists need to decide what to do. There are no final answers, but it is important to address the questions.

In your action group, is it ever beneficial to lie to other members? When is it wise to lie to authorities? If a member of your group has done something wrong, is it better to be open about it now or keep it hidden in the hope that outsiders will never know? What are the pros and cons of infiltrating opposition groups to collect information about harmful activities? Should we wear masks at rallies? There's lots of research showing that lying is an everyday occurrence in most people's lives, and furthermore that lies can be beneficial in some circumstances. But they can also be very damaging, especially lies by authorities.

Order from:

www.lulu.com/spotlight/johansen_jorgen

www.ingramcontent.com/pod-product-compliance
Lightning Source LLC
Chambersburg PA
CBHW050134240426
43673CB00043B/1662